John Calvin and Roman Catholicism

Critique and Engagement, Then and Now

Edited by
Randall C. Zachman

Foreword by Lawrence S. Cunningham

Baker Academic
a division of Baker Publishing Group
Grand Rapids, Michigan

Published by Baker Academic
a division of Baker Publishing Group
P.O. Box 6287, Grand Rapids, MI 49516-6287
www.bakeracademic.com

Printed in the United States of America

Library of Congress Cataloging-in-Publication Data
Calvin Studies Colloquim (2007 : University of Notre Dame)
    John Calvin and Roman Catholicism : critique and engagement, then and now / edited by Randall C. Zachman.
        p.   cm.
    Includes bibliographical references and index.
    ISBN 978-0-8010-3597-5 (pbk.)
    1. Calvin, Jean, 1509–1564—Congresses. 2. Reformed Church—Relations—Catholic Church—Congresses. 3. Catholic Church—Relations—Reformed Church—Congresses. 4. Reformed Church—Europe—History—16th century—Congresses. 5. Reformed Church—Europe—History—17th century—Congresses. I. Zachman, Randall C., 1953– II. Title.
BX9418.C368 2007
280'.042—dc22   2008003418

In memory of
the Reverend George H. Tavard, AA, 1922–2007
Teacher, author, and ecumenist extraordinaire

Contents

Foreword   7
  Lawrence S. Cunningham

Introduction: Why John Calvin and Roman Catholicism?   9
  Randall C. Zachman

List of Contributors   19

Abbreviations   21

1. Roman Catholic Lives of Calvin from Bolsec to Richelieu: Why the Interest?   25
   Irena Backus

2. Calvin and the Nicodemites   59
   George H. Tavard, AA

3. Friend and Foe: Reformed Genevans and Catholic Neighbors in the Time of Calvin   79
   Karen E. Spierling

4. Rules of Engagement: Catholics and Protestants in the Diocese of Geneva, 1580–1633   99
   Jill Fehleison

5. *In partibus infidelium*: Calvinism and Catholic Identity in the Dutch Republic   119
   Charles H. Parker

6. John Calvin, Accidental Anthropologist   145
   Carlos M. N. Eire

7. Revising the Reform: What Calvin Learned from Dialogue with the Roman Catholics   165
   Randall C. Zachman
8. Calvin and Sacramentality: A Catholic Perspective   193
   Dennis E. Tamburello

Name Index   217
Subject Index   221

Foreword

Theology, as Saint Anselm famously asserted, is "faith seeking understanding." That "seeking" takes place for individuals, within communities, and rightly among theologians. Again, the "seeking" assumes faith, and that is what distinguishes theology from religious studies. The essays collected in this volume constitute a fine example of theology done from within the context of a community—in this case, an academic one, for it is within the university, as John Henry Newman observed in the last century, that mind clashes with mind. The precise focus of this particular exercise is to inquire into the "catholicity" of John Calvin. The topic, as these essays amply demonstrate, is not so much in the form of a "clash" but rather in the manner of a conversation and a dialogue. It is quite clear that the conversation goes well beyond the centuries of polemic, apologetics, and *parti pris* that have patinated Catholic-Reformed exchanges over the centuries. Indeed, the tone of these studies is fair, searching, and "seeking" in the best sense of the term.

One of the nodal themes uncovered in this conference is the issue of the Church itself. To what degree was Calvin separated from and united to the ancient tradition of Christianity? Obviously, the Catholics and Reformers of the time vigorously debated that question. The merit of seeing that discussion from the vantage point of time and free from the controversial context in which it was first undertaken is not only a fruitful step forward but also a firm foundation for building further strategies for finding a greater unity among the churches now so lamentably separated. One can only hope and pray that the results of these colloquia will bring us further into that community where when gathered together as brothers and sisters we will meet our common Lord, Jesus Christ.

Lawrence S. Cunningham
John A. O'Brien Professor of Theology
University of Notre Dame

Introduction

Why John Calvin and Roman Catholicism?

Randall C. Zachman

The following chapters were originally presented at the Calvin Studies Colloquium held in April 2007 at the University of Notre Dame. A. N. S. Lane suggested the theme of the colloquium at the previous colloquium held at Notre Dame in 2003.

The theme of "John Calvin and Roman Catholicism" was chosen for several reasons. First of all, it is an acknowledgment that Calvin did not envision himself as the founder of a new tradition called "Calvinism," but rather as one who sought to restore the Catholic Church to what he called its "purer form" under the apostles and early church writers. Calvin thought of himself as belonging to the "orthodox and evangelical" tradition, which associated him not only with Martin Luther, Philipp Melanchthon, Martin Bucer, and Heinrich Bullinger, but also with Cyprian, Ambrose, Chrysostom, and Augustine. One of the concerns of this volume will therefore be to assess the degree to which Calvin might be seen as a Catholic theologian, as surprising as such a claim might appear to be at first glance.

Second, as a consequence of his desire to restore the Catholic Church of his day, Calvin's engagement with his contemporary Roman Catholics was not tangential to his concerns, but was directly related to the task he was called to carry out. By placing Calvin and his followers within the context of their wider interactions with Roman Catholics in Geneva and its environs, and in places like Holland, we can gather a better grasp of what the real issues were that both united and divided them, and we will be able to see more clearly how members of the old church regarded the work of Calvin and his colleagues. As each author indicates in his or her own way, it is not possible to study the Reformed and Roman Catholic communities in isolation from each other. Calvinists and Roman Catholics had continual interaction with each other and were constantly seeking to come to an understanding of each other, at times in an apologetic and polemical way, and at other times in a surprisingly objective and impartial manner. As Jill Fehleison rightly points out, the Roman Catholic and Reformed communities need to be studied in concert because in many ways they remained one community.

Third, the theme of this volume highlights the remarkable fact that a good deal of the best scholarship on Calvin has been done by Roman Catholics, substantiating the importance of understanding one's own tradition through the eyes of others outside that tradition. Roman Catholic scholars such as Alexandre Ganoczy, George Tavard, Lucien Richard, Killian McDonnell, Carlos Eire, and Dennis Tamburello have greatly enriched our understanding of Calvin and his theology by highlighting aspects of his work that could only be seen with Catholic eyes. It is essential that Protestant Calvin scholars listen to what our Roman Catholic colleagues see in the thought of Calvin and the movement he so deeply influenced. As Carlos Eire reminds us, Protestantism and Catholicism cannot be fully understood in isolation from each other. It is our hope that this volume will give further impetus to these efforts at ecumenical understanding, which help us to overcome unfortunate stereotypes and to come to a richer understanding of the Christian tradition we all share.

The volume begins with two essays that set Calvin's relationship to Roman Catholicism in its French context. Irena Backus explores the interest shown by French Roman Catholics in the life of Calvin, showing how their pictures of Calvin have changed with the development of increasingly objective and critical historical methodologies, which were yet never quite able to displace the ideologically driven pictures of Calvin developed by his followers and opponents. French Roman Catholics were horrified by what Calvin had done to their beloved

France, especially in the Wars of Religion, while being simultaneously impressed by his undoubted success. The first French Catholic biography of Calvin, by Jerome Bolsec, proved in many ways to be the most enduring, even though it was based on fabrication, rumor, and hearsay. Bolsec located Calvin in a tradition of heresy going back to the Pharisees and Sadducees and introduced several unfounded rumors about Calvin, especially regarding his alleged sexual sins, that endured for centuries.

In spite of this inauspicious beginning, French Roman Catholics did develop increasingly critical biographical skills, especially in the work of François Bauduin and Jean-Papire Masson, which would undermine the credibility of the lives of Calvin written by Bolsec and by Calvin supporters Beza and Colladon. Remarkably, Masson presents his account of Calvin as neither his friend nor his foe, thereby stepping decisively in the direction of a historical criticism that would seek to rise above confessional polemics and apologetics. Masson's biography enjoyed the status of being the sole authoritative biography of Calvin in the seventeenth and eighteenth centuries, and both Calvinists and Catholics used it. Ironically, Protestants would appeal to Masson's work as a corrective to the negative myths perpetuated by Bolsec, and later by Richelieu. Unfortunately, Richelieu added further impetus to the polemically negative image of Calvin by reproducing all the negative stereotypes of Calvin in the previous lives of Calvin.

Fr. George Tavard, AA, locates Calvin within the context of the French Catholic Evangelicals, with whom he once identified and from whom he decisively broke; Calvin came to portray them negatively as "Nicodemites." Over against Calvin, Tavard argues that these former associates of Calvin were not "Nicodemites," but instead were sincere reforming Catholics who thought that their adherence to justification by grace through faith did not entail a break with the historic episcopacy, as Calvin came to claim. Tavard frames this issue in light of Calvin's friendship with Louis du Tillet, which came to be tragically broken due to du Tillet's shock at his friend's willingness to be called to the ministry by the City Council of Geneva, and not by the apostolic bishops of Rome. Calvin saw his friend's willingness to return to the bishops and priests of the Roman Catholic Church in France as an abandonment of the gospel, whereas Du Tillet believed that Calvin had entered into an illegitimate form of ministry, though he did not accuse him of schism.

According to Tavard, Du Tillet's position was not unique: it was shared in France by Roussel, Marguerite d'Angoulême, and Stapulensis; in Italy by Ochino, Contarini, and Colonna; and in Spain by Valdès and Gonzaga, among others. All of them sought to teach and preach justification by faith alone in the context of episcopal authority and papal primacy; they did not accept Calvin's description of them as "Nicodemites," limping under two opinions out of fear of persecution. Rather, they could not see why their adherence to justification by faith alone in the work of God in Christ should require joining a new church. Tavard challenges us to think of what might have happened if Calvin had come to agree with Du Tillet and had returned home to France, to the Roman Catholic Church that had baptized him.

The next three chapters examine the relationships between the Reformed and Roman Catholics in the city of Geneva at the time of Calvin, in the environs of Geneva at the time of François de Sales, and in the Dutch Republic after the Synod of Dort. Karen Spierling begins this section by pointing out how historical descriptions of the city of Geneva still tend to read Roman Catholics out of the narrative, focusing instead on the successes and failures of Reformed pastors, and especially of Calvin, in institutionalizing their vision of a godly community. However, an understanding of the various interactions between the Reformed and Roman Catholics is essential for understanding the actual life of the Reformed in Geneva. Spierling is especially interested in highlighting the porousness of the civic and religious boundaries of the day, due to the need of Geneva to be an open city, and due to the relationships that Genevans had with their Roman Catholic friends, families, and business associates. As is clear from cases brought before the consistory (council of ministers), many Genevans did not share their pastors' view that one's commitment to the gospel should be the defining aspect of all human relations; they were unable to see why they should not go to Mass while visiting their Catholic neighbors, even as they went to sermon and the Lord's Supper while in Geneva.

The pastors sought to immunize their congregations against Roman Catholic influences by having them internalize the gospel through catechesis and preaching, so that they would of themselves avoid doing in Catholic territories what they already avoided doing in Geneva. They also sought to impress on their congregations the mutually exclusive nature of Reformed and Roman Catholic worship. However, Spierling convincingly shows that the pastors had good reason to be anxious that the religious distinctions between Reformed and Catholic that the pastors wanted to draw did not weigh as heavily on the minds of many of their parishioners.

By the end of the sixteenth century, Geneva came to see itself as an island in a sea of Roman Catholicism. Thus interactions between Reformed Genevans and their Roman Catholic neighbors were unavoidable. Jill Fehleison poses the question of how the two confessional communities perceived each other, and whether the increasing contact between them brought greater understanding or greater conflict. Fehleison shows how the Treaty of Nyon in 1589 made it possible for Roman Catholics to travel through the city of Geneva, shown most dramatically in the visit of François de Sales to Geneva to debate the elderly Theodore Beza in an attempt to convert him. There was even a Capuchin named Maurice who tried to preach in St. Pierre. As these stories indicate, not only was there increasing Roman Catholic and Reformed interaction during this period, but the momentum also appears to have been clearly on the side of the Roman Catholics, who succeeded in putting the Reformed in the position of defending the status quo.

Many Genevans were drawn to the affective and symbolic rites of the Catholics in the Mass and in the Forty Hours Celebrations, much to the consternation of their pastors. The Catholics also made much better preachers and debaters, appealing effectively to the emotions of the audience, over against the intellectual and doctrinal orientation of the Reformed pastors, who preferred the written text to live debate. Not surprisingly, the Genevans participated in only one debate with the Catholics, in spite of the repeated efforts of Père Chérubin de Maurienne to have more, and the Genevans appeared to be outperformed in this debate through their representative Herman Lignaridus, a professor of theology. Fehleison confirms the portrayal given by Spierling, that in spite of the efforts of each community to present the other as anathema, the Roman Catholics and the Reformed continued to interact and shape each other's communities, which in many ways remained one community after all.

Charles Parker completes the historical examination of Reformed and Roman Catholic interaction by examining this dynamic in the

Dutch Republic after the Synod of Dort. Even though the Reformed achieved their political victory in the Dutch Republic after 1619, the marginalized Roman Catholic community experienced a remarkable revitalization during this period, so that the number of Roman Catholics rivaled the size of the Reformed in the latter part of the century. The Dutch faced the daunting challenge of creating a public polity that was Reformed, while also allowing freedom of worship to Roman Catholics, Lutherans, Mennonites, Spiritualists, and Remonstrants. At the beginning of the seventeenth century, the Roman Catholics had no bishops, no property, no canonical parishes, and only a few priests in the Dutch Republic.

To address the pastoral needs of the Roman Catholics, Rome restored the model of the vicar apostolic from the early church, and viewed him as the successor of the archbishop of Utrecht. The opening of two seminaries in the Dutch Republic placed the reforms of ministry at Trent and in the Jesuit order at the foundation of priestly formation, far in advance of other locales in Europe. The priests were trained in apologetics to try to convert the Reformed to Catholicism, and used catechesis and other devotional literature to ground the laity in the Catholic faith so that they would not succumb to Protestant attacks. The shortage of priests necessitated the increased role of laity in many functions of the Catholic Church, such as catechesis, poor relief, patronage, and visitation of the sick. The sense of being a persecuted minority also strengthened the commitment of Roman Catholics to their church. In sum, Parker details the great irony that the victory of the Reformed in the Dutch Republic had the unintended but real effect of strengthening and revitalizing the Roman Catholic community there, even as it remained marginalized from the mainstream of Dutch civic life.

The final three chapters address the theological relation of Calvin to Roman Catholicism, both of his day and of our own. Carlos Eire addresses the question of the degree to which Calvin might be seen as a Catholic theologian by examining an issue that seems to bring out Calvin's most anti-Catholic theological stance: his analysis and critique of idolatry. Eire notes how Calvin unintentionally became one of the first anthropologists of the modern era by means of his ability to detach himself coldly from his Roman Catholic past, so that he could view Roman Catholicism as essentially "other," as the false religion that was antithetical to the true religion of the gospel. Thus Eire argues that Calvin's dichotomous way of speaking of true and false religion was deeply Catholic, while his description of false religion was quite modern and anti-Catholic. Eire sees the modernism of Calvin's analysis of idolatry as lying in his grounding of idolatry in human nature itself, and not in satanic or demonic deception, which Eire claims to be the Catholic understanding of idolatry. Fallen human nature of itself is a factory productive of idolatry, as we all invent our own deities to worship.

The sense of divinity or seed of religion that Calvin insists is in all people does not provide a link to the self-revelation of God, as Catholics would claim, but rather serves as the fountainhead of idolatry. Eire claims that Calvin builds on the insights of Erasmus, Zwingli, and Bullinger but goes beyond them in grounding idolatry in human nature, and not in a misunderstood encounter with the divine. One may still see Calvin as Catholic by viewing his diatribe against idolatry in concert with Roman Catholic diatribes against the gods of the native peoples in the New World, but Calvin is nonetheless radically un-Catholic in his refusal to root idolatry in satanic deception. According to Eire, Calvin began the divorce of religion from the supernatural that was carried forward first by Hume and later by Durkheim. In sum, Calvin is Catholic in thinking of true and false religion, and anti-Catholic in the way he defines each.

Randall Zachman returns to a question first posed in this volume by George Tavard: Calvin's understanding of his relationship to the Roman Catholic Church, in which he claimed that the true church was still present, though in a hidden way. In particular, Zachman explores whether Calvin actually revised his position on baptism, the holy Supper of the Lord, the laying on of hands, and the order of the church; he examines this possibility in light of Calvin's participation in the dialogues between the evangelicals and the Roman Catholics between 1539 and 1541, with particular attention to the 1543 edition of Calvin's *Institutes*. Zachman details how Calvin's view of baptism changes in 1543 to accentuate the way baptism incorporates the faithful into the family of God and the body of Christ in the church, along with his increasing willingness to describe baptism as an instrument used by the Holy Spirit.

Calvin's understanding of the holy Supper of the Lord increasingly accentuates the bestowal of the reality signified in concert with the sign, and he also begins to build on the ancient eucharistic prayer that exhorts the faithful, "Lift up your hearts." However, Zachman finds the most dramatic changes in Calvin's teaching to be located in his understanding of the laying on of hands. Calvin moves from describing the laying on of hands in ordination as a foolish "aping" of the apostles in the 1536 *Institutes*, to it being a sacrament that conveys the Holy Spirit in the 1543 *Institutes*. Calvin similarly reverses his position on the orders of the church. In 1536, Calvin sarcastically insists that the distinction between priests and bishops was taken from paganism. By 1543, however, Calvin claims that the early Catholic polity of deacons, priests, bishops, archbishops, and patriarchs is as rooted in the Word of God as the orders of pastor, teacher, elder, and deacon. He also describes the bishop as superior to priests and as having the authority to ordain. Even though the evidence is circumstantial, Zachman suggests that Calvin's experience of dialogue with the Roman Catholics may well have led him to make such dramatic revisions in his previous theology.

The concluding chapter of the volume assesses the degree to which one, from a contemporary Roman Catholic perspective, might consider Calvin to be a sacramental theologian. Fr. Dennis Tamburello, OFM, draws on his experience, both as a Calvin scholar and as a participant in Roman Catholic and Reformed dialogue, to frame the issue in terms of contemporary Roman Catholic understandings of sacramentality, especially as set forth by Edward Schillebeeckx and David Tracy, as well as Protestant understandings in Paul Tillich and Donald Baillie. All of these theologians speak of the visible self-manifestation of the divine in a sacramental way, even if Tracy and Tillich seek to combine such manifestation with the proclamation of the Word. Then Tamburello turns to Calvin's theology per se, especially his descriptions of creation, humanity, and the person of Christ, to see if he might detect the theme of sacramentality in his theology.

Tamburello finds the most compelling evidence for sacramentality in Calvin's theology of creation, as Calvin speaks of the way God reveals himself and daily discloses himself in the whole workmanship of the universe. Calvin therefore describes the universe as the "mirror" or "theater" in which the invisible God becomes somewhat visible in God's works. Tamburello notes how Calvin combines this visible self-manifestation of God with the Word of God, thereby anticipating Tracy and Tillich. The visibility of God also appears in Calvin's description of the image of God in humanity, especially in his description of humans as a microcosm. Finally, Calvin's descriptions of the eternal Son of God as the one in whom the invisible Father becomes somewhat visible seems to strike a chord similar to Schillebeeckx's claim that Christ is the primordial sacrament in whom grace became fully visible. In sum, Tamburello claims that the Catholic theme of sacramentality is most clearly present in Calvin's description of creation as the mirror, spectacle, or theater in which the invisible God becomes somewhat visible, whereas for contemporary Roman Catholics sacramentality is primarily rooted in Christ and then in the sacramental life of the church.

All of these studies show how fruitful it is to place John Calvin and the Reformed in the context of their ongoing and dynamic interaction with their Catholic neighbors. Historians and theologians are often tempted to think of John Calvin and the Reformed tradition in silo-like fashion, tracing their history and development in isolation from others who surrounded them. All of our authors have illustrated the need to study John Calvin and Roman Catholicism together, both to come to a better understanding of the traditions bequeathed to us by the Reformation, and also for the mutual benefit and enrichment of one another's traditions.

List of Contributors

Irena Backus (DD, Oxford; Honorary DD, Edinburgh) is professor of Reformation history and ecclesiastical Latin in the Institute of Reformation History at the University of Geneva. Among her most recent publications are: *Historical Method and Confessional Identity in the Era of the Reformation*; *Life Writing in Reformation Europe: Lives of Reformers by Friends, Disciples, and Foes*, and an edited collection entitled *Théodore de Bèze (1519–1605): Actes du colloque de Genève de 2005*. While Anglican by affiliation, she comes and writes from a mixture of religious traditions.

Carlos M. N. Eire (PhD, Yale University) is the T. Lawrason Riggs Professor of History and Religious Studies at Yale University and chair of the Renaissance Studies program. He is the author of *War against the Idols*; *From Madrid to Purgatory*; and co-author of *Jews, Christians, Muslims: An Introduction to Monotheistic Religions*. His memoir of the Cuban Revolution, *Waiting for Snow in Havana*, which won the 2003 National Book Award in nonfiction, has been translated into many languages but is banned in Cuba. He is a Roman Catholic.

Jill Fehleison (PhD, Ohio State University) is assistant professor of history at Quinnipiac University. She completed her dissertation, entitled "Visitor and Villager: Communal Dynamics and the Status of Local Religion in the Diocese of Geneva-Annecy during the Time of Catholic Reform 1579–1640," in 2001.

Charles H. Parker (PhD, University of Minnesota) is associate professor of history at Saint Louis University. His research interests focus on the religious history of early modern Europe, and his publications include *Faith on the Margins: Catholics and Catholicism in the Dutch Golden Age* and *The Reformation of Community: Social Welfare and Calvinist Charity in Holland, 1572–1620*.

Karen E. Spierling (PhD, University of Wisconsin–Madison) is visiting associate professor of history at Ohio State University and author of *Infant Baptism in Reformation Geneva: The Shaping of a Community, 1536–1564*. She was raised in the Presbyterian Church (USA).

Dennis E. Tamburello, OFM, is a Roman Catholic theologian who belongs to the Order of Friars Minor (Franciscans). He is a professor of religious studies at Siena College in Loudonville, New York.

George H. Tavard (STD, University of Lyons) was a Roman Catholic ecumenical theologian who was a member of the Augustinians of the Assumption and professor emeritus at the Methodist Theological School in Ohio. His most recent works were *The Starting Point of Calvin's Theology* and *From Bonaventure to the Reformers*.

Randall C. Zachman (PhD, University of Chicago Divinity School) is professor of Reformation studies at the University of Notre Dame. He is the author of *The Assurance of Faith: Conscience in the Theology of Martin Luther and John Calvin*; *John Calvin as Teacher, Pastor, and Theologian: The Shape of His Writings and Thought*; and *Image and Word in the Theology of John Calvin*. He is Episcopalian with a strong interest in a number of Christian communions.

Abbreviations

BPU	Bibliothèque publique et universitaire (Geneva)
Catechism	I. John Hesselink, *Calvin's First Catechism: A Commentary; Featuring Ford Lewis Battles' Translation of the 1538 Catechism* (Louisville: Westminster John Knox, 1997)
CNTC	John Calvin, *Calvin's New Testament Commentaries*, ed. David W. Torrance and Thomas J. Torrance, 12 vols. (Grand Rapids: Eerdmans, 1959–72)
CO	*Joannis Calvini opera quae supersunt omnia*, ed. W. Baum, E. Cunitz, and E. Reuss, 59 vols., Corpus reformatorum (Braunschweig: Schwetschke, 1863–1900)
Comm.	*Commentary*
CTS	John Calvin, *Calvin's Commentaries*, various translators, 30 vols. (Edinburgh: Calvin Translation Society, 1844–48); www.ccel.org/ccel/calvin/commentaries.i.html
CTT	*Calvin: Theological Treatises*, trans., intro., and notes by J. K. S. Reid, Library of Christian Classics 22 (Philadelphia: Westminster, 1954)
Fr.	French; also, Father

Inst. 1536	John Calvin, *Institutes of the Christian Religion*, 1536 ed., trans. and annotated by Ford Lewis Battles, rev. ed. (Atlanta: John Knox, 1975; repr., Grand Rapids: Eerdmans and the H. Henry Meeter Center for Calvin Studies, 1986)
Inst. 1960	John Calvin, *Institutes of the Christian Religion*, ed. John T. McNeill, trans. Ford Lewis Battles, 2 vols., Library of Christian Classics 20–21 (Philadelphia: Westminster, 1960)
MS	manuscript
no.	number
OBC	Het Utrechts Archief. Apostolische Vicarissen Hollandse Zending en hun Secretarissen, 1579–1728
OE	*Ioannis Calvini opera omnia*, ed. B. G. Armstrong, Series 2, *Ioannis Calvini opera exegetica* (Geneva: Librairie Droz); vol. 16, *Ad Galatas, ad Ephesios, ad Philippenses, ad Colossenses*, ed. Helmut Feld (1992); vol. 19, *Ad Hebraeos*, ed. T. H. L. Parker (1996)
OS	*Johannis Calvini opera selecta*, ed. Petrus Barth and Guilelmus [Wilhelm] Niesel, 5 vols. (Munich: Chr. Kaiser, 1926–52)
PH	Pièces historiques, manuscript housed at the Archive d'État de Genève
R. Consist.	Registre du Consistoire, manuscript housed at the Archive d'État de Genève
R. publ.	Registre des publications, manuscript housed at the Archive d'État de Genève
RC	Registres du Conseil, manuscript housed at the Archive d'État de Genève
RCP	Gabriella Cahier and Michel Grandjean, eds., *Registres de la Compagnie des pasteurs de Genève au temps de Calvin*, vol. 7, 1595–1599 (Geneva: Droz, 1984)

SDG 2	Émile Rivoire and Victor van Berchem, eds., *Les sources du droit du Canton de Genève*, vol. 2, *De 1461 à 1550* (Arau: H. R. Sauerländer, 1930)
SDG 3	Émile Rivoire, ed., *Les sources du droit du Canton de Genève*, vol. 3, *De 1551 à 1620* (Arau: H. R. Sauerländer, 1933)
LWZ	*The Latin Works of Huldreich Zwingli*, ed. S. M. Jackson et al., 3 vols. (New York: G. P. Putnam's Sons, 1912–29)
TTRC	John Calvin, *Tracts and Treatises on the Reformation of the Church; with a Short Life of Calvin by Theodore Beza*, trans. Henry Beveridge, notes and intro. by T. F. Torrance, 3 vols. (Grand Rapids: Eerdmans, 1958; repr., Eugene, OR: Wipf & Stock, 2004)
ZSW	*Huldreich Zwinglis sämtliche Werke*, 14 vols. (Berlin: C. A. Schwetschke und Sohn, 1905–)

1

Roman Catholic Lives of Calvin from Bolsec to Richelieu

Why the Interest?

Irena Backus

Calvin was a controversial figure in his lifetime, and he continued to be controversial after his death. One of the characteristics of keeping alive the memory of the reformer is the number of negative and sometimes even slanderous biographical accounts that his religious adversaries devoted to him. I am going to examine just the ones that proved to be the most influential, starting with Bolsec and ending with Richelieu. My aim is to establish his biographers' motives as well as to investigate their methods.[1] Perhaps because of its controversial nature, the figure of Calvin constitutes a fruitful ground for testing the biographical genre as it developed in the sixteenth and seventeenth

1. This essay relies partly on material used in my monograph *Life Writing in Reformation Europe* (Aldershot, UK: Ashgate, forthcoming in 2008).

centuries, evolving from being an exercise in negative image creation to something resembling a modern biographical account.

Jerome Bolsec

Jerome Bolsec wrote his *Life* of Calvin in 1577 as a response to Beza's first *Life* of the reformer, a hagiographical account of 1564, reprinted several times, which I shall refer to as the *Discours*.[2] I do not propose to introduce Bolsec. It is enough to remember here that in his last years he returned to the Catholic Church, settled in France, and published his *Lives* of Calvin (1577) and Beza (1582).[3]

Although Bolsec spent much of his life in conflict with Calvin, these two *Lives* (of Calvin and Beza) were intended to strike at Beza rather than at the author of the *Institutes*, who had been dead since 1564. What is significant about his *Lives* is not that they were hostile but that they were published as full-scale biographical accounts, as opposed to short biographical notices on Calvin such as those by (e.g.) Dupréau, Lindanus, Florimond de Raemond, or Laurentius Surius, which were concealed within larger works of history of heresy. This suggests that Bolsec saw the threat of the Reformers, Calvin in particular, attaining to the status of saints, thanks to their biographies by Beza and others, and that he wanted to strangle the idea at birth. His image of Calvin, Beza, and the Genevan Reformation was to prove as pervasive in the centuries to come as the image of the Christian hero or Protestant saint promulgated by Beza and de la Faye respectively. Bolsec wanted to destroy the image of Geneva as quickly and effectively as possible, which is no doubt why he published a biography of Beza while the latter was still alive.

Whether Bolsec's works are factually true or false is not something that needs to concern us here. Declaring that they arose in a polemical context is saying little. It is far more important to recognize that any hint of the existence of Protestant saints posed a threat, at least

2. See Frédéric Gardy, *Bibliographie des œuvres de Théodore de Bèze* (Geneva: Droz, 1960), no. 173, p. 105.

3. On Bolsec, see, e.g., Philip Holtrop, *The Bolsec Controversy on Predestination from 1551 until 1555*, 2 vols. (Lewiston, NY; Lampeter, UK: E. Mellen, 1993), and literature cited therein.

in some Catholic circles; otherwise Bolsec's works would not have enjoyed enduring success.

Although always treated in isolation, Bolsec's *Life* appeared in a particular literary context, as part of a collection titled *Histoire des vies, meurs, actes, doctrine et mort des quatre principaux heretiques de nostre temps, à scavoir Martin Luther, André Carlostad, Pierre Martyr et Jean Calvin, iadis ministre de Geneve: Recueillie par F. Noel Talepied, C. de Pontoise et H. Hierosme Bolsec . . .*, first published in 1577 (Paris: Jean Parant). Despite the common title page, the Taillepied part and the Bolsec part were two separate publications and were simply sold together. The volume with the common title page does not contain Calvin's *Life* by Bolsec, only the *Lives* of Luther, Carlstadt, and Vermigli by Noël Taillepied (or Talepied), a Capuchin of Pontoise.[4] Bolsec's account, although appended to it, had its own title page and a different printing address: *Histoire de la vie, moeurs, actes, constance et mort de Iean Calvin, iadis ministre de Geneue, recueilly par M. Hierosme Hermes Bolsec . . .* (Lyon: Jean Patrasson, 1577). Like Taillepied's anthology, it was dedicated to Pierre d'Espinac (1540–99), archbishop and count of Lyon and primate of France, who had links with the Holy Catholic League, the extreme Catholic party, led by the House of Guise. In his preface Bolsec shows full awareness of ancient biographical genre and his own distortion of it. Indeed, he admits that hostile biographies were not practiced in antiquity and that lawyers of the classical era preferred to exercise their rhetorical skills in their clients' defense rather than as attorneys for the prosecution. Of Cicero's extant prosecuting speeches, he singles out those against Verres, a governor of Sicily notorious for his avarice and lasciviousness.[5]

---

4. On Noël Taillepied, see his *Les antiquités et singularités de la ville de Pontoise: Réimpression de l'ouvrage de F. Noël Taillepied, lecteur en théologie des Cordeliers de cette ville; Edition revue et annotée sur les manuscrits des Archives de Pontoise et collationnée sur l'imprimé de 1587 par A. François. Précédée d'une notice biographique et bibliographique sur l'auteur par Henri le Charpentier* (Pontoise: A. Seyes; Paris: H. Champion, 1876).

5. The preface is included in the Latin translation of the *Life* of 1580 (*De Ioannis Calvini magni quondam Geneuensium ministri vita, moribus, rebus gestis ac denique morte: Historia ad reuerendissimum archiepiscopum et comitem Lugdunensem per Hieronymum Bolsecum medicum Lugdunensem conscripta et nunc ex gallico eius Parisiis impresso exemplari Latine reddita* (Coloniae [Cologne], apud Ludouicum Alectorium et haeredes Iacobi Soteris, anno 1580), 3–7 (hereafter, Bolsec, *Calvin*, 1580), but it disappears from later editions and translations. I have consulted the 1580 Latin version after ascertaining that it is a faithful rendering of the French original of 1577 (cf. 1577 pagination in parentheses).

As well as deviating from the antique biographical style, Bolsec knows that he is flouting the basic rhetorical rule of not speaking ill of the dead.[6] However, he considers that one way to avoid that accusation is to reinterpret the proverb "praise is to be bestowed after death" so as to mean "not that we should praise all men once they are dead but that men who did perform great and illustrious deeds in their lifetime should not be given excessive praise while still alive in order not to encourage adulation and more importantly because it is only at the end of their lives that we can say what they did that was good or bad."[7]

Bolsec feels that he thus justifies himself in the eyes of many people who will hold it against him that he "wanted to bring out into the open the many vicious deeds of John Calvin after his death," in contrast with Beza and his laudatory *Discours*.[8] He also cites Plato, according to whom "he who is immersed in sordid deeds and nonetheless passes for a good man and is elevated to the highest public position, wreaks more damage upon the common weal than all those citizens generally acknowledged as bad, of whom nothing is expected."[9]

He is the first of Calvin's hostile biographers to insist on the reformer's calamitous influence on France and on his role in the wanton destruction of his native country "and the neighboring lands." According to Bolsec, Calvin was directly responsible for turning countless simple souls away from the Roman Catholic Church. However, his real adversary is, as we already said, not so much Calvin as Beza. According to Bolsec, Beza dares to contend in the *Discours* that Calvin was more important and led a purer life than all the apostles, doctors, and their successors put together.[10] With its hagiographical tone, the *Discours* could have influenced some Catholic faithful to defect to the Protestant camp; hence comes Bolsec's determination to "counter Beza's lies."[11]

6. Bolsec, *Calvin*, 1580, 3: "Et surdo maledicendum etiam non esse vulgo iactatum prouerbium est, quod de absente vel de vita functo potest intelligi. Atque huc etiam pertinet quod non minus vulgo dicitur, nimirum vt post funera atque mortem laudes" (cf. 1577, 3–4: "C'est aussi un proverbe commun en la bouche de plusieurs qu'il ne faut medire d'vn sourd, par lequel mot se peut entendre l'absent et le passé de ce siècle").

7. Bolsec, *Calvin*, 1580, 3–4 (cf. 1577, 4). All translations are my own unless otherwise credited.

8. Bolsec, *Calvin*, 1580, 4 (cf. 1577, 4).

9. Ibid.

10. Bolsec, *Calvin*, 1580, 4–5 (cf. 1577, 4–5).

11. Bolsec, *Calvin*, 1580, 5: "Silentium abrumpere coactus sum vt eodem zelo atque spiritu qui me anno 1552 incitabat vt praesens praesenti in eo ipsi Geneuae coegerant

One obvious question arises at this point: why did Bolsec wait so long before publishing his *Life* of Calvin? He justifies the delay by claiming that he had planned to do this for some years but that God's ancient enemy had put all sorts of hindrances and impediments in his way so that the first opportune moment did not come until thirteen years after Calvin's death.[12] The moment was indeed well-chosen since it coincided with the time when France was at its weakest after the Seventh War of Religion, which ended with the Treaty of Bergerac in June 1577. It was also the time of hardening of positions. D'Espinac, who had links to the League and introduced Tridentine reforms in his diocese as well as having undoubted political influence (he was Henri III's ambassador to England), was the perfect dedicatee. Moreover, his claims to the contrary notwithstanding, Bolsec was seeking revenge not so much on Calvin himself but on his disciples who conspired to blacken his (Bolsec's) name. As he put it: "The followers and servants of the Calvinist sect have not only set all sorts of deadly traps against my person but have also waged and do to this day wage a war against me, aiming to make me the object of hate of everyone. Not only do they write vicious invectives against me and spread all sorts of rumors about me with various fabrications, . . . but they also secretly send clandestine letters against me to their comrades, as has frequently come to my knowledge."[13] What better way to counter his enemies and clear himself than to blacken the reputation of the leader of the Calvinist Reformation against whom he had stood out over twenty years previously?

On what sources is Bolsec's account based? He swears to their soundness; yet if we examine his statement, we see that he all but openly admits to relying on fabrication, rumor, and hearsay. This is how he describes them: "And I call the same God to witness that I am not aware of having written anything that goes against my knowledge of the facts and my conscience, but that what I write is based on truth.

---

coetu atque concilio palam resisterem etiam nunc permotus et instigatus manum calamo admouerem et Bezae me obuium obiicerem eiusque mendacia confutarem quibus in magnum diuinae gloriae praeiudicium et ad ecclesiae domus Dei euidentem, qui malitiosissimus Sathanae minister fuit, eum syncerum ac praecellentem Dei seruum fuisse asserere ac praedicare est ausus" (cf. 1577, 5).

12. Bolsec, *Calvin*, 1580, 5–6 (cf. 1577, 6–7).
13. Bolsec, *Calvin*, 1580, 6 (cf. 1577, 6).

I have taken it either from the official documents and accounts in Calvin's own hand or gained knowledge of it from the oral accounts of men of highest authority or saw it with my own eyes and touched it with my own hands."[14]

Bolsec's *Life* of Calvin falls into twenty-six chapters. As we saw, it is difficult to situate it in any genre, given that his intention is to write a purportedly historical account that flouts the convention of "not speaking ill of the dead," for which no literary models were established. In practice, Bolsec anticipates the accusation of "speaking ill of the dead" by situating Calvin in the long line of heresies going back to the Sadducees and the Pharisees and continuing in an unbroken line to Calvin's Geneva. By definition, within the Christian tradition, a heretic—and even less a heresiarch—dead or alive could not be portrayed in a favorable light. He had to be persuasive, hypocritical, acting for his own glory while leading numerous souls to perdition, an ignoble life that ended fittingly with an ignoble death.

Bolsec therefore opens his work with an extremely superficial and brief account of ancient heresies, Jewish and Christian, without worrying too much about the chronological order.

He presents Calvin as the reincarnation of all heresies, an impersonal tool of the devil rather than a consenting accomplice. Like Beza in his *Discours*, he concentrates on the reformer's morals, actions, and death on one hand and his doctrine on the other, achieving the obverse effect to Beza. Bolsec's *Life* is of special importance because it is the origin of several completely unfounded rumors about Calvin. Although those were to be refuted soon enough by the Protestant and the Catholic camps, they nonetheless played an important part in generating a certain image of Calvin and Geneva that proved extremely tenacious. Indeed, Bolsec's work encountered considerable success if we go just by the number of editions and translations it received at the time. The French version was published simultaneously in Lyon and

---

14. Bolsec, *Calvin*, 1580, 5: "Iam hoc quoque eundum testor Deum nihil me hoc tractatu complexum quod contra meam conscientiam scriptum esse mihi conscius sim, sed quae scribo, omnia veritate niti et vel ex tabula ac testimoniis ea me manu ipsius Calvini conscriptis desumpsisse vel referentibus maximae auctoritatis viris cognouisse vel meis oculis conspexisse manuque palpasse" (cf. 1577, 5–6: "Semblablement que je n'escry chose aucune en ce traicté qui soit contre ma conscience, mais selon verité approuvée par tesmoignages d'escrits de la main mesme d'iceluy Caluin: par relaticn de personnages dignes de foy et selon que j'ay veu de mes yeux et touché de ma main").

in Paris in 1577 and reprinted in Paris in 1582. It was translated word for word into Latin by an anonymous translator in 1580 and 1582 and published in Cologne. James Laing, Scottish doctor of the Paris Faculty of Theology, incorporated the Latin version, with some revisions as well as considerable additions and marginalia, into his *Vitae haereticorum* published in Paris in 1581 and 1585. As the example of *Histoire des trois principaux hérétiques* shows, it was also the Bolsec account of Calvin that was included in French-language Catholic biographical anthologies of the late sixteenth and early seventeenth centuries. The work's existence in Latin from 1580 onward also meant that it could be and was translated into other vernacular languages. The German translation appeared in 1580 and was reprinted in 1581 and 1631, Dutch translation was published in 1581, and a Polish version came out in 1583. Although rapidly discredited, the book continued to be printed in Catholic circles until 1875.

As has been shown by other sixteenth- and particularly seventeenth-century Catholic biographers, Bolsec's account of Calvin's youth conflates at least two people from Noyon called Jean Cauvin.[15] To this conflation he adds a certain amount of rumor and fiction to give his reader a full portrait of Calvin's iniquitous youth, the hallmark of any heretic. Bolsec further claims that as a young cleric in Noyon, Calvin was convicted of sodomy, a crime for which he would have been burned at the stake if the sentence had not been commuted at the last moment to branding with a fleur-de-lis on the shoulder. Under the weight of this opprobrium, according to our biographer, Calvin sold his benefices and left for Germany and Ferrara. In this account, his morals never improved. Not content with the charge of sodomy, considered a heresy in itself, Bolsec accuses the reformer of having intercourse with most of Geneva's married women under the cover of pastoral guidance. Although admitting that he has no proof of the reformer's promiscuity, Bolsec weaves together rumors circulated by "several people of sound judgment" and calculated to make Calvin appear as the local lecher and his home as a seat of depravity. Interestingly enough, he makes no mention of the reformer's marriage.

---

15. Cf. also Théophile Dufour, "Calviniana," in *Mélanges offerts à M. Émile Picot, membre de l'Institut, par ses amis et élèves* (Paris: Librairie Damascène Morgand, 1913), 1–16, esp. 13–16.

What may seem surprising is not so much the fact that Bolsec accuses Calvin of sexual depravity but that his image of the reformer encountered success even though he openly admitted that he founded it on rumors. However, his aim was basically to contradict Beza's *Discours*. Whereas Beza praised Calvin's chastity and austerity, Bolsec charged him with total licentiousness. To Beza's praises of the reformer's zeal and capacity for hard work, Bolsec opposes an obsessive interest with the rewriting of one work, in itself a proof of inconstancy. Where Calvin's successor expounded on Calvin's marriage as a model of what a pious marriage should be, the ex-Carmelite does not even advert to it in his treatment of Calvin as the local seducer of married women. Whereas Beza praised Calvin's good death, Bolsec has him die a miserable death in solitude, as behooves a heresiarch who embodied all early heresies. While Beza exalted Calvin's kindness to heretics, Bolsec has him bear the entire responsibility for the death of Servetus, a myth that turned out to have an astonishingly long life despite many attempts to disprove it. When he reacted against Beza's *Discours* with his *Life of Calvin*, Bolsec did not know Beza's 1575 *Life*, in which Calvin's successor explicitly lays down criteria for truthfulness in writing biography.[16]

Had Beza decided to lay down these criteria in 1564, Bolsec's job would have been much more difficult. As it was, however, Beza's first *Discours* seemed to augur the birth of exaggeratedly laudatory Calvinist hagiography, an impression that Beza and Colladon strove to wipe out with their subsequent attempts at the Genevan reformer's biography. Bolsec's *Life*, which constituted a response to Beza's first *Discours*, inevitably assumed the form of a sort of upside-down saint's *Life*. All he had to do was critique where Beza praised. As we shall see, other biographies of Calvin, notably that of Jean-Papire Masson, were oriented using quite different criteria.

François Bauduin as Source for Calvin's Biography: The *Vita Calvini* of Jean-Papire Masson

Although Bolsec nowadays is something of a household name in matters of biography hostile to Calvin, he was by no means the

16. See Gardy, *Bibliographie*, no. 200, p. 119.

biographer who was taken the most seriously by the Catholic or the Protestant camps in the seventeenth and eighteenth centuries. Curiously, Jean-Papire Masson's Latin *Vita Calvini* has not been the object of study since Pierre Ronzy's biography of Masson, which appeared in 1924.[17] Ronzy devotes just a couple of pages to the work, noting in passing the possible influence of Bauduin on Masson.

To appreciate fully the significance and orientation of Masson's work, a brief presentation of both him and Bauduin is necessary.

François Bauduin (1520–73) has been an object of studies in fairly recent years and is the better known of the two. He therefore requires a minimal introduction.[18] Son of a Flemish lawyer, he studied law at Louvain at the time when *mos gallicus* (French custom of interpreting Roman law) was introduced. He became a disciple of Calvin in 1545 and was his private secretary in 1546–47.

Unlike many of Calvin's French disciples, Bauduin did not settle in Geneva; he left for Lyon in the autumn of 1547, never to return. In 1548 he went to Bourges as professor of law and stayed there until 1555, when he fell victim to quarrels between the *mos gallicus* and the *mos italicus* camps. At the same time he began to voice his irenic views and to criticize Calvin's lack of tolerance for religious positions other than his own. He spent some time in Strasbourg, where he encountered Vermigli, Sleidan, Jean Sturm, and others.

In 1556 Bauduin was appointed professor of law at Heidelberg, and during his years there (1556–61) he produced his most important works on history, law, and religious tolerance.[19] He left Heidelberg in 1561, when the Elector Friedrich III officially went over to Calvinist faith, and by May 30 of that year was back in Paris. His conflict with Calvin broke out well and truly over the publication of George Cassander's *De officio pii viri*, a plea for the via media in religion.[20]

In 1563 Bauduin returned to the bosom of the Roman Catholic Church. After some time spent in Paris and in the Netherlands, he

17. Pierre Ronzy, *Un humaniste italianisant: Papire Masson (1544–1611)* (Paris: Édouard Champion, 1924).

18. See Michael Erbe, *François Bauduin (1520–1573): Biographie eines Humanisten* (Gütersloh: Mohn, 1978); and Mario Turchetti, *Concordia o Toleranza? François Bauduin e i Moyenneurs* (Geneva: Droz, 1984).

19. See Erbe, *François Bauduin*, 103–22, 210–24.

20. See ibid., 140–44.

joined the University of Angers in 1569 as professor of law. Here he had Papire Masson among his students. He held the post until 1573, the year of his death.

Though Bauduin's relations with Calvin show that one would hardly expect him to be a source of information favorable to the reformer, we should weigh this against Bauduin's view of history, which would have influenced Papire Masson as much as or more than the personal issue of his mentor's relations with the Genevan reformer. According to Gregory Lyon, Bauduin thought that in historical research it would not do to rely on the authority of the testimonies to determine the fact. Rather, the fact itself had to be interrogated by the testimonies available. In this way a historian could establish the reliability of testimonies.[21] Bauduin was also a firm believer in the principle of the *similitudo temporum*, the capacity of historical situations, if correctly analyzed and studied in context, to yield a message that would make history instructive for the future. He saw the age of Constantine as providing an answer to the religious conflict of his own era and argued that Charles V should follow Constantine's example and convoke an ecumenical council. One would thus expect a disciple of Bauduin to pay close attention to sources as elucidating facts and to espouse the *similitudo temporum* principle.

Masson was born in 1544, son of a merchant family in Forez. After a period of classical study in Lyon, he joined the Jesuit order and spent four years studying theology in Rome and Naples. On his return he broke with the Jesuits and theology and took a post for teaching philosophy at the Collège du Plessis in Paris. At about that time Masson acquired as patron Philippe Hurault de Cheverny, chancellor of the duke of Anjou, who in 1569 obtained the chair of law for him at the University of Angers. According to Christophe de Thou's *Life* of Masson,[22] Masson and Bauduin got to know each other in Paris before the latter's departure for Angers. They remained in correspondence during 1570 and 1571, when Masson could finally join Bauduin and become his student.[23] According to Ronzy

21. See Gregory B. Lyon, "Bauduin, Flacius, and the Plan for the Magdeburg Centuries," *Journal of the History of Ideas* (2003): 253–72, esp. 265n43.

22. See Ronzy, *Un humaniste italianisant*, 124n1.

23. This correspondence is no longer extant. See ibid., 124–25n4. For a full bibliography of Masson's printed and MS works, see Ronzy, *Bibliographie critique des œuvres imprimées et manuscrites de Papire Masson, thèse complémentaire pour le doctorat* (Paris: Édouard Champion, 1924).

and Erbe,[24] it was under Bauduin's influence that Masson finally gave his preference to history and began to aspire to combining his theological and historical knowledge and method with the study of law.

There are several indications that Bauduin's approach to history and biography influenced Masson, judging by the excerpts of their lost correspondence that Masson cites in his *Historia calamitatum Galliae*, written in 1600 but not published until 1636. Bauduin was especially concerned to draw his disciple's attention to the importance of weighing sources in forming historical judgments. He expressly warned Masson against works such as the three imperial panegyrics of Sidonius Apollinaris, which he considered as suspect in matters of historical accuracy, just as Cicero thought funeral orations to be suspect.[25]

His extant literary production shows Masson to have been first and foremost a biographer[26] of antique and contemporary scholars, writers, philosophers, statesmen, and others. Among his best-known works are his *Elogia* (eulogies) of various figures, some of which were published singly before being anthologized posthumously by Jean-Baptiste Masson, the author's brother. More important, however, Masson was probably the first early modern author to make a distinction between a biography (*Vita*) and an *Elogium* (posthumous praise in declamatory form). His *Vitae* tended to contain remarks (not necessarily on the hero) that would not do in an *Elogium*, a discourse sharply focused on the hero and composed of undiluted praise. A good example here is the contrast between his portrayal of Christophe de Thou in the *Elogium* on him and in the *Vita Caroli Molinaei*. In the former, de Thou comes across as a model of kindness to his lawyers. In the *Vita Molinaei*, on the other hand, Masson mentions that as president of the *parlément de Paris*, de Thou was prone to brief and quickly regretted outbursts of bad temper.[27]

Masson's *Vita Calvini*, despite Ronzy's insistence to the contrary,[28] is something of an "odd man out" since it is his sole biographical work

24. Erbe, *François Bauduin*, 129; Ronzy, *Un humaniste italianisant*, 124–25n2.

25. See Ronzy, *Un humaniste italianisant*, 125nn1–2. For Cicero on funeral orations, see Cicero's *Oration* 2.84.341.

26. Ronzy, *Bibliographie*, shows that most of Masson's literary production consisted of biographies of some kind.

27. See also Ronzy, *Un humaniste italianisant*, 312n3.

28. Ibid., 313–15.

devoted to a religious adversary. Masson composed it in 1583, during his last years in Paris, after he had had ample opportunity to gather information on the reformer from the late Bauduin. However, it was not published until nine years after his death, by his brother Jean-Baptiste Masson, who added some information on Calvin's year in Angoulême and a very short postface. The work itself is also very short, thirty-four small (ca. 3 × 4 inches) pages in octavo format (eight leaves per gathering produces sixteen pages), and copies of it are scarce.[29] We do not know its original imprint, but we do know that it largely escaped the attention of most theologians and historians who took an interest in Calvin's life.[30] Jean-Baptiste Masson was opposed to incorporating the *Vita* in the full edition of his brother's *Elogia* that he was planning. However, he never carried out his plan for the edition of eulogies, and they did not come out as a collection until 1638. This edition was the work of the bibliophile Jean Balesdens. Balesdens did not distinguish between *Elogium* and *Vita* any more than had Jean-Baptiste Masson, and so he collected both types of writing under the heading of *Elogia*. He was persuaded to include the *Vita Calvini* by Gui Patin (1601–72), the well-known physician and man of letters, of libertine persuasion, who was professor at the Collège Royal de France from 1655. The publisher, who found himself under pressure from the Jesuits, put up opposition, but Patin and Balesdens got their way.

Given the situation, Jean-Baptiste Masson's postface was excised; only his appendix on Calvin's passage in Angoulême was maintained. The *Vita* thus appeared with Jean-Papire Masson's name but without any hint of its ideological orientation. As early as 1656, Masson's authorship was put in doubt, and the text was henceforth attributed frequently (but not invariably) to the Gallican Jacques Gillot.[31] Among

29. I have used the copy held by the Bibliothèque de Sainte Geneviève in Paris (shelfmark: 4Q 897 [3] Inv. 358): Jean-Papire Masson, *Vita Ioannis Calvini auctore Papirio Massono* (Lutetiae [Paris], 1620).

30. See Ronzy, *Un humaniste italianisant*, 635–36.

31. *Cl. viri Jo. Papirii Massonis, . . . Elogiorum pars prima, quae imperatorum, regum, ducum, aliorumque insignium heroüm . . . vitam complectitur Accessit ipsius P. Massonis vita, authore . . . Jacobo Augusto Thuano. . . . Omnia haec . . . e musaeo Joan. Balesdens, . . . Cl. viri Jo. Papirii Massonis, . . . Elogiorum pars secunda, quae vitam eorum complectitur qui . . . dignitatum titulis vel eruditionis laude . . . claruerunt. [Accesserunt Simonis Pietrei patris, doctoris medici parisiensis, elogium, auctore G. Patin, et Vita Johannis Calvini, auctore J. Gillot.]* Omnia haec . . . e musaeo Joan. Balesdens, . . . Parisiis, apud S. Huré: 1656.

seventeenth- and eighteenth-century historians, Pierre Bayle particularly[32] questioned this outright and attributed the *Vita* correctly on the
basis of internal evidence. The reason for the widespread misattribution
was partly the seventeenth-century image (shared by Bayle) of Jean-
Papire Masson as a conservative Catholic who could not possibly have
written an objective *Life* of Calvin. Without Jean-Baptiste's caveat, the
text seemed to suggest that Jacques Gillot, editor of the *Traictez des
droits de l'Eglise gallicane* and coauthor of the *Satire ménipée*, was a
much more likely author. The misunderstanding was finally dispelled
in 1913 by Théophile Dufour, who discovered a copy of the 1620 edition with Jean-Baptiste's postface.[33]

This is how the latter closes his brother's *Vita Calvini*:

> Having collected as many *Elogia* or *Vitae* of famous men and women
> written once upon a time by my brother, I would like to publish them
> shortly as a collection. However, I thought it most inappropriate to
> include in that collection his *Life* of Calvin in nineteen chapters lest the
> pious and Catholic reader take offense at the unpleasant odor or rather
> stink that exudes from it. For this reason I am sending it to Calvin's
> fellow-citizens and comrades who inhabit the region of the Lake Leman,
> which the Swiss call the "Genfer-See," so that the memory of him can
> drown and perish. I shall add just a few facts about him that I learned
> from several authoritative and rather aged citizens of Angoulême when
> I served there as a canon.[34]

Jean-Baptiste Masson obviously did not fully understand his
brother's distinction between *Elogium* and *Vita*. Also, he made it
quite clear that he did not publish the *Vita* to either praise or blame
the reformer but to bury his reputation in the waters of Lake Leman.

32. See Pierre Bayle, *Dictionnaire historique et critique*, 5th ed. (Amsterdam, n.p.,
1740), 19, s.v. "Calvin."

33. See Dufour, "Calviniana," 1n1.

34. Masson, *Vita Ioannis Calvini* (1620), 33: "Collectis quamplurimis illustrium vir-
orum ac foeminarum vitis seu elogiis a fratre meo olim scriptis eas in lucem breui mittere
cupio. Vitam autem Ioannis Calvini haeresiarchae 19 capita continentem operi miscendam
minime duxi ne pius ac catholicus lector ingrato quodam odore aut foetore offendatur.
Idcirco eam mitto ad conciues suos segreges lacum Lemanum inhabitantes quem Heluetii
'Genfer Zee' vocant vt ibi demergatur pereatque memoria eius. De quo pauca referam
quae dum canonicus essem ecclesiae Engolismensis a pluribus ciuibus, senioribus scilicet
et doctis accepi."

There is no record of the 1620 edition making any impact on seventeenth-century Geneva, and as we said, whatever the number of copies printed, it had apparently disappeared from booksellers' shops by 1638. During the seventeenth and eighteenth centuries, it became as popular among Catholics as among Calvinists and seems for a while to have enjoyed the status of the sole authoritative biography of the reformer. Even more interestingly, most of those who cited it between 1620 and 1650 tended to attribute it to Masson without going into the finer points of the question of authorship. Some of these writers obviously still had access to the 1620 edition. Most, however, relied on the text in the 1638 edition of Masson's *Elogia*. How does it differ from the standard hostile Calvin biographies of the period, and what does it tell us about the author's use of sources and Bauduin's possible role?

As Jean-Baptiste Masson says, the *Vita* is divided into eighteen short chapters plus a conclusion. Jean-Papire did not append a preface worthy of the name, just one prefatory sentence: "It is important to make the life of John Calvin publicly known so that posterity may know what sort of man was he who challenged the authority of the Roman Church and who came close to overturning ancestral faith in France."[35]

He then subdivides the *Life* into the following chapters: Calvin's ancestry and home; his birth and childhood; his studies in the liberal disciplines; his departure from Paris; exile; his departure to Italy, Geneva, and Germany; his activities in Germany; return to Geneva; his activities in Geneva; his writings; his adversaries; the harm he did to his native country; his death and burial; his will; his morality; his vices and reproaches made to him; some of his sayings; his virtues; conclusion. Within this framework, four features characterize the *Vita* and point to Bauduin as inspiration. One is Masson's quite careful evaluation of his sources and unhesitating dismissal of some of them (e.g., Bolsec and other "authores plebeii") as unreliable. Another is his awareness of the usefulness of publishing Calvin's *Life* so that posterity can learn from it according to the "similitudo temporum [resemblance of times]"

---

35. Masson, *Vita Ioannis Calvini* (1620), 3: "Vitam Ioannis Calvini mandari literis publice interest vt posteri sciant a quo homine oppugnata Romanae ecclesiae dignitas ac pene euersa religio maiorum in Gallia fuit."

principle. The third is the frequent mention of Bauduin as source. The fourth is Masson's portrayal of Calvin as a tyrannical, vindictive, and bad-tempered despot, an image he would have inherited directly from his former teacher, Bauduin. However, unlike a modern biographer, Masson does not cite his sources with any precision. He gives no specific references to documents consulted.

We are not told where he obtained the very detailed and exact information about Calvin's studies, any more than who informed him about Calvin's movements until 1536 and his arrival in Geneva, or about his exile in Strasbourg and the rest of his career. The only sources Masson mentions *explicitly* are Calvin's own works (of which he shows very thorough and impartial knowledge, which cannot be anything other than firsthand), and François Bauduin, who is mentioned as a source no fewer than eight times in what is a quite short text. These references are sufficiently detailed to throw a light on Bauduin as Masson's main source or at least one of his main sources, as the following examples illustrate:

1. Sensation-seeking writers reproach him with worldly pleasures and debauchery. However, no one seems to have hated adultery more than he, even though his own family was not immune to it. For adultery was the reason why Antoine his brother took a second wife, even though his first wife, whom he divorced, was still alive, and Calvin and his colleagues approved the divorce.[36] And Bauduin taxed Calvin with this . . .[37]

2. Although he appeared modest and disposed to expose his thoughts simply, the appearance concealed pride and self-love. This is a vice that all founders of sects are prone to, regardless of whether the sect is good or bad. Therefore Bauduin says quite rightly: "Your colleagues complain about your arrogance and unbelievable haughtiness."[38]

36. For full account of the adultery involving Calvin's sister-in-law, see Robert Kingdon, *Adultery and Divorce in Calvin's Geneva* (Cambridge, MA: Harvard University Press, 1995), 71–97.
37. Masson, *Vita Ioannis Calvini* (1620), 25–26: "Antonius enim Calvini frater ob eam [26] causam, viuente priore vxore quam repudiauit, alteram duxit, Calvino et collegis repudium probantibus. Quod ei Balduinus obiicit."
38. Ibid., 26: "Facie cum modesta videretur ad omnemque simplicis animi figuram compositus, tegebat latentem intus superbiam et filautian. Quo vitio sectarum auctores carere nequeunt, seu bonae seu malae sint. Itaque non immerito Balduinus ait: 'Collegae tui conqueruntur de tua intolerabili arrogantia et incredibili fastu.' "

3. [Many writers reproach Calvin with having pretended to raise from the dead a man who was in fact alive.] I find it amazing that he should have done such a thing, seeing as he had already written what follows in the preface to his Institutes: "They are wicked who demand miracles from us. For we are not forging a new gospel but maintaining the very one whose authority rests on what was done by Christ and the apostles." As for the false miracle, whether there is any substance to it or not, both Lutherans and Catholics have reproached Calvin and his disciples with it. But Bauduin, who after all was hostile to Calvin, never accused him of it, and he certainly would not have omitted it, had he known for certain that Calvin had done such a thing.[39]

Despite the absence of chapter-and-verse references, Masson's account shows that, apart from Calvin's and Bauduin's works, he had knowledge of all the hostile biographies or biographical notices of Calvin and also of Beza's and Colladon's biographies, which would be the most likely source for the summary he gives of Calvin's will. Given his indebtedness to Bauduin, Masson inevitably inherits Bauduin's perception of Calvin as a cruel, arrogant, tyrannical, hard-working insomniac. However, because of his reliance on Bauduin and Bauduin's historiographical method, he also does away with a large number of myths about Calvin much more authoritatively than Beza or Colladon did in their more-or-less idealized accounts. At the same time, be it under Bauduin's influence or simply on the basis of his own reading, Masson does lavish a certain amount of approval on the reformer, as we shall see. He concludes his account by saying: "We have given this account of Calvin's life as neither his friend nor his foe. I will not be lying if I say that he was the ruin and destruction of France. If only he had died in childhood or had never been born. For he brought so much ill to his country that it is legitimate to hate and detest his origins."[40]

39. Ibid., 27–28: "Id quomodo ab eo factum sit miror, cum locum illum in praefatione Institutionis christianae pridem scripserit: 'Et quod miracula a nobis postulant improbe faciunt. Non enim recens aliquod [28] Euangelium cudimus sed illud ipsum retinemus cuius confirmandae veritati seruiunt omnia quae umquam et Christus et Apostoli ediderunt.' Illud tamen, siue verum est siue ab aliquo confictum versum est in fabulam, Lutheranique et Catholici id veluti gestum deinceps et Calvino et discipulis eius obiecere. Quod ne Balduinus quidem, Calvino infensus, vnquam obiecit, non obmissurus profecto si gestum scire potuisset."

40. Ibid., 31–32: "Conclusio. Haec de vita Calvini scribimus neque amici neque inimici, quem si labem et perniciem Galliae dixero, nihil mentiar. Atque vtinam aut nunquam natus

Although negative, to say the least, once the reader has understood that the mentioned "ill" refers to the French Wars of Religion (1562–98), this judgment turns out to have nothing especially Roman Catholic about it and could well express the opinion of Bauduin or any advocate of the via media.

The Profile of Masson's *Vita Calvini*

What then is the ideological profile of the *Vita Calvini*, and how does it differ from the standard Roman Catholic image of Calvin propagated by Bolsec and others? First and foremost, Masson ignores the myth of branding and substitutes for it the well-supported account of Calvin's brother Charles's unfortunate end (excommunication).[41] He devotes some attention to Calvin's Parisian period and lavishes a certain amount of praise on the care he took to learn Greek, Latin, and Hebrew. He considers as "elegantissimi" Calvin's comments on Seneca's *De clementia*, published in 1532. Although he underlines the anti-Roman tone of the first edition of the *Institutes*, he does not see it as impious or blasphemous and, in contrast with Bolsec, does not think that the endless revisions it underwent argue for inconstancy in religious matters. On the contrary he points out: "In the *Institutes*, often augmented and published for a thousand times, he devotes 104 chapters to rejecting most of the teaching we receive from the Roman Church, but he also strikes down the errors of Servetus and his like and refutes very astutely the impious baptismal teaching of the Anabaptists."[42]

Again in contrast with Bolsec, Masson does not see Calvin's first sojourn in Geneva as a seditious attempt to overthrow civil powers.

---

esset aut in pueritia mortuus. [32] Tantum enim malorum intulit in patriam vt cunabula eius merito detestari atque odisse debeas."

41. Ibid., 5: "Is patris concilio ecclesiastico ordini destinabatur vt Carolus eius frater et presbyter qui Nouioduni mortuus noctu et clam sepultus est et inter quatuor columnas furcae publicae quia eucharistiam sumere noluerat. Et duo sacerdotia quae habebat Ioanni Calvino affini suo et presbytero dari conferrique procurauit; parociam scilicet Pontis Episcopalis—sic enim Nouiomenses appellant vicinum vrbis suae oppidum ad Oesiam amnem situm—et capellam beatae Mariae Virginis de Partu, vulgo de la Gesine, in templo Virginis Maximo ad Leanam Ostii chori deseruiri solitam."

42. Ibid., 11: "Illa Institutione saepe aucta et millies excusa capitibus 104 magnam partem receptae a Romana et Catholica ecclesia doctrinae reiicit, obruit quoque Seruetianos errores et Anabaptistarum impias de baptismo sententias acutissime refellit."

Although he does describe him (not unjustly) as a "self-styled theologian," he attributes Calvin's and Farel's expulsion simply to the desire on part of the community to restore ancestral worship and rituals, which had been abolished only recently.[43]

His description of Calvin's activity in Strasbourg is equally impartial. He correctly reports that, thanks to Bucer, "the great defender of Lutherans," Calvin was given the freedom of the city and that his job was to look after the French-speaking congregation. Masson is not averse to recognizing that Calvin's fame at that time began to spread throughout "Germany," especially after the publication of his *Commentary on Romans*, which he dedicated to Simon Grynaeus, "eruditissimus Germanorum." He is full of praise for Calvin's converting work among the city's Anabaptists ("genus hominum superstitionis nouae et maleficae"), including the first husband of Idelette de Bure, Calvin's future wife.[44]

Equally sound and impartial is his account of Calvin's return to Geneva after the failure of the opposition. He stresses that the establishment of ecclesiastical discipline was the reformer's first and foremost concern, but he does not mention the Sadolet affair presumably because he had no knowledge of it.[45]

Masson's judgment on Calvin's writings and his style are particularly interesting as being probably the only impartial literary judgment we have by a near-contemporary humanist and man of letters who had good knowledge of Calvin's early education and who considered his commentary on Seneca as "extremely elegant." He does not criticize any of the reformer's literary production, and he echoes Beza's judgment on Calvin's capacity for hard work: "Practically not a day went by when he did not preach to the citizens. Three times a week for as

43. Ibid., 12–13: "Diu vero in Italia esse non potuit, ne forte agnitus ad supplicium religionis causa raperetur etsi clericum sacerdoti inseruientem agebat. Igitur per Pennas Alpes in Galliam reuersus Geneuae ad lacum Lemanum pedem fixit, precibus G'i Farelli qui veteribus sacris muncipio illo fugatis, nouos ritus introducere coeperat.

"Ibi Christiani theologi nomen adeptus, intermissum Catechismi vsum reuocauit, hac ratione et facili methodo simul docens persuadensque elementa ac principia nascentis sectae. At vero enata inter ciues discordia sententiis dictis, Farellus Caluinusque vrbe excedere iubentur cupientibus quibusdam reuocare ritus et ceremonias maiorum, non multo ante depulsas. Caluinus secundum exul Basileam, mox Argenti [13] nam se contulit quae est ciuitas Galliae ad Rhenum flumen."

44. Ibid., 13–14.

45. Ibid., 15–16.

long as he lived, he lectured in theology. He was industrious and always active, writing or planning something. He used to reread the works of Cicero once a year, although his style does not resemble that of Cicero in any way. Rather, he seems to have imitated Tacitus and Seneca and the ancient theologians."[46]

Although a humanist such as Masson would certainly regard the Ciceronian ideal as something to strive for, his remark on the resemblance between Calvin's Latin and that of the later Roman writers has the merit of being correct and should not be seen as a criticism. Indeed, as the following paragraph shows, Masson was fully aware of the strengths of Calvin's style: "He wrote as much and as well as any secretary, if we consider the quantity, the conciseness, the sting, the rhetorical stress, the vigor of expression. He published commentaries on nearly all the books of the Old and the New Testament. However, out of all his books he particularly recommended his treatise the *Institutes of the Christian Religion*, and he also boasted that his commentaries on the Minor Prophets would always be considered as good as any patristic commentary."[47]

In the chapter on Calvin's adversaries, he notes the reformer's outstanding polemical gifts. More interesting to us are his remarks on Servetus since they show that neither Masson nor (we surmise) Bauduin disapproved of the execution:

Another of his adversaries was Michael Servetus, a Spaniard by race who impiously compared the Trinity to Cerberus. When he came to Geneva, he was arrested and burned at the stake. Calvin wrote a remarkable book on the errors of this individual of infinite viciousness, and he includes a very brief summary of his observations on this in book one of the *Institutes of the Christian Religion*. Catholics taxed Calvin with this

46. Ibid.: "Nulla fere dies praeteriit, qua non ha [16] buerit concionem ad ciues de rebus sacris. Ter in octiduo quamdiu vixit theologiam professus est, operosus et semper aliquid scribens ac moliens Ciceronisque Opera quotannis relegens etsi stylus eius nihil minus quam Ciceronem sapuit. Tacitum enim et Senecam potius et veteres theologos imitari videtur."

47. Ibid., 16–17: "Scripsit nec pauciora nec minus bene quam segregus quisquam, si numerum, si breuitatem, si aculeos, si emphasin, si argutias spectare volumus. Extant eius Commentarii ad omnes fere veteres ac Noui Testamenti libros. Caeterum ex omnibus scriptis Opus de Institutione christianae religionis praecipue commendabat et gloriabatur ad minores Prophetas quos ediderat Commentarios nullis [17] patrum interpretationibus vnquam cessuros."

issue and affirmed that he, Calvin, was thus justly punished as an enemy of the gospel for having abandoned the religion of his forefathers.[48]

Masson does not use Servetus's execution to tax Calvin with cruelty, despotism, arrogance, and so forth. Yet as a matter of course, he is, as we shall see, quite liberal with examples of all these vices, relying on information provided by Bauduin. More interesting, he does not automatically suppose, in contrast to most of his Catholic contemporaries, that the Reformation entailed the rise of heresies such as antitrinitarianism.

However, this absence of standard invective does not make Masson into a totally objective biographer. His chief aim, as we said, is to draw his countrymen's attention to all the ills that Calvin brought to France. This is why an entire section is titled "Caluinus quantum nocuit patriae [The harm Calvin did to his native country]." According to Masson, Calvin's harmfulness consisted initially in the persuasiveness of his propaganda and his capacity to disseminate it. As might be expected from a disciple of Bauduin, it is not the issue of corruption of the innocent faithful or their damnation in large numbers that preoccupies Masson. The Wars of Religion are the real ill that Calvin brought to France.

Masson notes that Calvin's works first began to circulate in France in the reign of Henry II despite a ban on them, for "the greed of peddlers was responsible for procuring them in large quantities." That meant that educated people read them, were converted, and in their turn influenced the unlearned. Masson finds Calvin's errors infinitely greater and more harmful than those of Berengarius, whose teaching in any case gained few disciples, unlike Calvin's doctrines. He sees the role of Antoine de Navarre during the reign of Charles IX as definitely

---

48. Ibid., 17–18: "Horum plurimi quidem aduersus eum scripsere, nemo tamen pari grauitate scribendi pondereque verborum et aculeis ad eius principia respondisse visus est. Pighium ipse de libero arbitrio disserentem et Sadoletum pene terruit. Ipsi silentium Balduinus Iurisconcultus imposuit seni, magno dolore Calvini quem ille patrem et praeceptorem saepenumero appellasset. Aduersarium quoque habuit Michaelem Seruetum genere Hispanum. Hic Trinitatem cerbero impie comparans, Geneuam cum venisset, comprehensus atque igni crematus est. De erroribus tam scelerati hominis librum singularem [18] scripsit Caluinus, idemque summam speculationum eius breuissime complectitur lib. 1 de Institutione Christianae religionis. Hoc exemplum Catholici Calvino obiecere vt assererent non iniuria punitum quasi hostem Euangelii qui defectionem a veteribus sacris antea fecisset."

a low point in this process. Among other things, it resulted in several of Calvin's ministers arriving in France, especially Beza ("a poet turned theologian").[49] Although, according to Masson, Calvin himself could not come precisely because he wanted to avoid the burning of his ministers and his own death, things turned out otherwise: "For an incredible number of people turned out to hear Beza and his associates, armed defense of the sect was mounted, and a civil war broke out bloodier than any France had ever seen."[50]

Unlike all other biographers of the period, Masson is not at all interested in whether Calvin's death was "good" or "bad." He categorically asserts that Calvin never sought personal advancement or financial gain and echoes Beza's point about the reformer never seeking rich patrons, despite the fact that he was in touch with many heads of state. He is equally categorical in affirming (against Bolsec) that Calvin did not defect from the Roman Catholic Church because he wanted to constitute himself as head of his own church, but because he genuinely disagreed with the Roman religion over the number and nature of the sacraments, worshiping (or honoring) images, rituals, and biblical interpretation.[51]

Although Masson's *Life* of Calvin did not displace Bolsec's among the Catholics or Beza's among the Protestants, it certainly dented the

49. He is referring to the period 1560–62 and the events that terminated in the outbreak of the first War of Religion in September 1562. On the role of Beza as councillor to the vacillating Protestant Antoine de Bourbon, king of Navarre, on the increase in the numbers of Protestant parishes in France, and on the outbreak of the first War of Religion see, e.g., Alain Dufour, "Théodore de Bèze," in *Histoire littéraire de la France*, vol. 42 (Paris: distributed by de Boccard, 2002), 359–77. See ibid., 359–72, for analysis of 1561–62 as the period when Protestantism was a "fashionable" religion in France.

50. Masson, *Vita Ioannis Calvini* (1620), 19–20: "Aliter tamen accidit et valde praeter opinionem piorum hominum. Incredibili enim numero concursus factus ad audiendum Bezam et socios, parata arma ad defensionem sectae exortique motus ciulis belli quo nullum vnquam funestius in Gallia fuit."

51. Ibid., 24–25: "Et timidum fuisse natura ipse non negat, intrepidum tamen sese exhibuit in magnis reipublicae negotiis ac bis terue in graui discordia ciuium per strictos enses nudus penetrans voce ac vultu seditiones sedauit. Deferebant ei collegae et discipuli vt doctori suo. Munera ipse publica neque ambiit neque aliis inuidit, contentus ea laude quam docendo [25] scribendoque ad principes, ad reges consequi poterat. Scribebat enim vltro magnis principibus non expectata occasione scribendi nec responso quo illum raro honorarunt, neque defectionem tam a papa fecit vt alibi maior fieret, quam quod de numero reque sacramentorum, de imaginibus, ceremoniis, ritibus, interpretatione verbi Dei et similibus aliter sentiebat."

credibility of both accounts. It is not without significance that the first objective *Life* of the reformer was so heavily marked by Bauduin's method and by the latter's knowledge and perception of Calvin.

Post-Masson Views of Calvin: Catholic Images of Calvin in the Seventeenth Century

Although the accounts I shall be examining do not fall within the literary genres of *Vitae* or *Elogia*, they are of some importance as they illustrate the rise and fall of a more-critical approach to Calvin in some French Catholic circles in the seventeenth century. I have chosen Desmay, Le Vasseur, and Richelieu as some of the most distinctive Catholic authors who best illustrate this.

Jacques Desmay

There is very little information available about Jacques Desmay, who was vicar general of François de Harlay, archbishop of Rouen, dean of the collegiate church of Notre Dame d'Escouys, and doctor of theology of the Sorbonne. He authenticated a miraculous healing in 1618 and sanctioned the publication of its account so as to stop the faithful from turning away from saint worship.[52] In 1614 Charles de

---

52. *Miracle advenu à Andely la veille de la Pentecoste derniere, le second jour du mois de Juin, mil six cens dix-huict: Par l'intercession de saincte Clotilde Reyne de France, femme de Clovis, premier Roy Chrestien des François.* —A Rouen, Chez Nicolas Le Prevost, près les Jésuites [1618]. —8 p., in 12, p. 8: "Nous Jacques Desmay Prestre Docteur en Theologie, de la société de Sorbonne, Doyen de l'Eglise Collegialle de nostre Dame d'Escouys, & Vicaire general de mondit Seigneur, ayant examiné honorable homme Jean Grivet maistre de la maison du grand Dauphin parroisse de sainct Paul au fauxbourg de Martainville de Rouen, aagé de soixante et quinze ans ou environ, sur la subite santé par luy recouverte la veille de Pentecoste derniere: Et ayant recogneu par son examen de bouche, & deux autres tesmoings qui ont signé au procez verbal sur ce dressé, qu'apres huict ans de maladie & perclusion de ses membres il avoit fait vœu à saincte Clotilde, & l'avoit esté accomplir en sa Chappelle érigée dans l'enclos du Cimetiere de nostre Dame d'Andely, le second jour de ce present mois veille de Pentecoste, auquel jour il avoit entierement recouvert sa santé, la fonction naturelle de ses membres, & le mouvement progressif; ainsi que nous l'avons veu marcher. Nous de l'authorité que dessus pour ne point taire les merveilles de Dieu en ses Saincts, avons permis le narré du miracle estre imprimé, comme un tesmoignage evident que Dieu veut que le nom de ses Saincts et Sainctes soient honorables devant luy, & qu'ils soient reclamez, & invoquez par les hommes en leurs necessitez; en vertu dequoy

Balzac, bishop of Noyon and peer of the realm, invited him to preach there during the Advent of 1614 and Lent of 1615. During his time there, he conducted an extensive inquiry into Calvin's early years. In 1621 he published his *Remarques considérables sur la vie et moeurs de Jean Calvin, hérésiarque: Et ce qui s'est passé de plus mémorable en sa personne depuis le iour de sa naissance . . . iusq'au iour de son deceds . . . tirées des registres de Noyon par Jacques Desmay.*[53] Desmay gives a general description of his sources but does not provide detailed references or exact citations. He carefully distinguishes between the information in the *Registers* of the Dean and Chapter of the Noyon Cathedral[54] and information from oral sources, which are unnamed. Among his written sources, he singles out the records of the inquiry by M. de Mesle (to which Le Vasseur will also refer), as well as the chapter *Registers* put at his disposal by the dean Philippe de Gourlay and the other canons. He apparently used five chapter *Registers* in all. The first volume covered the years 1516–20, and the second the years 1522–24. Both were written by the notary Jean Quentin. The third volume began on January 16, 1525, and the fourth in 1530. These two volumes were the work partly of Quentin and partly of Trémon and Morlet, notaries under the two successive deans, M. Randoul and M. Antoine de Chermoluë. The fifth volume covered the years 1534–36 and was the work of Martin Morlet.

Despite his extravagant claims in the title, Desmay turns out to have quite scant knowledge of what happened to Calvin once he left Noyon. Indeed, his aim is not to produce a *Life* of Calvin in any sense but simply to inform his readers about the reformer's youth and childhood. Of particular interest to Desmay is the issue of benefices Calvin is supposed to have held. Calvin's works, however, are of no interest at all to him. Even so, his *Remarques* mark a turn in Roman Catholic

---

nous avons signé à ces presentes ce vingtdeuxiéme de Juin mil six cens dix-huict. Signé J. Desmay Vicaire General, avec un paraphe."

53. Copies of the original edition are extremely rare. I have used a reissue (which omits both the first few pages on Calvin's ancestry and Desmay's list of sources used) published in *Archives curieuses de l'histoire de France, depuis Louis XI jusqu'à Louis XVIII . . . publiées d'après les textes conservés à la Bibliothèque Royale et accompagnées de notices et éclaircissements . . .* par L. Cimber [pseudonym of L. Lefaist] and F. Danjou, 1st series, book 5ᵉ, no.26 (Paris: Beauvais, membre de l'Institut historique, rue Saint-Thomas du Louvre, 1835), 387–98.

54. They are no longer extant.

biographies of the Genevan reformer, which will be accentuated by Le Vasseur a few years later, with details corrected and added. Both aim to show that Calvin was never a good Catholic and that his dereliction of his clerical duties shows him to have set a poor example to priests and holders of benefices generally. In other words, he provides an *exemplum horrendum* of a dissolute pre-Tridentine cleric, a warning to post-Tridentine clergy as well as lay believers. At the same time, these early seventeenth-century Catholic biographers, Le Vasseur even more than Desmay, continue the trend set by Masson (whose work Le Vasseur cites) and disassociate themselves tacitly from the Bolsec image. They find it more important to indict Calvin on the basis of what they consider to be sound evidence than to repeat or create myths. Desmay's aim is first and foremost to show, using the evidence in the Cathedral *Registers*, that Calvin, when young, compounded all the vices of a bad pre-Tridentine cleric. These are plurality of benefices when far too young to be put in charge of a parish, absenteeism, simony, and nepotism. In all this, young Calvin was aided and abetted by his father, Gérard.

Thus according to Desmay, in 1521 Calvin obtained the "chappelle de Gésine," not from his brother Charles, as Le Vasseur was to assert later, but from the vicars of Charles de Hengest, bishop of Noyon, following the resignation of one Michel Courtin, who had exchanged the chapel of Gésine for Charles's chapel of La Madeleine.[55] Thus, as his biographer does not fail to point out, he was only twelve years old when he obtained this first living. In 1523, according to Desmay and Le Vasseur after him, Gérard Cauvin obtained leave for his son to flee the plague epidemic, following the example of the Cathedral canons. Permission was granted "iusques à la feste de Saint-Remy suivants."[56]

---

55. Desmay, *Archives curieuses de l'histoire de France*, 388: "Le 29 mai 1521, maistre Jacques Regnard, secretaire de révérend père en Dieu messire Charles d'Angestée, évesque de Noyon, rapporta en chapitre que les vicaires généraux de mondit Seigneur avoient donné à Jean Calvin, fils de Gérard, aagé alors de 12 ans, vne portion de la chapelle de Gesine vacante par la pure et simple resignation du maistre Michel Courtin, suivant la procuration passée à vénérable homme, maistre Antoine d'Estrée, procureur fondé et nommé pour ceste fin. Alors lecture fut faicte par Jean Calvin des statuts et serment par luy presté suivant la coustume et fut mis en réelle possession de ladicte chappelle par celuy qui presidoit en chapitre. Le susdit Courtin avoit en ceste portion de la chappelle de la Gésine par la permutation qu'il avoit faicte avec Charles Cauvin pour sa chappelle de la Magdelaine."

56. Ibid.: "En l'an 1523 une grande peste régnit en la ville de Noyon, qui fit abandonner la vie à plusieurs chanoines. Girard Cauvin, pour ce qu'il aimoit son fils Jean

At that point young Jean Cauvin went to study in Paris, where—still according to Desmay yet with no mention of source of information—"his mind, rather like his father's, was without any discretion or decorum and became easily carried away by the license of his youth."[57] Again like Le Vasseur a few years later, Desmay dwells on Calvin's conviction for absenteeism from his charge in January 1526: "Since there was absenteeism, it is easy to see that this young viper was already beginning to gnaw at the entrails of his mother the holy church, who nurtured him; his libertinism was already making him forget the oath he had sworn on being received as chaplain."[58]

As if this were not enough, on Monday, May 6, 1527, Calvin and his brother Charles were again condemned for absenteeism. However, continues our chronicler, Gérard persisted in seeking ecclesiastical advancement for his children and would not rest until he obtained a presbytery for Jean.[59] Thus on September 27, 1527 (Desmay cites folio 3, page 1 of the *Registers*), Gérard appeared before the chapter to present a resignation of one Jean Havart from the presbytery of Saint-Martin de Martheville. Antoine Fauvel, the canon who was doing his turn presenting candidates to benefices, immediately presented Jean Calvin in absentia to the general approval of the other canons. It was also Fauvel who was delegated by the chapter to present Calvin to the bishop or to the vicar general. Desmay finds this shocking and says so: "The same man that they condemned for absenteeism in two of their chapters, they receive as one able to take care of souls without making him make amends for his past, and him not even a full clergyman,

---

Cauvin pour ce qu'il le voyait de bon esprit, d'une prompte naturelle à concevoir et inventif en l'estude des lettres humaines, luy procura un congé de s'absenter et sortir de la ville, tel qu'on avoit accordé en chapitre aux chanoines, ainsi que nous voyons au chapitre tenu le 5 d'aoust auquel requeste se voit presentée par Girard, à ce que son fils Jean Cauvin obtint congé d'aller où bon luy sembleroit durant la peste, sans perdre ses distributions; ce qui luy fut accordé iusques à la feste de Sainct-Remy suivants. Ce fut alors que Calvin s'en alla à Paris estudier dans l'Université, aagé seulement de 14 ans, où son esprit sans conduite et retenue, semblable à celuy de son père, se porta facilement à la liberté de jeunesse."

57. See preceding note.

58. Desmay, *Archives curieuses de l'histoire de France*, 389: "Puisqu'il y a de la contumace, il est facile à juger que desjà ce petit vipereau commençoit à ronger le ventre de sa mère saincte église, de laquelle il recevoit sa nourriture; ses libertez luy faisoient desjà oublier le serment qu'il auoit faict le iour de sa réception au nombre de chapelains."

59. Ibid.

simply a tonsured clerk and not yet of age, a mere eighteen-year-old, full of the folly and libertinism of youth."[60]

While portraying Calvin as the wolf, the dissolute cleric, the thief, and the adherent of the "new sects," Desmay at the same time sees him as rather much a lost soul, who left the church too late to return to its bosom. Thus he cites the dean of Noyon Cathedral as saying that Calvin's nephew (who apparently died during Desmay's visit) once visited his uncle in Geneva and asked him whether he thought that Catholics were damned. To this the reformer replied no. What is more, he apparently never put pressure on his nephew to convert to Protestantism. Indeed—here Desmay cites an aged canon as his source—Calvin wanted to return to the bosom of the church but, faced with the canon's attempt to reconvert him, he simply replied that it was too late. Moreover, according to the dean of the cathedral who had known the reformer's valet, Calvin nearly reconverted on his deathbed and asked the valet to bring him the Book of Hours of Our Lady as used in Noyon.[61]

Desmay's Calvin is quite fragmentary. However, he does show certain distinctive traits that do not feature in any of the other biographies. First, Calvin emerges as a restless youth, forever seeking change and novelty. This, so Desmay implies, is the immediate cause of his straying from the straight and narrow, regardless of whether it takes the form of pluralism, absenteeism, nepotism, or "joining the new sects." At the same time, as I mentioned above, Calvin with his traffic of benefices, his supposed stealing, and his absenteeism serves any young clergyman as a model of how not to behave. In another register, far from being the "devil's disciple," he is shown as one regretting his departure from the

60. Ibid., 389–90: "Le vendredy 27 septembre 1527 ainsi qu'il est enregistré au feuillet 130, page 1, Girard se présenta en chapitre, porteur d'une procuration ad resignandum de maistre Iean Havart, curé de l'église paroissiale de Sainct-Martin de Marteville, diocèse de Noyon, par laquelle ledit Havart résignoit purement et simplement entre les mains du chapitre sa cure de Marteville. Alors maistre Antoine Fauvelae, chanoine, qui estoit en tour ad praesentandum, présenta à la dicte cure Iean Calvin, laquelle présentation fut acceptée de messieurs de chapitre. On voit par là que c'est d'un corps à plusieurs testes. Celuy qu'ils avoient condamné de contumace en deux divers chapi-[390]tres, ils le recoivent à prendre charge des ames sans correction du passé, n'estant promeu à aucun ordre sacré, n'ayant que simple tonsure et en un aage incompétent, n'ayant encore que dix-huict ans, remplis de follies et libertez de jeunesse. Le mesme Fauvel fut député en ce chapitre pour présenter Jean Calvin à monsieur l'evesque ou à son grand vicaire."

61. Ibid., 396–97.

Catholic Church, especially as he finds that it is too late to return. While the parts of the account that adhere strictly to the Noyon *Registers* are obviously reliable, given that they resurface with some minor corrections in Le Vasseur's *Annals*, the parts based on verbal testimony contain a fair amount of fiction. However, Desmay carefully distinguishes between written historical records and mere hearsay.

Le Vasseur

Jacques Le Vasseur was born in 1570 in Wismes, not far from Abbeville, and became archdeacon at Noyon. He also taught at Orléans and Paris, whence he fled in 1608 because of the plague. As well as compiling the *Annals* of Noyon Cathedral, he is known as the author of *Le Bocage de Jossigny, ou est compris le verger des vierges, et autres plusieurs pièces sainctes, tant en vers qu'en prose. / Antitheses ou contrepointes du ciel et de la terre.* This collection of religious poetry was printed in Paris by Fleury Bourriquant, 1608. Le Vasseur composed it while seeking refuge from the plague at Jossigny (Brie). He also wrote, among other things, *Antithèses ou contrepointes*, a work of 111 quatrains of reflections on God, the fight between the flesh and the spirit, and so forth. His *Annals* show him to have been particularly devoted to propagating the image of Noyon as a city unscathed by Calvin's heresy.

Indeed, it was a source of great pride to the French Catholics in general and to the civil and ecclesiastical powers of Noyon in particular that despite having given birth to a heretic of Calvin's caliber, the city itself remained resolutely loyal to Rome. Already in 1570 the controversialist Antoine de Mouchy, one of the canons of Noyon cathedral, addressed the city's inhabitants in these glowing terms in the preface to his *De veritate Christi*:

> For at no point, although you knew Calvin from childhood and although many of you knew his mother and father, did you take him seriously enough to believe rashly what he wrote and did, which would have meant deserting your own faith, nor did you follow his example and abjure the true God, the Catholic religion, and the Christian teaching of the holy fathers. On the contrary, when you first sensed that he had defected from our true religion, you shrank from him as if he were

51

worse than a dog or a serpent, and you wisely averted your eyes from his writings when they were first forced upon you against your will, lest your very eyes be contaminated by the sight of them as they might be by the sight of a basilisk. And you were afraid to pollute your clean hands by their very touch.[62]

Since Bolsec's time, however, rumor was about that Noyon was just as much a seat of iniquity as Geneva or any other place connected with Calvin. With this in mind, Jacques Le Vasseur, when he was writing his *Annals*, searched the Noyon Cathedral Chapter *Registers* for mentions of the reformer, intending to sharply distinguish once and for all between him and the city that gave him birth.[63] He fully acknowledged that he was not the first historian to attempt a portrait of Calvin on the basis of the evidence provided by the *Registers*. Indeed Le Vasseur had read Desmay's "petit liure" on the reformer's life and refers to it several times in the text of the *Annals*.[64] However, it would be a mistake to suppose that Le Vasseur copies Desmay. Although, as I mentioned, he does echo his account on several points, on other occasions he passes it over in silence, adds to it, or diverges from it. He

62. Preface cited by Jacques Le Vasseur, *Annales de l'Eglise de Noyon, jadis dite de Vermand ou le troisiesme liure des Antiquitez, Chroniques ou plustost Histoire de la Cathédrale de Noyon*, Par M. Jacques Le Vasseur, docteur en théologie de la Faculté de Paris, doyen et chanoine de ladite Église, 2 vols. (Paris: Robert Sara, 1633), 2:1179; "Non anim aliquando tanti fecistsi Caluinum quem a teneris annis, sicut patrem et matrem eius plerique vestrum cognouistis, vt statim dictis, scriptis suis ac actis temere crederetis, deserta fidei receptae pietate aut huius instar Deum verum, catholicam religionem et christianam sanctorum patrum institutionem perfide abiuraretis. Sed contra, vbi primum hunc a nostra et vera defecisse religione subolfecistis, vt cane et angue peiorem abhorruistis et a librorum suorum quos vobis nihil minus cogitantibus gratis obtrudebant lectione, velut a basilisco, ne visu inficerentur, oculos sapienter auertististis, sicut et horum tactu puras manus vestras pollui caute timuistis."

63. Le Vasseur, *Annales*, 2:1162: "Noyon n'est pourtant ce qu'aucuns l'ont fait estre à son suiet: vne Paneropole, vne carriere venimeuse et la sœur des cinq villes comprises sous le nom de Pentapole. Ce sont les tiltres que quelques estrangers luy donnent, escriuans de Caluin et en haine de luy, comme ci ce n'estoit assez de le rendre immonde, si on ne faisait quant et quant de Noyon, ville innocente, vne cloaque publique et sentine generale de toutes ordures, au prejudice de sa bonne renommée, du Royaume et de la Chrestienté. C'est ce qu'ont fait plusieurs de temps en temps."

64. See ibid.: "Maistre Iacques Desmay (maistre Iacques Desmay en son petit liure de la vie de Caluin, imprimé à Rouen, chez Richard l'Allement 1621 auec priuilege du Roy et approbation des docteurs) docteur en theologie mentionné cy-dessus, qui preschant Aduent et Caresme à Noyon en 1614 et 1615 y fit tres-exacte recherche des vies et vices de ce decrédité, n'a rien découuert dauantage."

is also infinitely more damning than Desmay, who confined himself to the minimum of comment over and above what he had read in the *Registers* or heard from witnesses. Le Vasseur also admits to having extensively consulted the *Vita* of Papire Masson, to which he refers as another highly reliable source, while correcting it occasionally when it is contradicted by documentary evidence.[65]

As a whole, Le Vasseur's account is far more comprehensive than Desmay's digest of the Cathedral *Registers* and of the local, oral tradition surrounding the reformer. Although Le Vasseur's portrait of Calvin emerges as extremely hostile, it is also the first to draw a clear distinction not just between written and oral sources but also between sources and commentary. Le Vasseur also carefully compares printed sources, especially Masson's *Vita*, with the manuscript evidence available. To us, the value of the *Annals* thus lies in their careful listing of all the documentary evidence about John Calvin and his family that was available in the Noyon *Registers* before they burned down later in the seventeenth century. Just as important, perhaps, the *Registers* show that the method of comparing sources advocated by Bauduin and, in his wake, Masson found fruitful ground among French Catholic clergy and theologians; and that, from the early seventeenth century onward, those who wrote about Calvin no longer wanted to portray him as a

---

65. Ibid., 2:1152: "La seconde fille de Gerard suiuit son frere Iean à Genèue où il l'attira par ses inductions. Papire Masson en sa Vie de Caluin en nomme d'autres de ceste race [Cauvin]. Car apres auoir fait mention des deux benefices que Gerard procura à Iean son fils, fait suiure ces mots: 'Haec causa fuit cur pater eum quam doctissimum fieri caperet mitteretque Lutetiam et Ricardo fratri commendaret in vico diui Germani Altissiodorensis, fabro ferario fratrique eius Iacobo, qui nunc anno 1583 eandem artem Parisiis prope sanctum Medericum, via Vulpis dicta exercet etc.' S'en informe qui voudra, en voilà les enseignes." Evidently the Noyon Registers did not contain any information on Gérard's brother Richard and his children. Otherwise Le Vasseur would have spotted the anachronism and corrected "fratri" to "filio," as Théophile Dufour would do some three hundred years later; cf. above, n. 15. Le Vasseur, *Annales*, 2:1161: "Le lundy 4 iour de May 1534 il resigna la chappelle susdite à maistre Antoine de la Marlière et sa cure du Pont-l'Evesque à Caïm. Et de là, après quelques courses se retira à Genèue, où il fut suiui de son frère Antoine. Tout ce que dessus auéré par l'information de feu M. Antoine de Mesle, docteur es droit, thrésorier et chanoine de l'Eglise de Noyon, iuge ordinaire en l'audience episcopale du lieu, mon tres honoré deuancier et par le tesmoigange de Papire Masson, duquel entr'autres sont ces mots: 'Duo illa supra memorata modici prouentus beneficia vendidit, Antonio Marlero vnum, alterum Gulielmo Bosio, presbyteris Nouiomensis ecclesiae. Antonius religionis causa exsul postea ad venditorem Geneuae se contulit.' Mais le Masson prend Bosius (ou du Bois) pour Caïm."

scourge unless they could back up their assertions with documentary evidence. Religious biography, even hostile religious biography, thus entered the sphere of history, but without fully inhabiting it. Le Vasseur is not above repeating rumors. However, as we said, he carefully distinguishes between oral and written sources and is as intent on destroying Bolsec-type myths as Masson before him.

Thus, alongside the Bolsec image, new images of Calvin—unbranded and innocent of sexual crimes, but above all source-based and historically founded—were taking shape in accounts of his life that his Roman Catholic adversaries devoted to him in the early seventeenth century. This was going to change in 1651 with the publication of Richelieu's *Traitté* on the one hand and with the flood of Jesuit anti-Calvin satirical literature on the other hand.

The Influence of Richelieu on Calvin Biography

Richelieu's *Traitté qui contient la méthode la plus facile et la plus asseurée pour conuertir ceux qui se sont séparés de l'Église* appeared posthumously in 1651.[66] This three-volume treatise was obviously not a biography of Calvin. Richelieu's aim was to expose every single aspect of Protestant belief and practice. Only one chapter, chapter 10 in book 2, touches on biographies of Reformers. The cardinal's aim was to show in twelve brief pages that the "debauched lives of the first instigators of the so-called Reformation make it clear to us that the church they founded cannot be the true church of Jesus Christ."[67] He contrasts the sinful and wicked lives of the Reformers with the holy lives of Christ and the apostles and notes that God, who first founded the church by the agency of "very holy people," would not have recourse to depraved individuals to reform it. Calvin is not the sole object of his attack. He runs through Luther, Zwingli, Calvin, and Beza, showing each to have been of loose morals and therefore heterodox. His knowledge of their lives is scant, to say the least, and he relies on excerpts extracted

66. I have consulted the copy held by the Bibliothèque Sainte Geneviève in Paris (shelf-mark: FOL D551 INV 621 RES): Cardinal Richelieu, *Traitté qui contient la méthode la plus facile et la plus asseurée pour conuertir ceux qui se sont séparés de l'Eglise* (Paris: Sebastien et Gabriel Cramoissy, 1651).

67. Ibid.: "Que la vie déréglée des premiers autheurs de la pretendue reforme nous fait connoistre que l'Eglise qu'ils ont fondée ne peut estre la vraye Eglise de Jesus Christ."

from their writings to show the symmetry between loose morals and wicked convictions.

Calvin constitutes an exception, however. Richelieu does not append extracts from his writings or say much about his teaching. He concentrates entirely on the reformer's sexual degeneracy, his taciturnity, and his tyrannical nature. The printed marginalia, or shoulder notes, show that he was familiar with the Bolsec and the Masson images and biographies of Calvin. It is less certain that he had also read either Desmay's or Le Vasseur's account of Calvin's youth, based on the Noyon *Registers*. If he did, he certainly does not share their view that a biographer's job is to remain as close as possible to his sources. He does, however, show knowledge of Bauduin's *Responsiones* to Calvin (possibly via Masson's *Vita Calvini*) and of Edmund Campion's controversy with Whittaker about the Genevan reformer. The result, as we are about to see, is an amalgam of all the negative remarks any of Calvin's adversaries had ever made about the reformer, combining the most pejorative of the Bolsec and the Bauduin-Masson tradition.

The cardinal devotes only three of the twelve pages to Calvin. However, the three pages were to raise a veritable storm of controversy and therefore deserve to be examined in detail. Basing himself quite loosely on Masson, Richelieu notes that Calvin was born in Noyon in 1509 and that he held benefices: Martheville, which he exchanged for Pont l'Evesque as well as a chapel in Noyon. He also stresses that Calvin was barely eighteen when he obtained his first living (twelve according to Le Vasseur!). More significantly, he conflates Jean with his father, Gérard, as he tells his readers: "While he held these benefices, he was reprimanded several times for his bad debts and for his depraved morals, but having finally been condemned for his debauchery, which took him to the extreme limits of vice, he moved away from the region of Noyon and at the same time from the Roman Church."[68]

68. Ibid., book 2, chap. 10, 291: "'Il naquit en la ville de Noyon en 1509. Il eut vne chapelle dans Peronne et vne dans Noyon. La premiere cure estoit celle de Martheville et la seconde celle du Pont l'Evesque; à 25 ans il se défit de la cure et de la chapelle' Calvin fut nourry dès son bas âge pour estre ecclésiastique. N'ayant encore que 18 ans, par la licence du siècle il fut dès lors pourveu d'vne cure, laquelle deux ans apres il permuta auec vne austre. Pendant qu'il possedoit ces beefices il fut plusieurs fois repris et de la liberté de sa créance et de la deprauation de ses mœurs mais ayans esté enfin condamné pour ses incontinences qui le porterent mesmes jusqu'aux dernieres extremitez du vice, il se retira et des enuirons de Noyon et de l'Eglise romaine tout ensemble."

As further evidence for Calvin's dissolute morals, he refers to the dispute between Edmund Campion and William Whittaker, where Campion accuses the Protestants, among other excesses, of having had a leader (Calvin) who was a fugitive branded with a fleur-de-lis. Whittaker replies that Saint Paul was also branded. In his apology for Campion, Dury replies in turn, "It is impious to compare St. Paul branded for his faith in Christ with Calvin branded for his crimes."[69]

Indeed, about a half of the short notice is devoted to Calvin's purported branding. The best proof for the authenticity of the fact, according to Richelieu, is that the Geneva Church never denied it, not even when Philibert Berthelier brought back with him a document signed by the most prominent men in Noyon attesting to the branding. It is this document, still according to Richelieu, that states that the capital punishment normally incurred for sodomy was commuted to branding by Calvin's bishop. "And the Genevan Church," Richelieu adds, "does not belie this information about Calvin's *Life*, and it would certainly have done so if it had thought this would be possible without bending the truth."[70] What is more, he concludes, Berthelier himself never denied this information, and he had the opportunity to do so since he was still alive when Bolsec's *Life* of Calvin appeared.[71]

Richelieu acknowledges using Bolsec as a source for this completely fictitious account. As is well known nowadays, Philibert Berthelier was exiled after being excommunicated and never occupied the position of the city clerk or secretary that Bolsec attributes to him, and the

69. Ibid.: "Campianus qui mourut en Angleterre sous le regne de la royne Elisabeth (en 1581) reprochant à nos aduersaires la vie infame de Caluin et vsant de ces termes: 'que leur chef auoit esté fleurdelisé et fugitif,' Witaker en sa Reponse n'en a point d'austre que celle-ci: 'Caluin a esté stigmatisé mais S. Paul l'a esté, d'autres l'ont esté aussi.' A quoi Duraeus repartant en la replique qu'il fait pour Campianus dit: 'que c'est vne chose impie de comparer Caluin marqué par ses crimes à S. Paul marqué pour la confession de Iesus-Christ.'"

70. Ibid., book 2, chap. 10, 291–92: "Est que depuis qu'il a esté chargé de ceste accusation l'Eglise de Genèue non seulement n'a pas justifié le contraire mais mesmes n'a pas nié l'information que Berthelier enuoyé par ceux de la mesme ville fit à Noyon. Cette information estoit signée des plus apparens de la ville de [292] Noyon et auoit esté faicte auec toutes les formes ordinaires de la iustice. Et dans la mesme information on void que cet Heresiarque ayans esté conuaincu d'vn peché abominable que l'on ne punit que par le feu, la peine qu'il auoit meritée fut, à la prière de son euesque moderée à la fleur de lys. Et l'Eglise de Geneue qui ne desauoue pas cette information touchant à la vie de Caluin, n'eut pas manqué de la déauouer, si elle eut cru le pouuoir faire sans blesser la vérité."

71. Ibid., book 2, chap. 10, 292.

Council of Geneva never sent him or anyone else to Noyon to seek any documents about Calvin's early misdemeanors.

To this image of Calvin the dissolute clerk, the cardinal adds the strictures passed on the reformer's character by Jean-Papire Masson, whose account he had read with some care, carefully extracting what he considered to be the most damaging information while omitting anything that did not contribute to tarnishing the reformer's reputation. Stressing its objectiveness, he misquotes extensively and out of context Masson's account of Calvin's choleric temperament, vindictiveness, arrogance, chronic bad temper, dislike of being contradicted, and an invincible superiority complex. Completely ignoring Masson's remarks on Calvin's sincerity, he points out: "This is what Papirius says, quite rightly in my opinion, about Calvin's vices, which were all the more detestable since their starting point was the greatest vice of all, and that is pride and ambition to be considered intellectually superior to all other men, leading to contempt of God, Jesus Christ, and his church."[72]

Richelieu was not interested in Calvin's life but only in portraying the reformer as a thoroughly wicked, debauched, and unpleasant megalomaniac, who passed himself off as a religious leader. After all, first and foremost the *Traitté* was meant to convert. Richelieu was fully aware of his goal and of the means to achieve it and made selections from Bolsec, Masson, and one or two other accounts and writings quite consciously. The result was a thoroughly libelous portrayal of this reformer's morals and character without even paying some symbolic homage to searching for the truth about him. As a historical account, it constituted a setback to the French Catholic historiography of Calvin.

Conclusion

An analysis of Protestant responses to Richelieu's slanderous account would require an essay in itself, as would the Protestant

---

72. Ibid., book 2, chap. 10, 293: "C'est ce qu'écrit Papyrius, judicieusement à mon avis, touchant les vices de Caluin, qui ont été d'autant plus détestables qu'ils ont eu pour origine le plus grand de tous, qui est l'orgueil et l'ambition d'exceller sur les autres hommes dans les auantages de l'esprit jusqu'au mépris de Dieu, de Jésus-Christ et de son Eglise."

reception of Masson.[73] As for the Roman Catholic *Lives* of Calvin we have examined here, they point to a certain number of significant facts about the reformer. First, they show that most myths about Calvin's depravity, tyrannical nature, and so forth arose already during his lifetime and were not, as has often been thought, a twentieth-century invention. Similarly, the Protestant rehabilitation of Calvin began immediately after his death with Beza's first *Life* and was to receive its second impetus from reacting to Richelieu's work. These factors are of some significance as attempts to varnish or tarnish the reformer's reputation partly persist in Calvin biographies up until the present day, if we think of the work of Zweig, Stauffer, Bouwsma, or more recently Cottret.[74]

Finally, partly to answer the question I asked at the beginning about the whys and wherefores of Roman Catholic interest in the life of Calvin in the late sixteenth and early seventeenth centuries, we might say that Calvin's early Roman Catholic biographers were without exception French. Their reactions to the reformer were naturally divided between shock that one of their countrymen should inflict so much damage on the established order, on the one hand, and admiration of his undoubted success, on the other hand. The very ambivalence of this attitude allowed them to develop a historicocritical space for a better founded and more modern assessment of the reformer as witnessed by the biography of Masson, which was often to be used by later Catholic biographers and also to be cited by Protestant theologians as antidote to the Bolsec myth, which Richelieu did his best to keep alive.

73. For an extended discussion of both these topics, see my monograph *Life Writing in Reformation Europe*.

74. Stefan Zweig, *Castellio gegen Calvin: Ein Gewissen gegen die Gewalt* (Vienna: Reichner, 1936); Richard Stauffer, *L'humanité de Calvin* (Neuchâtel: Delachaux & Niestlé, 1964), 9–17; William J. Bouwsma, *John Calvin: A Sixteenth-Century Portrait* (New York: Oxford University Press, 1988); Bernard Cottret, *Calvin: A Biography*, trans. M. Wallace McDonald (Grand Rapids: Eerdmans, 1998).

2

Calvin and the Nicodemites

George H. Tavard, AA

I n the writings of Calvin the expression *Nicodemites* covers several different cases. In his pamphlet *Excuse à Messieurs les Nicodémites*, composed in 1544, Calvin distinguishes four kinds of Nicodemites. The first teach a little bit of the true doctrine and stop there. In his words, they "sing the Mass, which they know to be an abominable sacrifice." Calvin nonetheless adds: "I am fully persuaded that some do this with a good zeal, seeking God's honor and the salvation of the people, and not their own profit."[1] The second are "officials [*protono-taires*] who discuss the gospel lightly with the ladies," without trying to apply it, or jolly young men at the court, or ladies who care only about their makeup [*mignardées*]. The third treat Christianity as a philosophy

---

1. Eberhard Busch, Alasdair Heron, et al., *Calvin-Studien Ausgabe*, vol. 3, *Reformatorischen Kontroversen* (Neukirchen-Vluyn: Neukirchener Verlag, 1999), 230; Bernard Cottret gives a good short treatment of the Nicodemites in *Calvin: Biographie* (Paris: J. C. Lattès, 1985), 275–80.

and never take it to heart. The fourth are "merchants and common people,"[2] who do not wish to be disturbed in their habits.

Some ten years later, in Calvin's *Commentary on the Gospel of John*, the allusion to Nicodemus has become entirely negative. There are people who know that they should abandon the idolatry of the papal church, but they do not do it out of fear of persecution. These hypocrites believe one thing and do another: "Today we see several who say they are like Nicodemus, and wearing this mask, think that they will remain unpunished while they mock God."[3]

In this essay I will first look at several early friends of Calvin: Nicolas Duchemin and Gérard Roussel, the original "Nicodemites," and Louis du Tillet. All three agreed with the central ideas of the Reformation yet decided to remain in the episcopal/papal system. None of them completely fits in the four categories mentioned, even though Calvin had the first two in mind when he composed his *Excuse à Messieurs les Nicodémites*. After presenting the exchange of letters between Calvin and Du Tillet, I will then present several prominent women, especially Marguerite de Navarre in France, Renée de Ferrare in Italy and France, and Vittoria Colonna in Italy. Each of them animated a circle where the ideas of Calvin were largely accepted. Yet most of the persons who frequented these circles remained under the pope. The appellation *Nicodemites* was not applicable to them in any of the four meanings itemized by Calvin.

Nicolas Duchemin and Gérard Roussel

Two priests whom Calvin regarded as friends, and who shared the basic ideas of the reforming movement, accepted promotion to higher ecclesiastical office. Nicolas Duchemin had studied law in Orléans with Calvin. Like Calvin he had moved to Bourges to study classical scholarship with the Italian humanist Andrea Alciati. He had composed an *Antapologia*, in which he defended Alciati from various accusations. Calvin had written an introduction to this essay and had supervised its publication in Paris in 1531. When Duchemin was invited to become

2. Busch and Heron, *Reformatorischen Kontroversen*, 238.
3. John Calvin, *Comm. on the Gospel of John* (1553), on John 7:50 (*Commentaires sur le Nouveau Testament: Evangile selon saint Jean* [Geneva: Labor et Fides, 1968], 230).

officialis to René du Bellay (ca. 1496–1546), bishop of Le Mans, he asked for Calvin's advice. Calvin answered unequivocally with a long letter, really a treatise against the pope and his church, which he made public in 1537 as the first of his two letters "against the Nicodemites."[4] In it he argued that a true Christian cannot possibly collaborate with a bishop, for bishops are responsible for the idolatry that is pervasive under the pope. Duchemin did not respond. He does not seem to have had major problems in his subsequent career in Le Mans.

Gérard Roussel (1480–1555),[5] a canon of Meaux, was active in the humanist circle around Bishop Briçonnet and had contributed to introducing Luther's writings and ideas in France. He was chosen by Marguerite d'Angoulême, queen of Navarre (see below), to be her chaplain at Nérac. In the Lent of 1533 he openly preached justification by faith alone at the court of François I in Paris, though in the absence of the king. How far he went in the direction of the Reformation is difficult to know. He is likely to have contributed to a proposed reform of the Mass, *La Messe à sept points*, which, if the later writer Hilarion de Coste (1595–1661) is right,[6] was occasionally used at Nérac. Calvin met Roussel when he visited Nérac in the Lent of 1534. In February 1536, Pope Paul III (1534–1549) promoted Roussel to the diocese of Oloron (today, Oloron-Sainte Marie) at the request of Marguerite d'Angoulême, and he became a bishop. Calvin's indignant letter to Roussel when he heard of this promotion forms the second part of *Epistulae duae*. It can be read as a tractate against the priesthood as practiced under the pope. As a bishop, Roussel maintained some of the reforming ideas. It is reported that, one day in 1550 while he preached against the cult of saints, an angry parishioner attacked the wooden pulpit with an axe, the pulpit collapsed, and Roussel was severely crippled for the rest of his life.

4. These two letters are in *OS* 1:288–328, 329–62. The titles of the letters are significant: *"De fugiendis impiorum illicitis sacris, et puritatis Christianae religionis observanda"* and *"De Christiani hominis officio in sacerdotiis papalis ecclesiae vel administrandis vel abiiciendis."*

5. These dates are given in Conrad Eubel, *Hierarchia catholica medii et recentioris aevi summorum pontificum*, part 3, *Saeculum XVI ab anno 1503 complectens* (Regensburg: Manz, 1923); P. B. Gams gives different dates: episcopate in Oloron, 1542–60; death, 1568 (*Series episcoporum ecclesiae catholicae* [Regensburg: Manz, 1873]).

6. Hilarion de Coste, of the Order of the Minims, wrote several volumes presenting biographies of famous women.

George H. Tavard, AA

Louis du Tillet and the Controversy over Calvin's "Ordination"

Another case touched Calvin more personally and deeply than the promotions of Duchemin and Roussel. In January 1534, Calvin left Paris in a hurry because of the hostile reaction to a speech that Nicolas Cop delivered at the University of Sorbonne on November 1, 1533. He eventually took refuge in Angoulême, where he was the guest of Louis du Tillet (born ca. 1509), a priest, canon of Angoulême, and since 1532, the pastor of Claix, a small village in the vicinity. Louis was the youngest of four brothers, who were all conversant with the writings of the Renaissance.[7] The Tillet house in Angoulême contained a sizable library, which Calvin put to good use. He visited the aging humanist Jacques Lefèbvre d'Etaples (ca. 1455–1536), who was a guest of the queen of Navarre in nearby Nérac, though he could not see the queen herself, for she was at the time visiting her lands in Normandy. In May 1534, Calvin traveled by way of Poitiers to Noyon, where he officially renounced his ecclesiastical benefices. Louis du Tillet seems to have gone with him as far as Paris.

In the night of October 17/18, 1534, posters against the Mass (*les placards*), which summed up the theology of François Antoine Marcourt, a Frenchman from Lyon, appeared on walls all over France, including one that was nailed to the door of the king's bedroom in his palace at Amboise by one of the king's servants. To a devout Catholic, the text could only sound blasphemous. This angered the king profoundly, and a savage persecution of Protestants soon began. This *affaire des placards* was the immediate reason why, at the end of October, Calvin and Louis du Tillet left Paris for Basel, by way of Strasbourg. In January 1535 they arrived in Basel, where Calvin finished writing his first *Institutio christianae religionis* and had it published in March 1536. In February or March they paid a visit to the Duchess Renée de Ferrare (1511–75), daughter of the late King Louis XII of France (king, 1489–1515), and therefore a cousin of the present King François I. The duchess openly favored the Reformers. In Ferrara, Calvin wrote his Latin letters to Duchemin and Roussel. He left Ferrara, it seems, in late April because of the duke's hostility to the Reformers. After a

7. Louis's brothers were Séraphin, *greffier* (registrar) of the Parliament of Paris; Pierre, also *greffier* of the Parliament; and Jean (d. 1570), who became bishop of St-Brieux and later of Meaux; there were also two sisters.

quick trip to Noyon after the Edict of Coucy (July 16, 1535), he traveled back toward Basel by way of Geneva because war in the province of Champagne made it impossible to reach Strasbourg. There, Louis du Tillet, who was already in Switzerland, informed Guillaume Farel (1489–1565) of Calvin's presence, and Farel persuaded Calvin to remain as a lecturer in the New Testament.

During most of this period, Du Tillet supported Calvin financially. But, assailed by scruples for abandoning the old church, Du Tillet was despondent in Geneva. In August 1537, he left the city for Strasbourg, where he remained for several months and had talks with the Alsatian reformers Martin Bucer and Wolfgang Capito. In October or November he crossed the border into France and returned to the Catholic Church. At first he lived in the house of his brother Séraphin in Paris. Calvin, expelled from Geneva in May 1538, went to Strasbourg, where Martin Bucer persuaded him to take up the ministry of the numerous French-speaking exiles. He wrote to Du Tillet from Strasbourg.

Six letters remain from the correspondence that followed. Compared to Du Tillet's letters, those of Calvin seem quite short. The letters are universally courteous, and it is clear that each writer deeply cares for the other, though they contain pointed barbs. They also carry a subdued tone of secrecy, Calvin being somewhat hidden under one of his many pseudonyms, Charles d'Espeville.[8]

(1) The first letter, dated January 31, 1538, is from Calvin. It is a five-page answer to a letter, long lost, that he had received from Du Tillet. In it his friend must have explained why he had returned to the jurisdiction of the pope, for this is the subject of all the correspondence. Calvin admits that in Geneva he treated Du Tillet in such a way that his "presence could not have been very agreeable to him." What this alludes to we do not know, but Du Tillet's response shows that his despondency in Geneva was not caused by Calvin. At any rate, Calvin is shocked at what he sees as his friend's abandonment of the gospel, for until then he had seen Du Tillet "firm and resolute,"

---

8. Espeville was the name of a land attached to one of Calvin's benefices in his youth. Calvin used several more pseudonyms; the six letters of the correspondence with Du Tillet are in A. L. Herminjard, *Correspondance des Réformateurs dans les pays de langue française*, 9 vols. (Nieuwkoop: De Graaf, 1965–66), vol. 4, no. 680 (pp. 354–59), no. 692 (pp. 384–400); vol. 5, no. 722 (pp. 43–45), no. 742 (pp. 103–9), no. 754 (pp. 161–65), no. 759 (pp. 186–200).

showing "constancy and firmness." He does not now find Du Tillet's reasons persuasive (*péremptoires*), and his conscience says the exact opposite of Du Tillet's conclusions. Calvin suspects that those with whom Du Tillet talked in Strasbourg, the unnamed Bucer and Capito, may have contributed to Du Tillet's decision by their own lack of firmness. Besides, if Du Tillet followed his action to its logical conclusion, he would accuse Calvin and his side of being schismatics. Would he really go as far as that? Whatever is said for the papal system, Calvin assured his correspondent, "I know well that our assurance is too certain to give way before vain objections."

(2) Du Tillet's response is formulated at length in three much-longer letters, of March 10 (sixteen pages), September 7 (six pages), and December 1, 1538 (fifteen pages). The perspective of the first is essentially ecclesiological. Abuses have occurred under episcopal and papal authority, but they have not ruined the nature of the church. The abuses must be repressed, and the church must be reformed, yet without destroying its God-given structure. Both he and Calvin have the evidence of its fruitfulness in their lives, for it is from this church in its traditional form that they received baptism and were nurtured in the faith. When he thought about this in Geneva, Du Tillet was so struck, as he says, by such "an affliction of conscience" that he found himself unable to function properly. Devoted as he was to "the word of God and purity of religion," he could not ignore the growing impression that it was not God who had called him out of France and its churches, and that he had been misled by merely human arguments. He is convinced that the churches where he previously lived and ministered in France do remain true churches of God: "If we recognize that we received the efficacy of the baptism of Jesus Christ in the churches where we were baptized, and thus through the ministry that was in them, . . . it is necessary that we confess the ministry of these churches to have been a true ministry of God, which perseveres and continues in them. If you think sufficiently about it, you cannot, in my opinion, say the opposite in your conscience." Du Tillet affirms that no other reason could have persuaded him to come back to France. He now perceives that his "affliction of conscience" in Geneva was the way in which "our Lord wanted to warn and correct me." He would like Calvin to reflect on this conviction, for Calvin also is indebted to the churches of France for his baptism and for the faith that he prizes so much.

(3) Calvin's brief reply (four pages), dated July 10, 1538, does not allude to his friend's scruples or to his present conviction. It simply gives news of Calvin's current situation and concerns in Strasbourg. His excuse is that he has a lot of things to say, and that he spoke of them to a certain Johan, who came from Strasbourg to Paris and must have visited Du Tillet. He does not wish to return to Geneva, where he ministered when he felt bound to it by God's call. He now waits in the hope "that our Lord will lead me in so ambiguous a deliberation, all the more so as I will pay heed to what he will show me rather than to my own judgment." Delayed by the illness of Calvin's messenger, this letter reached Du Tillet on August 19, 1538.

(4) Louis du Tillet was evidently surprised by the brevity of Calvin's response and his avoidance of the question raised in Louis's letter of March 10, 1538. In his letter, on September 7, 1538, Du Tillet takes Calvin's recent difficulties in Geneva as a divine warning,[9] just as he had understood his own despondency when he was in that city. He points to the danger of not recognizing one's errors: "It can very often happen that we do not understand the faults we commit, even if they are very great and heavy; and often what seems to us the best, and [seems] so certain that nothing is better in our opinion and judgment, is simply against the truth of God and the judgment of his Spirit." Going further, Du Tillet draws attention to the nature of a vocation to ministry. Reflecting on what this should be, he doubts that Calvin's call to minister in Geneva came from God. It came from men who themselves had no divine mandate (Guillaume Farel and Pierre Viret, but they are not named). Besides, Calvin's judgment on what is a true church is seriously mistaken: "I am quite sure that you keep an extreme position in not considering [as] churches of God those in which you received the beginning of your Christianity and the progress you made in them for more than fifteen years, and you condemn in them things that are not condemnable, which an infinity of persons use for good and according to God's will with zeal and knowledge of God, with the good testimony of the Spirit in their consciences."

9. Calvin was expelled from Geneva on Easter (April 21) 1538. He then went to Basel, where he was invited to Strasbourg by September 1538. He ministered in Strasbourg until he returned to Geneva on September 13, 1541.

The testimony of the Spirit was not a major topic in Calvin's first *Institutio*, though it may have been in his conversation. In any case Du Tillet may have thought that it was in the logic of Calvin's orientation. Moreover, he stresses another point that was familiar to Calvin: the presence of evil in the human condition. It is easy to be misled by evil desires, *concupiscentia*. And no one should think that, "if there is in us some beginning of the Spirit of God, we are the only one who has some of It, or we have more of It than others." Accordingly, Du Tillet invites Calvin to "examine himself." Indeed, "the spiritual man judges all things," but only if the Spirit of God guides him. Personal humility should be a rule of our conduct: "It is necessary for every one of us to be suspect to himself and to restrain his judgment in great fear, humility before God, in order not to pronounce and judge too boldly of the things of God, especially as they concern one's calling; therefore one must abstain from inconsiderately and summarily rejecting the judgment of others, even if at first sight it is contrary to ours."

With an open allusion to Calvin's writing, Du Tillet urges his friend not to make the present debates worse, whether "through published books or otherwise." Knowing that Calvin has practically no income, he offers to send whatever money is needed, even though he himself has no personal resources for the time being and relies entirely on his brother's generosity.

(5) Calvin writes back on October 20, 1538, less briefly than previously, with a letter that is quite friendly and moderate in tone. The confession of his own frailty takes up most of the letter's first half. He nevertheless strongly defends his vocation: "If the question were to discuss my calling, I think that you have no such [good] reasons for impugning it that the Lord does not give me better ones to confirm me in it." He also invites Du Tillet to apply his recommendations to himself: "I would like you to take some of these exhortations for you. For by calling *tenebras lucem* [darkness light] in all your letters, you condemn those who walk in this more straight than all of yours. . . . I take what you say in this matter as proceeding from a good heart, but I ascribe it to another spirit than that of God." Calvin clearly cannot return to France. This would be entering hell. He had indeed wished to lead the quiet life of a scholar, but he bowed to the judgment of "persons who are not contemptible to me and must not be to you." He gratefully acknowledges Du Tillet's generous offer of

money, but he does not need it now. Calvin regrets that Du Tillet does not "forgive the truth of God or God's servants." Because of this, he has made his letter short. He nonetheless wishes that God keep his friend "in his holy protection, so leading you that you do not veer from his way."

(6) Du Tillet's last letter, the longest, begins with an apology: he has unintentionally hurt his friend Calvin. The letter is at the same time a small treatise on the church and its legitimate ministry, a personal plea that Calvin will listen seriously and examine his conscience, and a rather sophisticated analysis of Calvin's character. Du Tillet's argument is focused on the authenticity of the churches in France as true churches of God, and on the nature of ministry, which one cannot take on by oneself, but to which one must be called by legitimate pastors, the bishops, and into which one must be introduced by the sacrament of orders. Unfortunately, Calvin believes himself to be infallible, does not see his serious defects, and is blinded by impatience. He has gratuitously accused Du Tillet of calling *tenebras lucem*, and he should not have answered as he did. I take this to mean that he should have taken Du Tillet's arguments more seriously.

Indeed, Du Tillet admits that Calvin has all the personal qualities that are needed by a good minister, but he simply has not been called, for one must be called "in the way approved by God," and this "true way is by the apostles." Du Tillet cites 1 Timothy 4:14 and 2 Timothy 1:6. He insists that "no one can . . . have vocation from God to the ministry, to minister licitly, and to be accepted in it, if he is not called and constituted by the one or the ones who have God's authority and responsibility for it in the church."

This is the true tradition. The old church has the only "legitimate and ordinary way" to ministry. Du Tillet therefore knows that Calvin's ministry did not proceed in that way: "I do not see that you ever had calling and constitution in that way in the order of the ministry that you exercise now." Furthermore, the "noncontemptible persons that you speak of," who induced Calvin to take up his present ministry in Strasbourg, Bucer and Capito, had no authority to do so. Therefore, Du Tillet concludes: "I cannot see (if all I have said and that for the present I can accept in regard to God's calling and institution to the ecclesiastical ministry is true) that you have been called to it and instituted in it by God, since you have not been, by them or by others, called to or installed in the order of this ministry through the sacrament and form that our Lord (as I understand) wanted to be in his church."

Calvin's view of the sacrament of orders was, in the first *Institutio christianae religionis*, purely negative. Ordination is one of the false sacraments (chap. 5). After making fun of the minor orders, Calvin finds no proper basis in Scripture for the unction with oil or the imposition of hands. Ministers should simply be chosen by the magistrates in the name of the people. Their function is to announce the gospel and to administer the sacraments. There is no need of an ordination: *Ordo est ipsa vocatio.*[10] Church authority is not essentially different from political administration; both are examined as side issues of the more fundamental topic of Christian liberty (chap. 6, "De libertate christiana, potestate ecclesiastica, et politica administratione"). The *Brève instruction chrétienne*, composed in Geneva in 1536 or 1537 as a summary of the *Institutio*, taught that "there must be ordained pastors in the churches to teach the pure doctrine to the people, to administer the sacraments, and to give to everyone the good example of a pure and holy life."[11] But it gave no explanation as to how a pastor should be ordained. "The Lord," it said, did not make the promise of Matthew 18:18 ("What you will bind on earth will be bound in heaven . . .") "to the men, but to the Word," of which men must be servants. Ministry is a fruit of the Word authentically proclaimed. It is manifest in the preaching of the Word. The Word itself is not defined by ordination or by the ministry. Rather, it defines the ministry. In the *Institutio* of 1539, published after the exchange with Du Tillet, the one chapter of 1536 grew to three (chaps. 13–15); and these remained totally negative concerning traditional ordination.

Du Tillet, however, has come to trust the Catholic doctrine. Individual churches cannot create ministers outside of the regular process that has been practiced since the beginning of Christianity: this can be seen in the Scriptures, in the early Christian writings, and in the decisions of councils. Calvin has entered an illegitimate ministry. And Du Tillet, as a close friend, judges that he acted out of a "carnal and ambitious desire," which made him consent to what others wanted, and easily led him to esteem that God had called him, through his

---

10. *Institutio christiana* (1536), in *OS* 1:212, 244.
11. Calvin, *Brève Instruction chretienne* (Paris: Les Bergers et les Mages, 1957), 72.

servants, who, however, had no authority to do so. Du Tillet would have preferred not to regard this as a fault, but the evidence is too strong. Of course, if Calvin will not confess his fault, Du Tillet can only pray for him. He did not himself call *tenebras lucem*. And the messenger—Johan, whoever he was—did not report anything on that matter, even if Calvin had spoken of it with him. "If you believe, you and those who agree with you, that you are walking the right path, your belief does not make it to be so." That Du Tillet has no ministry at the moment does not stop him from seeing and reflecting. "It is not said that a person who preaches his doctrine in public cannot fail, and that whoever knows him should not tell him privately in good equity." Du Tillet condemns abuses and impieties as much as Calvin does. Calvin has correctly felt that it was from a good heart that Du Tillet wrote "regarding your view that the churches of this country are not churches of God and your condemnation of several things that are not condemnable." It was also "in conformity with the truth of God." He will not respond to Calvin's boast that the rule of his conscience is more certain than du Tillet's. In spite of all this, Calvin can still accept his offer of financial assistance.

If Calvin still considers Du Tillet a friend, he will be welcome to write and send news, as long as he does not do so in a spirit of contention, anger, and presumption, "with the desire to justify yourself too much before men." If this is not the case, however, Du Tillet tells him, "If you cannot use such modesty and temperance (until our Lord gives us the possibility to agree more), you will give me great pleasure in not writing, at least that sort of thing." It is not totally certain that this last letter of Louis du Tillet ever reached its addressee. In April 1539 Calvin wrote to Farel that he feared letters between himself and Du Tillet had been lost on the way. In any case, since no other letters have survived, one may assume that the correspondence ceased at that point.

In 1557, in the preface to his *Commentary on the Psalms*, published in 1558, Calvin alludes to an unnamed "individual who now basely apostatized and returned to the Papists."[12] This person is undoubtedly Du Tillet.

12. James Anderson, trans., *Commentary on the Book of Psalms, by John Calvin* (Grand Rapids: Eerdmans, 1949), xliii.

Calvin's Developing Theology of Ministry

Du Tillet's letters raise at least two serious questions. First, is there a necessary way of entrance into the ministry that derives from the apostles? Second, is it true that, whatever Calvin's great talents, God did not call him to the ministry of teaching in which he engaged in Geneva, or to the pastoral ministry he was now doing in Strasbourg? Because of their friendship and their close association over several years, Du Tillet expected Calvin at least to take his arguments to heart, if not to accept his conclusions.

Calvin, however, was caught between a rock and a hard place. On the one hand, he could hardly dismiss his friend's warnings if he wanted to keep his friendship. On the other, he could not forget the vehemence of Guillaume Farel, who had proclaimed in God's name that Calvin must remain in Geneva to explain the Scriptures to the people, or the persuasive insistence of Bucer that the French refugees in Strasbourg needed a shepherd, and that he, Calvin, was perfectly qualified for this task. What is the more important fact? Is it the order that is apparent in the history of the church, based on a special sacrament and on ordination by bishops? Or is it the undeniable fact that pastors are needed in the churches that no longer wish to be run by the bishops? Calvin was certainly familiar with Luther's *Babylonian Captivity of the Church*, with its downgrading of episcopal ordination. He had presumably suffered due to the excommunication of his father. He was not inclined to look favorably on bishops. But Du Tillet had a point when he complained that his arguments were not taken seriously.

Calvin's understanding of the ministry did evolve toward a more traditional view. In his *Homilies on the Minor Prophets*, Calvin clearly taught both that the whole company of believers is indeed a royal priesthood consecrated to praise and thanksgiving, and that God also chooses particular persons to be priests. "What is a priest?" he asks in his seventy-fourth *Homily on Malachi*. A priest, he replies, is "a messenger of God and his interpreter. It hence follows that the office of teaching cannot be separated from the priesthood."[13] This, in Calvin's

---

13. Cited in T. F. Torrance, "Legal and Evangelical Priests: The Holy Ministry as Reflected in Calvin's Prayers," in *Calvin's Books: Festschrift Dedicated to Peter De Klerk on the Occasion of His Seventieth Birthday*, ed. Wilhelm H. Neuser, Herman J. Selderhuis, and Willem van't Spijker (Heerenveen: J. J. Groen, 1997), 63–74.

eyes, does not give a priest "power," as he thinks ordination is understood in the Roman doctrine. Rather, the priest is sent to preach the gospel and to intercede for the people. Further, in a letter of December 5, 1554, to Sigismund II, king of Poland (1520–72, king in 1548), Calvin distinguishes between an ordinary way of entering the ministry and an extraordinary, prophetic way that is outside the ordinary norms. He meant that the latter was his own ministry.

The rather unequal exchange between Du Tillet and Calvin raises another fundamental question: Did acceptance of the Reformers' central emphasis on justification by faith justify a total break with the old church? Why not preach justification by faith alone in the context of episcopal authority and papal primacy, when it is possible?

Calvin certainly did not reject all church authority. Since the church is "the mother of all the faithful,"[14] it should be obeyed. In the first *Institutio*, Calvin taught that the church is kept in the truth when it is truly gathered in the name of the Lord. Then indeed, as his adversaries argued, "the church cannot err in those things that are necessary to salvation."[15] But this is not because of traditions, pastors, or general councils. Rather, the church cannot err "when it is taught by the Holy Spirit through the word of the Lord." Though Calvin despised the superstitions and idolatries that he thought flourished under the papacy, he still regarded the church of Rome as somehow a church. In 1561 he wrote a "response to a certain werewolf," toward the end of which he mentioned "those who falsely call themselves Nicodemites."[16] The werewolf was George Cassander (1513–66), and his piece was *De officio pii ac publicae tranquillitatis vere amantis viri in hoc religionis dissidio* (1561), an irenic writing in which he tried to bridge the gulf between Catholics and Protestants. Calvin's response, however, could well have been a final answer to Du Tillet. He acknowledges the baptismal argument. Calvin himself was indeed baptized under the pope: "Our baptism, though administered to us in the papacy, must be, like a flag, transferred from disorder to the worship of Christ."[17] In any case, Calvin maintains, "No sane person has

---

14. Torrance, "Legal and Evangelical Priests," 71.

15. "Errare non posse ecclesiam in iis quae sunt ad salutem. Sed hic etiam plurimum sensu variamus. Errare non posse ida sentimus, quod, abdicata omni sua sapientia, a Spiritu Sancti doceri se per verbum Domini patitur" (*Institutio christiana*, chap. 6, in *OS* 1:244; see 239).

16. *Responsio ad versipellem quondam*, in *CO* 9, col. 555.

17. Ibid., col. 544.

ever said that Christianity was completely extinct wherever the tyranny of the pope flourished. Hence, one gathers that in some part the church remains there. One only wonders, to what degree? Our answer rests on a solid reason: Although the ordinary ministry of baptism remains among the bewitched pastors who preside there, nevertheless they deserve no more authority than the sacrificers of Cybele."[18]

Nicodemites or Evangelical Roman Catholics?

Undoubtedly, there were Catholic theologians who accepted the doctrine of justification by faith alone as a truly Catholic doctrine. Their situation was not always easy. The strange case of Bernardino Ochino (1487–1564) illustrates the double difficulty, first, of holding Protestant convictions in the Catholic system of government, and second, of remaining in a stable doctrinal position once all church authority has been rejected. Cardinal Gasparo Contarini (1483–1542, cardinal in 1535), who at the Colloquy of Regensburg (1542) tried to find a compromise with Melanchthon, became persona non grata with Pope Paul IV (1555–59). What Calvin did not acknowledge, though he certainly knew it, was that many prominent personages remained in good standing in the episcopal/papal system of government while publicly professing that justification is by faith alone. I will give the example of two prominent and influential women, one in France, one in Italy.

In France, Marguerite d'Angoulême (1492–1549), sister of the king of France François I, queen of Navarre by her second marriage, was a distinguished humanist, writer, and poet. She was no less at home in the description of human love (*Les quatre dames et les quatre gentilshommes*) and in the profane episodes, largely inspired by her observation of the royal court, of her *Heptameron*, than in spiritual and even mystical verses. She was also politically competent. She assisted her mother in the administration of the kingdom when her brother was captured at the battle of Pavia, by the fault, it would seem, of Marguerite's husband, who failed to maneuver on the battlefield as he was expected. She herself traveled to Madrid and successfully negotiated the release of François I.

18. Ibid., col. 543.

Prompted at first by personal sorrow at the death of her beloved niece Charlotte de France (1516–24) when she wrote *Dialogue en forme de vision nocturne*, Marguerite's religious poetry evoked the redeeming power of faith in her *Miroir de l'âme pécheresse* (published 1531). This is a long scriptural meditation on the work of the Redeemer, which includes a plea for toleration of different religious views. Placed on the index of the Sorbonne through the influence of Noël Béda (1470–1537), it was promptly removed from it when her brother the king intervened.

Marguerite undoubtedly regarded the superiority of faith over works as the authentic and old doctrine. As she says in one of her *chansons spirituelles*:

Si quelqu'un parle de la Foy	If someone speaks of the Faith
En la mettant quasi à rien	Making it as though nothing
Au prix des oeuvres de la Loy,	Compared to the works of the Law,
Les estimant les plus grands biens,	Thinking these are the greater goods,
Sa doctrine est nouvelle.	His doctrine is novelty.
Laissez-le là, passez avant;	Leave him there and go beyond;
Autant en emporte le vent.[19]	As much does the wind blow away.[19]

Again Marguerite opposes the law and the faith:

Le Fidèle dedans la Loi	In the Law the Faithful
Tout caché, tremblant et peureux	Hiding, trembling, and fearful,
Par la lumière de la Foy	Through the light of Faith
Voit clair, et devient amoureux	Sees clearly, and falls in love
De Dieu qui le connaît:	With God who knows him:
Voici nouvelle joie.[20]	Here is new joy.[20]

19. "Si quelque injure l'on vous dit" (poem), in *Chansons spirituelles*, included in *Marguerites de la Marguerite des Princesses*, Classiques de la Renaissance en France (Paris: Mouton Editeur, 1970), 492.

20. "Voici nouvelle joie" (poem), in *Marguerites*, 482.

Marguerite understood the concern for doctrine. But she was not interested in rejecting old articles of faith or formulating new ones. Her abundant spiritual poetry is mostly focused on the incarnation of the eternal Son of God, and on the Christian experience of grace and salvation. It is also devoted to the praise and glory of, as she put it, "Dieu tout en tout, un seul en Trinité [God all in all, one in Trinity]."[21] Profoundly spiritual, she spent a great deal of time in the abbey of Tusson, of the Order of Fontevrault, where she wrote much of her poetry. She was eager to respect and protect the various ways and forms of religious experience, which is not surprising for a reader of Nicolas of Cusa. Marguerite was deeply saddened by the killing of heretics, including Anabaptists. She frequently corresponded with the bishop of Meaux, Guillaume Briçonnet (1472–1534), whose influence on the religious Renaissance in France was considerable. She is said to have made a deep impression on Pope Paul III when she met him in May and June of 1538 in Nice, where the pope was negotiating a truce between King François I and Emperor Charles V. Whatever her appreciation of the Reformers and her willingness to experiment with an unauthorized liturgy (*la Messe à sept points*), Marguerite persevered in the Catholic Church.

Her daughter, Jeanne d'Albret (1528–72), though she had been educated mostly under the supervision of her uncle, the king of France, freely attended sermons preached by ministers from Geneva. On Christmas day of 1560, she declared herself a Protestant, though her indecisive husband, Antoine de Bourbon (1518–62), kept wavering. Her son, Henri de Navarre (1553–1610), raised Protestant, joined the Catholic Church when, in 1589, he became king of France as Henri IV and Paris would not open its gates to a Protestant sovereign. "Paris," he is said to have declared, "is worth a Mass."

Vittoria Colonna (1490–1547), marchioness of Pescara by her 1509 marriage to Marquis Antonio Ferrante, was also a distinguished religious poet. She lived chiefly in Rome and Viterbo and was a familiar figure in a circle of remarkable religious personalities connected with the Oratory of Divine Love, who were eager to modernize piety and to ensure that outward ceremonies did not stifle inward religion. After

---

21. This is the last verse of *Le Navire*, in Abel LeFranc, *Les dernières Poésies de Marguerite de Navarre* (Paris: Armand Colin, 1896), 439.

the death of her husband in 1525 from wounds received at the battle of Pavia, where he fought in the army of the Emperor Charles V against the king of France, she wrote quite sad poetry about him; he had been, she said, "the Sun" of her life. When she overcame her grief, she turned to religious poetry, with Jesus as now the true Sun of her life. Henceforth she lived mostly in convents. She had a profoundly traditional piety, focused on the passion of Jesus and the Virgin Mary. Her prose work, *Pianto sopra la passione di Christo*, composed, it seems, at the request of Bernardino Ochino, includes profound reflections on the mother of Jesus, who is also the topic of another piece, *Meditazione sopra l'Ave Maria*. Likewise, her long christological poem, *Capitolo del trionfo di Cristo*, ends with praise of the mother of Christ, present at the cross.[22]

The circle she frequented and often animated gathered at first in Naples around the person and the writings of the Spaniard Juan de Valdès (d. 1541), a spiritual author influenced by the Alumbrados of Spain. After the death of Juan de Valdès, this circle, later called the "Italian Evangelicals," at first met chiefly in Viterbo around the English cardinal Reginald Pole (1500–59, cardinal in 1536). Among the many distinguished personages who frequented the circle, one finds Cardinals Gasparo Contarini (1483–1542, cardinal in 1535) and Giovanni Morone (1509–80, cardinal in 1542). Both were members of the commission set up by Clement VII to advise him on reforming the church. Their report, "Consilium eminentium cardinalium de emendanda ecclesia," was issued in 1537 and denounced abuses in the Roman system of government. This largely political concern, however, stemmed from the religious ideals of the Italian evangelicals. The two cardinals presided over the first sessions of the Council of Trent, which opened in 1545. Morone presided also over the last sessions in 1563.

Other members of the evangelical circles were the artist Michelangelo Buonarrotti (1475–1564) and the Benedictine Benedetto Fontanini (ca. 1490–post 1555). In 1537 Fontanini composed a short book, *Beneficio di Christo*, which was inspired by Calvin's *Institutio*. The author

---

22. Eva-Maria Jung-Inglessis, "Il Pianto della Marchesa di Pescara sopra la passione di Christo," *Archivo Italiano per la storia della pietà*, vol. 10 (Rome: Edizioni di Storia e Letteratura, 1997): 115–203; idem, "La lirica di Vittoria Colonna come specchio dell'evangelismo italiano," *Archivo Italiano per la storia della pietà*, vol. 27 (Rome: Edizioni di Storia e Letteratura, 2005): 59–78.

took for granted both justification by faith and a strict predestination. His book became immensely popular. Another person, Marcantonio Flaminio (1498–1550), made no secret of studying the writings of Luther, Calvin, and Bucer. He worked on a second edition of Fontanini's *Beneficio*, and he wrote spiritual poems, *De rebus divinis carmina*, which were published after his death. In 1545, along with another person from the same circle, Alvise Priuli (1471–1560), Flaminio accompanied Cardinal Pole to the Council of Trent as his secretary.

There also was Bernardino Tomassini Ochino, who became vicar general of the Capuchins in 1538 before he found his way to Geneva rather than letting the Roman Inquisition interrogate him about his preaching. The Augustinian Pier Martyr Vermigli (1500–1562) also went to Geneva around the same time for a similar reason. However, they did not appreciate the strong hand of Calvin, for neither one remained in his vicinity. Vermigli went on to Zurich, and then he sought the more moderate reformers of Strasbourg and of England. Ochino traveled to permissive Poland, where he joined a small group of antitrinitarian Anabaptists, until in 1564 King Sigismund II expelled all foreigners who were not Catholic. A year later, Ochino died in Austerlitz, Moravia. His case illustrates the double difficulty, first, of holding Protestant convictions in the Catholic system of government, and second, of remaining in a stable doctrinal position, once all church authority has been rejected.

Less fortunate was the well-traveled Pietro Carnesecchi (1508–67). When still a young man, he was protonotary to Pope Clement VII (1523–34). Later he was a papal diplomat in France, where he had Flaminio's *Carmina* printed in 1550. Meanwhile, his mind and heart wavered between the old church and the new. In the fall of 1552 he was converted to Zwinglian doctrines by an Italian he met in Lyon, Lattanzio Ragnoni (1509–59), who ministered to Italian exiles in Geneva. After moving to Venice, Pietro Carnesecchi behaved like a Nicodemite: he pretended to be Catholic while he also started an underground Reformed community. Accused of heresy several times, condemned to death in absentia, he always found powerful protectors until, under Pius V (pope, 1566–72), he was arrested in Florence, judged in Rome, condemned to death, and beheaded on September 21, 1567.

Besides Vittoria Colonna, other highly educated women were familiar figures in the Oratory of Divine Love, where the doctrines of Calvin were widely accepted. To Giulia Gonzaga (1512–66), Valdès dedicated his *Alfabeto cristiano*, which is in the form of a dialogue between her and the author. Caterina Cibo (1501–77), duchess of Camerino, married to a nephew of Pope Leo X and herself a cousin of Clement VII (pope, 1523–34), intervened with Clement in favor of the foundation of the Capuchin Friars in 1528. When Ochino was called to Rome in 1538, he spent some time in her house before fleeing to Geneva. The influence of Renée de Ferrare on these ladies is certain. Like Calvin and Louis du Tillet, several of them visited her in Ferrara.

Under pressure from her husband, Duke Ercole, and from the Roman Inquisition, Renée rejected Protestantism in 1554. When she was widowed in 1559, however, she retired in France in the city of Montargis, where she openly protected Protestants and eventually she declared herself one of them.[23] Calvin, who above all cultivated clarity of thought and the conformity of life with thought, warned her in a letter of 1564 against educated women who cultivate ambiguity in order to keep, as it were, a foot in each camp. In Paris for the marriage of the Protestant Henry de Bourbon with the Catholic Marguerite de Valois, daughter of the king of France Henry II and Queen Catherine de Medici (August 18, 1572), Renée de Ferrare escaped the St. Bartholomew massacre (August 24) by remaining in the Hotel de Nemours, her Catholic daughter's residence.[24]

Calvin strongly disapproved of the people he perceived to be Nicodemites. He was shocked and angry when his friends Duchemin and

23. Renée de Ferrare had inherited the ladyship of Montargis. There are no recent books on her life and ideas, and an excellent dissertation is still unpublished: Charmarie Jenkins Webb, "Royalty and Reform: The Predicament of Renée de Ferrare, 1510–1575" (PhD diss., Tufts University, 1969). Several versions of Renée's last will and testament, in Appendix 3 (of ibid.), affirm her Calvinist convictions. Version E, from the State Archives in Turin, is the most elaborate: Renée affirms four principles: (1) salvation is "by faith, not by our works"; (2) Christ liberates us from the "malediction of the Law, . . . not from the moral Law in the ten commandments"; (3) we should often pray and ask for forgiveness; (4) there are only two sacraments, baptism and the Holy Supper (ibid., 587–89).

24. This was Anne (1531–1607), Renée's third child. Widowed from François de Guise in 1563, Anne in 1566 remarried, to Jacques de Savoie, duke of Nemours. All of Renée's children remained staunchly Catholic. Alfonso II d'Este (1533–97) in 1559 succeeded his father as duke of Ferrara. Louis (1538–86) became bishop-elect of Ferrara in 1550 and a cardinal in February 1561; he received the minor orders in June 1561, was administrator of the archdiocese of Auch, and finished his career in Rome.

Roussel accepted promotion under the pope. He was more puzzled than angry when Du Tillet returned to the church of his baptism after openly sharing Calvin's convictions and for a while acting as his collaborator in Geneva.

Equivocal as their position could be, the Italian evangelicals were totally sincere. The French Catholics who were sympathetic with Calvin's doctrines never formed a consistent group, and they have not received a generic appellation. Neither the Italians nor the French could see why a growing spiritual experience focused on the works of God in Christ, and on justification by faith alone, should require joining a new church. The alliance of a Reformed view of justification with the episcopal/papal ecclesial structure was for them a conscientious theological position, an alternative form of reformation. Many of them functioned quite well in the papal system, even if a fanatic like Pope Paul IV threw doubt on their orthodoxy. In spite of Calvin's strictures against the Nicodemites, and of Paul IV's aggressive orthodoxy, they did not doubt the legitimacy of their position.

The Joint Declaration on the Doctrine of Justification, which on October 30, 1999, was signed in the cathedral of Augsburg by representatives of the Catholic Church and the Lutheran World Federation, goes a long way toward giving evangelical Roman Catholics a belated recognition.

3

Friend and Foe

Reformed Genevans and Catholic Neighbors in the Time of Calvin

Karen E. Spierling

O n January 23, 1556, Pierre Authin, a Genevan resident and typecaster for printing presses, appeared before the members of the Genevan consistory to answer questions about his reported claims that "God is everywhere, elsewhere just as in Geneva, and that they have as good a church in Rome as in Geneva." When asked if he had in fact said this, Authin responded that he was referring to the groups of *faithful* Christians one could find in Rome. The consistory pressed further, asserting that he "had said that there is greater idolatry here than in other places." Authin protested that he had meant the usurers and fornicators who lived in Geneva (implying that he did not, certainly, mean the members of the consistory and leaders of the Reformed Church). He further said that he would like to hear from the people who had accused him of such things and that when he had returned from a trip to Lyon, where he likely had business with Lyon's printers, he would come back to the consistory to face their witnesses.[1]

A week later, on January 30, four witnesses, including a man named Guillaume Debosc and "his wife," appeared at the consistory's weekly meeting to give their testimony against Pierre Authin. Debosc explained that one time Authin had been a dinner guest at their house. In the course of conversation, Debosc's wife had said to Authin that she could not, in good conscience, live in the city of Lyon because of the idolatry there. According to Debosc, Authin had retorted that "the church was as good in Paris as in this city."[2] Unfortunately, I have found no mention of the final outcome of this case in the consistory records. It is quite possible that Pierre Authin never returned from his trip to Lyon and as a result never met with the consistory again. He had already been accused of being a fornicator himself several years earlier, had spent time in prison in Geneva, and had been excluded from the Lord's Supper. Perhaps this 1556 confrontation with the consistory was the last straw for Authin. In any case, the reported exchange between Pierre Authin and the Debosc couple illustrates the debate that recurred in Geneva, even after two decades of reform and after the defeat of Calvin's staunchest political opponents, regarding the nature of the "true" Christian church and the dangers that the Roman Catholic Church did or did not pose to Reformed Genevans.

In addition to Authin's comments about Catholic churches, his travel between Geneva and Lyon makes this a good case with which to begin our discussion. For both the city and church authorities of Geneva in

1. R. Consist. 10:87, January 23, 1556. Authin was a resident (*habitant*) of Geneva who worked for the printer Robert Estienne. In 1553 Authin appeared before the consistory on charges of fornication (*paillardise*). In 1555 he was imprisoned for that offense and excluded from the Lord's Supper. See Paul Chaix, *Recherches sur l'imprimerie á Genève de 1550 á 1564* (Geneva: Droz, 1954), 142. On the frequency of usury in Geneva during Calvin's lifetime, see Mark Valeri, "Religion, Discipline, and the Economy in Calvin's Geneva," *Sixteenth Century Journal* 28, no. 1 (Spring 1997): 123–42, esp. 127–34. For consistory records after 1546, I have used the unpublished transcriptions produced by the members of the Genevan Consistory publication project, under the direction of Robert M. Kingdon. I give the folio and date as listed in those transcriptions. Citations from 1545–46 are taken from the second published volume of that project; see below, n. 26. The original Genevan Consistory records are housed in the Archives d'État de Genève. All translations are my own unless otherwise credited.

2. R. Consist. 10:87v, January 30, 1556.

the 1530s–1560s, Catholicism threatened Geneva most immediately in connection to travelers. People who traversed the physical boundaries of the Genevan Republic, whether they were entering the city or leaving it, might carry with them ideas and convictions that could threaten both the piety and the liberty of Geneva. If it had been possible to seal off Geneva entirely—to make its boundaries impassable, so that neither people nor literature possessing Catholic ideas could enter the city—the concerns of the authorities would have been reduced immeasurably. Yet the Genevan reformers did not seek isolation from the world but rather continued participation in it.

This ongoing contact with the world beyond Geneva's borders significantly complicated the visions of the Genevan authorities regarding the future of their city. As Calvin scholars know well, the members of the Genevan City Council were determined to protect Geneva's independence at the same time that John Calvin and his fellow reformers were committed to transforming the place into a truly godly city.[3] The achievement of both these goals depended on the residents of Geneva internalizing the political and religious values of the city leaders. And both of these aims were constantly challenged not only by the influx of immigrants that Geneva experienced beginning in the 1550s, but also by the ongoing familial and business connections that a significant number of Genevans apparently maintained with neighboring Catholics.[4]

In recent decades, scholarship on Calvin's theology and on Reformation Geneva has provided an increasingly nuanced and complete

3. On the challenges involved in this double goal, see, for example, William Monter, *Calvin's Geneva* (New York: John Wiley & Sons, 1967); William G. Naphy, *Calvin and the Consolidation of the Genevan Reformation* (Manchester and New York: Manchester University Press, 1994); Henri Naef, *Les Origines de la Réforme à Genève* (Geneva: La Société d'Histoire er d'Archéologie de Genève, 1936); Robert M. Kingdon, "Social Control and Political Control in Calvin's Geneva," in *Die Reformation in Deutschland und Europa: Interpretationen und Debatten*, ed. Hans R. Guggisberg, special volume of the *Archiv für Reformationsgeschichte* (Gütersloh: Gütersloher Verlagshaus, 1993), 521–32.

4. For example, my preliminary investigation has shown that in the years 1546–47, the consistory heard three cases involving children going to school or living in Catholic areas; in 1558–59, the court heard twenty-five cases on the same topic. Even as Reformed doctrines and practices became well established in Geneva, residents continued to maintain relationships with Catholic friends and relatives. Cf. K. Spierling, "Good Christians or Good Neighbors? Protestant-Catholic Contact in Reformation Geneva," unpublished paper presented at the Sixteenth Century Society Conference, Atlanta, October 2005.

picture of the intentions of the Reformed Church; the contours of the ideal Reformed community as envisioned by Calvin and his colleagues; and the actual workings of the Reformed Church as embodied in Geneva.[5] A vital but still missing piece of this picture is a full understanding of the interaction between Reformed Genevans and Catholics. Elements of this topic are certainly found in most recent works on Geneva; it is impossible to consider the effects of the Reformation without considering the expulsion of Catholicism and Catholics from the city. Still, as of yet no one has produced a focused exploration of Genevan attitudes toward Catholics and interactions with them on a variety of levels—those of the state, the church, *and* the general population. Understanding this dynamic is essential to understanding the Reformed life as lived in comparison with the ideal Reformed life as pursued by pastors, consistory members, and other reformers. This chapter is a preliminary consideration of this issue and the beginning of a larger project. The specific questions I will consider are two: First, how did the Genevan authorities try to use legal measures to protect their inhabitants, city, and church from the dangers posed by the movement of people and ideas in and out of Geneva? And second, what are some of the specific ways that Genevan residents challenged those efforts?

An important concept in this discussion will be the idea of a porous religious and civic boundary. The question of defining religious and political boundaries has become increasingly popular among Reformation scholars in recent years. In applying the question of defining boundaries to Geneva, I am building most immediately on the work of Keith Luria, who has recently identified a variety of types of boundaries that, he argues, existed between Protestants and Catholics in France of the late sixteenth century and the seventeenth

5. Important contributions to this effort include, for example, Naphy, *Consolidation of the Genevan Reformation*; Robert M. Kingdon, *Adultery and Divorce in Calvin's Geneva* (Cambridge, MA: Harvard University Press, 1995); Thomas A. Lambert, "Preaching, Praying, and Policing the Reform in Sixteenth-Century Geneva" (PhD diss., University of Wisconsin-Madison, 1998); Christian Grosse, "Les rituels de la Cène: Une anthropologie historique du culte eucharistique réforme à Genève (XVIe–XVIIe siècles)" (PhD diss., Université de Genève, 2001); Jeffrey R. Watt, "Calvinism, Childhood, and Education: The Evidence from the Genevan Consistory," *Sixteenth Century Journal* 33, no. 2 (Summer 2002): 439–56. See also K. Spierling, *Infant Baptism in Reformation Geneva: The Shaping of a Community, 1536–1564* (Aldershot, UK: Ashgate, 2005).

century.[6] Most important for this chapter is Luria's description of a "permeable" boundary—that is, one crossed with relative ease. Luria identifies this type of traversable boundary as that most likely to have operated in relations between friends, relatives, or business associates—in cases where long-established social and economic ties motivated people to overlook or work around religious differences. In the case of Geneva, recognizing the permeability of the city's borders is vital to any accurate understanding of Genevan-Catholic relations. Both church and city authorities feared that any permeability of the city's physical boundaries might equate to, or at least encourage, flexibility in religious and political loyalties as well. And yet, despite this fear, the city never altogether outlawed contact with Catholics or travel to Catholic regions, nor did the Genevan reformers press for any such edicts. Instead, I argue, they relied on the impermeability of people's internal convictions: the personal boundaries of religious faith and of civic loyalty.[7] At the same time that both church and city placed their hope in the fixed nature of such internal boundaries, they worked persistently to establish guidelines, ordinances, and edicts that would shore up or correct any failure of individual piety or dedication to a Reformed Geneva.

To illustrate both the persistent porousness of Geneva's religious boundaries and the consistory and city council's strategies for fortifying those borders without sealing the city off from the outside, I will first discuss a number of the key edicts passed by the city council regarding Catholic practices and interactions with foreigners. If we are to understand the decisions that ordinary Genevans made when they chose to maintain Catholic connections, it is vital to have a sense of the established laws. The second part of my discussion will turn to

6. Keith P. Luria, *Sacred Boundaries: Religious Coexistence and Conflict in Early-Modern France* (Washington, DC: Catholic University of America Press, 2005), xxiii–xxxii. Luria identifies a model consisting of three types of boundaries: (1) the blurred line that could exist between Protestant and Catholic neighbors; (2) a negotiated boundary that separated the activities of Protestants and Catholics but allowed them to share the same civic space; and (3) the strictest barrier, constructed by church and state officials, that separated Protestants and Catholics completely.

7. See Luria on the complexities of individual conscience and conviction and the struggles of Catholic and Protestant authorities to control individual consciences. As he states, "In the end, individual conscience was not a refuge from but the definitive arena of the confessional struggle. It was the locus of religious truth, the place where God's will finally had to be acknowledged" (ibid., 246–47).

evidence from the consistory records. As I mentioned, the concerns of both city and church authorities regarding Catholicism were closely tied to travelers, to the *movement* of people and ideas across the physical boundaries of Geneva. To demonstrate this, I will discuss several specific examples from the consistory records involving people who did not simply relocate to Geneva or leave the city for good, but who moved back and forth between Reformed and Catholic territories. The willingness of such individuals to shift so easily between Catholic and Reformed territories, practices, and beliefs challenged the church and city's efforts to create an independent and purely Reformed city, invulnerable to the threats of Catholicism.

Edicts on Catholicism and Travelers

To understand the variety of concerns and priorities at play in Reformation Geneva regarding Catholicism and the movement of Catholic ideas and individuals, it is useful to look at some of the regulations passed by the Genevan City Council from the early years of the Reformation into the 1560s, near the end of Calvin's life. Although legal sources like this do not tell us how often such rules were enforced or precisely how the Genevan population reacted to them, they do give us a clear sense of the aims and the fears of both city and church leaders. Civic efforts to regulate foreigners, particularly merchants and the poor (*vagabonds*), had deep roots in medieval Europe, but the idea that self-identified *Christian* travelers could pose a threat based on their religious affiliation was a new development with the Reformation.[8] It was only starting in the 1520s and 1530s, in Geneva and in the rest of Western Europe, that Christians could be considered enemies of neighboring Christians based on religious doctrine and practices. The Genevan decisions and edicts collected in the *Sources du Droit* (see *SDG* 2; *SDG* 3) demonstrate that from the start of the Reformation in 1536, the city council had begun to draw such a connection between Catholicism and dangerous foreigners. It took several decades, however, to formulate the explicit tie between Reformed beliefs and political

---

8. For an overview of Geneva's treatment of poor foreigners in the early years of the Reformation, see Naphy, *Consolidation of the Genevan Reformation*, 121–25.

loyalty to Geneva that we see fully articulated in the edicts of 1560. Finally, these legal sources demonstrate that even as the city council and consistory codified the religious and political responsibilities of Genevan inhabitants within the city, they struggled to find an effective way to enforce those responsibilities when Reformed Genevans traveled beyond the city into Catholic regions.

In February 1536, just a few months before the city officially adopted the Reformation, the council declared that no inns should give lodging to any "unknown foreigner" for more than one day without notifying city officials.[9] In the previous decade, most legislation relating to foreigners or travelers had to do with either merchants or vagabonds, with the exception of a 1529 edict that had specifically prohibited any attacks on any foreigners in Geneva. In that case, the council had proclaimed that no one in Geneva should dare to "commit or have committed any annoyance, violence, outrage, injury, by action or by words, to any foreigners and neighbors [circonvoysins], whoever they may be, going, coming, trading [traffigans], and sojourning in this city and its limits; but they should let them go, come, trade, and sojourn peacefully, without reproaching them or committing any violence, outrage, injury, neither by acts nor by words."[10] While this 1529 decision was intended to protect travelers from Genevan inhabitants, for the rest of the 1530s and throughout the Reformation period, the council appears to have focused, instead, on protecting Geneva from potentially harmful travelers. In the decades following 1536, concerns about outsiders became inextricably tied to concerns about Catholicism. This apprehension was both religious and political: a Catholic traveler might endanger Geneva simply by sharing Catholic ideas with individual Genevans, potentially corrupting the godly community; or the Catholic might be part of a larger effort to overturn the independent, Reformed government of Geneva and return it to a state of subjection, both to the Catholic Church and to an overlord such as the duke of Savoy or the king of France.

Despite this perceived double threat, it was not until 1551, about the time that the number of immigrants from France began to increase

9. *SDG* 2:309 (PH 1161, February 29, 1536). Original date and source (housed in the Archives d'État de Genève) are given in parentheses. On the issue of suspicion of foreigners, see Naphy, *Consolidation of the Genevan Reformation*, 122–23.
10. *SDG* 2:270 (PH 1033, October 22, 1529).

substantially, that the city edicts explicitly connected the issue of unknown travelers to concerns about religion.[11] In August of that year, the council recorded a decision resulting from a discussion about "people who come into the city without being presented [to the council], whom one does not know and who could be suspected of not being here for *l'evangille*."[12] According to the edict, the council would not permit such people to stay in Geneva until they had been "duly examined about how and why they have come here by the council, and about their religion by M. Calvin or another preacher."[13] Two years later, in 1553, the council passed the longest set of edicts on foreigners up to that point. These included a new system for oversight of foreigners living in the city. While they did not specifically mention living according to the reform, the final item of these edicts concluded that any foreigners "suspected of heresy" would be thrown out of Geneva. In addition, these edicts ordered that all visitors had to turn over any weapons they had to the city during their stay in Geneva.[14] By 1555, the council had produced a new oath specifically for foreigners who had received permission to become residents of Geneva and who would be permitted to *keep* their weapons. Among a long list of required declarations, foreign residents now had to promise to "live according to the holy reformation."[15]

As these edicts demonstrate, as the Reformation progressed, the city passed increasingly strict laws, trying to prevent any Catholic presence from penetrating the borders of Geneva. This was a difficult task, to say the least, and their efforts were not entirely successful. But what was even more difficult was regulating Reformed Genevans' interactions with Catholics *outside* Geneva. Once again, the overarching concern here was one of repeated movement. If a Genevan resident decided to leave the city for good and move to a Catholic place, the authorities might decry the faithlessness and disloyalty of that individual, but they would not try to bring a person back unless he or she was fleeing legal

11. For useful introductions to the topic of French immigration into Geneva, see E. William Monter, "Historical Demography and Religious History in Sixteenth-Century Geneva," *Journal of Interdisciplinary History* 9, no. 3 (Winter 1979): 402–12; Naphy, *Consolidation of the Genevan Reformation*, 121–43.

12. *SDG* 3:9 (RC 46, 42, August 21, 1551).

13. Ibid.

14. *SDG* 3:12 (RC 47, 54, April 11, 1553).

15. *SDG* 3:29 (RC 49, 188v, September 23, 1555).

responsibilities, investigation, or prosecution in Geneva. The Genevans who caused Calvin and his colleagues the greatest consternation were those who, after making their promises to live according to the Reform, moved to Catholic areas, lived among Catholics, and then wanted to return to Geneva.

Despite their anxieties about the civic and religious dangers posed by such movement, neither church nor city ever went so far as to forbid Genevans from traveling to Catholic places to conduct business or visit their relatives. Since they were unwilling to take that extreme step to separate their godly and independent community from "papist" influences, the Genevan authorities resorted, instead, to a blanket command to any Genevans who traveled beyond the city's borders: in a 1546 declaration attempting to close the taverns of Geneva, the council ordered that "no one should do anything outside of Geneva that they would not dare to do inside the city."[16] Though this particular statement was connected to Calvin's ill-fated effort to shut down all the taverns in Geneva, the directive was repeated more broadly in the edicts of 1550: "No one should say, do, or contract anything outside of this city that he would not dare to do, say, and contract inside of it, according to the law of God and the reformation of the gospel."[17]

These edicts are outstanding examples of the church and city leaders' hope that their efforts within Geneva would lead to the internalization of the Reformation and the gospel. Their goal was not simply to mold individuals who were pious under the immediate threat of Genevan laws, but to create a city of inhabitants whose internal moral compasses were so strengthened by their faith and Reformed teachings that they would live according to the laws of both God and Geneva even when they were traveling. Calvin's whole system of education, including catechism and preaching, was constructed with this goal in mind. But even with that system of education in place, both the city's leaders and reformers clearly recognized the difficulty of achieving their ideal aim due to the overwhelming sinfulness and weakness of all humans. Thus the edicts illustrate both the hope that Genevan

16. *SDG* 2:478 (RC 41, 82v–83, April 29, 1546).

17. *SDG* 2:531 (R. publ. 1:61–66, March 10, 1550). This phrasing is repeated almost exactly in the Edicts of 1560; *SDG* 3:116 (original lost; printed version: *Les criées faites en la citée de Genève l'an mil cinq cent soixante* [Artus Chauvin], February 28–March 5, 1560).

inhabitants would internalize Reformed beliefs and values and the fear that they would not.

The first instance of this wording regarding behaving outside the city as one would inside had come in March 1536, shortly before the city officially adopted the Reformation. Initially this command was connected specifically to the matter of attending Mass and taking sacraments outside of Geneva—probably the most obvious change in regulations regarding travel outside the city. The editors of the *Sources du Droit* included as a supplement to their second volume a brief document dated March 26, 1536, that declared that no one "of any state or condition" should "go outside the city of Geneva to do what he would not dare to do in the city against the commandment and ordinance of God, unless he wants to stay there."[18] According to the editors' note, this declaration resulted from a small council meeting two days earlier, in which it had been decided that "in order to live in better unity and accord, one should announce in each district that no one should go to hear Mass or participate in a papal sacrament outside the city that they would not dare to do inside; unless they will stay there and will be reckoned enemies of the city."[19] This explicit connection between religious and political loyalty would not be stated so strongly again until the edicts of 1560. But the 1536 statement could not have been more forceful: they will be *reckoned enemies of the city*. This wording left Genevan residents with two options: they could either abandon their homes and be labeled as enemies of Geneva, or they could return to the city to face punishment from the council and consistory.

In addition to illustrating how quickly the political boundary between Genevans and non-Genevans was transformed into a religious boundary between Reformed Protestants and Catholics, the use of the phrase "enemies of the city" to describe people based on their religious practices highlights a fundamental aspect of the Genevan Reformation: the inextricable connection between the existence of Geneva as a godly city and Geneva as an independent republic. This correlation is, certainly, a long-established fact in the history of the Genevan Reformation.[20] But it is worth revisiting this important concept briefly in

18. *SDG* 2:543 (PH 1161, March 26, 1536).

19. *SDG* 2:543n1 (RC 29, 55v, March 24, 1536).

20. This connection is summed up in Monter's classic statement (*Calvin's Geneva*, 236): "Without the discipline and sense of mission instilled by Calvin, it is difficult to imagine

order to illuminate the religious and political context in which some Genevans chose to perpetuate their relations with Catholics. Repeatedly during the 1540s and 1550s, we find edicts and declarations that address the two problems of rebellion against the church and rebellion against the city within the same statement, but as separate items. For example, a 1547 document announced the "penalties against disturbers of the established order." The first item in this declaration states that no one should do anything "to make us renounce the laws and reformation of the gospel [*evangille*] of Jesus Christ [or] to return to the papist law and ceremony of the past, under pain of the confiscation and loss of his body and possessions." This is followed by a briefer statement prohibiting any words or actions against the "liberty and franchise of the city and its sovereignty." The same penalty applied to such political rebellion as to any religious conspiracy.[21]

This political-religious connection was repeatedly challenged during the 1550s.[22] The famous (or infamous) exiles and executions of Calvin's political opponents in 1555 are the outstanding example of the complicated relationship between religion and politics in Geneva in that decade. And while Calvin's victory may have strengthened the power and influence of the Reformers and the consistory, it did not literally make church and government one institution. Furthermore, while the showdown of 1555 eventually brought an end to a struggle among Genevans that had lasted over a decade, it did not resolve the problems facing Geneva due to the great influx of French immigrants

---

how so many men and so many talents could have been attracted to Geneva by the 1550's. Without this discipline, Geneva could not have managed her unique achievement as a sixteenth-century revolutionary commune that maintained her independence until the French Revolution." See also Amédée Roget, *Histoire du people de Genève depuis la Réforme jusqu'à l'Escalade*, 7 vols. (Geneva: John Julien, 1870–83).

21. *SDG* 2:489 (R. publ. 1:74, 1547).

22. These concerns of church and city were reiterated in a set of edicts from 1550, again in the same order: religious rebellion preceded political threat. But now the edict on religion was the briefer one. It stated that no one should do anything "secretly or overtly to abolish and cause to cease the word, preaching and sermon of God and of his holy gospel, nor to advance or bring back the papist law, under pain of the loss of life." The following item stated that "following the edict passed by the General Council," no one should do anything to transform the government of Geneva into anything "other than what God has ordained and she is at present." Not only this, but now Genevans were commanded to do everything in their power "to maintain the liberty and the franchises of this city"—also on pain of death; *SDG* 2:531 (R. publ. 1:61–66, March 10, 1550).

in the 1550s.[23] This was a different challenge to the connection between church and state. The majority of these immigrants arrived as religious refugees, seeking a place where they could live openly, in relative safety, as Reformed Protestants. But, aside from the fact that the existence of the Reformed Church was predicated upon Genevan independence, most of these newcomers were not dedicated to the liberty and sovereignty of the Genevan republic as a cause unto itself.

As William Monter made clear in 1979, the vast majority of French immigrants who arrived in Geneva from the 1550s to the 1580s were temporary residents, eager to return to their native France—and probably to cities with more economic opportunities than the strained Geneva could offer—as soon as possible.[24] Thus a paradox arose for the leaders of Geneva: the same immigrant population that had helped to reinforce the Reform in Geneva and solidify the political power of the reformers also posed a potential threat to the relatively fragile political liberty that city leaders were working so hard to preserve. The Genevan church was committed to protecting "true Christians," but how did one determine for sure that newcomers were faithful and truly converted? And the city government supported this religious commitment, but how could one be sure that refugees' familial and political connections in Catholic France might not turn out to be more important to them than their conversions to the Reformation?

An important facet of the authorities' answers to these questions was cementing the connection between the religious and political loyalty of Genevan residents, which the council finally made explicit in the city edicts of 1560. This document included a section of two items titled "Regarding the Reformation and Liberty of the City." The first statement reiterated the earlier edicts about not overturning the divinely ordained government of Geneva. But here an exhortation that all Genevans should protect the city included maintaining "the holy evangelical reformation" as well as the "liberty and franchises of this city." The following item ordered that anyone who knew anything about any actions "against the abovementioned principality, and likewise against the Word of God and his holy gospel," should tell the council

23. Naphy argues that Calvin's supporters did not solidify their political victory until 1557 (*Consolidation of the Genevan Reformation*, 213).
24. Monter, "Historical Demography," 411–12.

immediately or risk the penalty of death.[25] Thus, by 1560, to be a Reformed Genevan was officially and unquestionably to be a defender of Genevan independence, and vice versa. And yet Genevan citizens and residents continued to travel in Catholic regions and maintain Catholic contacts, in apparent contradiction to this official policy.

As I mentioned earlier, these edicts in and of themselves do not tell us how strictly they were enforced or how the people of Geneva reacted to them. But this overview of some of the key edicts and official city statements regarding the treatment of visitors to the city, the behavior of residents when outside of the city, and the responsibilities of Genevans toward both church and city provides us with a framework for analyzing the relationships between Genevans and Catholics during Calvin's lifetime. To complete our discussion, let me now turn to several specific examples of consistory cases involving individuals who crossed the city boundaries into the Catholic worlds beyond Geneva.

Consistory Cases on Travel to Catholic Areas

First, let me return briefly to the case I mentioned at the beginning of this chapter: the accusations that Pierre Authin—a Genevan resident and employee, not merely a visitor—had asserted that the Catholic churches in other cities were just as good as the Reformed Church in Geneva. This suggestion goes to the heart of the concerns underlying the various edicts I have just been discussing. One of the most basic premises of religion and politics in sixteenth-century Europe was that Protestant and Catholic churches were inherently unequal. Religious leaders on both sides of that divide believed that there was one true church; Protestants and Catholics could not be equally correct and equally faithful to God. But while the fundamental inequality of these churches in the sixteenth century is almost a truism, as we look beyond the level of religious and political leaders, we find that this inequality also is not always true.

Authin was hardly the only European to entertain the thought that going to church was still going to church, whether the doctrine of the

---

25. *SDG* 3:105 (Les criées faites en la citée de Genève, February 28–March 5, 1560).

church was Catholic or Reformed. But many governments, not only religious leaders, viewed this kind of religious tolerance as threatening. In the case of Geneva, where church and city together constructed a system for the assiduous oversight of residents' practices and beliefs, the limits of that supervision posed a particular challenge. Having given so much thought and effort to creating a Reformed and orderly society within Geneva, what power did they have to enforce their principles beyond the borders of Geneva, even in regard to their own inhabitants?

An examination of consistory cases involving people traveling to Catholic regions suggests, first, that the members of the Genevan consistory were especially concerned that such people moved too easily between Catholic and Reformed practice, without comprehending the gravity of their actions; and second, that in a number of cases, this fear that Genevan travelers did not appreciate the menace of Catholicism was grounded in reality. At least, interactions with Catholics did sometimes correspond to laxity in commitment to Reformed doctrine and practice. Whether this connection threatened Geneva in the ways that the authorities thought it did is a separate question that I hope to address in the course of my larger project.

In my preliminary investigations into the consistory records, I have found that Genevans traveled to and had contact with Catholic regions for reasons most commonly involving marriage, children (education, financial support, baptism of illegitimate children), servants, or business. In some cases Genevans also fled to Catholic regions in attempts to avoid confronting either the consistory or the city council—or both. I plan to explore all these contacts in the course of my larger project. Here I would like briefly to look at the most general types of consistory cases: those involving Genevans who moved back and forth across the Reformed/Catholic boundaries more than once, and sometimes on a regular basis.

An excellent example from the early years of Calvin's tenure in Geneva is the case of Pierre Goujon. The basic outline of Goujon's story, as related in the consistory records, is as follows: In February 1546, the consistory summoned Pierre Goujon to ask him if it was true that he was living in Geneva but was still attending "celebrations and other things in the papistry." Goujon responded that yes, this was true, and that he was "not in this city except as a servant, and that his household is still in La Roche. And that whenever it will please Messieurs, he will bring all of his household and will live according to the custom here." While the vast majority of consistory cases include general admonitions to the accused, in this case Calvin himself spoke to Goujon. The record states that "Monsieur Calvin remonstrated with him [saying that] as long as one allows that [behavior], we will have to permit everyone to live the way he wants to."

This is one of the relatively rare situations in which we do not have to surmise what Calvin thought of a consistory proceeding or how he influenced it. His words cut right to the heart of the matter, from the authorities' point of view: to allow people to straddle the border of Catholic and Reformed Christianity was to lose control not only of individuals in Geneva but also of the city as a whole. Sinful humans needed the guidance provided by the Reformed Church to help them live according to God's will. At the same time, that oversight was not enough to transform or control any individual who was not committed to the Reform in the first place. Thus even when Goujon protested a second time that, whenever it pleased the council to rule on his affairs (see below), he would be happy to move his family to Geneva, still the consistory concluded that "his confession is not sufficient." They required him to return a month later to demonstrate both his knowledge of Reformed beliefs and his commitment to those beliefs.[26]

Two months later, at the beginning of April, Goujon finally met with the consistory again. This entry opens with the observation that "he did not appear as he had promised to declare his conscience and scruple." But when he finally did present himself in April, Goujon asserted that "he is ready and wants to live and die in the reformation of the gospel." Still, the consistory admonished him that "it is not licit to live in two sects as he is doing and as the Jews once did." If he wanted to live in Geneva, they insisted, he needed to move there for good, with his entire

26. Thomas A. Lambert, Isabella M. Watt, Wallace McDonald, and Robert M. King-don, eds., *Registres du Consistoire de Genève au temps de Calvin, Tome II (1545–1546)* (Geneva: Droz, 2001), 134–35 (R. Consist. 2:29v., February 4, 1546). Cited hereafter as R. Consist. publ. 2; original archival citation given in parentheses. Pierre Goujon's case was further complicated by accusations that his brother, Antoine, had impregnated a servant, about which Pierre claimed to know nothing. In addition, Goujon was married to Nicoline Favre, sister of Gaspard Favre and daughter of François Favre, an important merchant in Geneva. Both Gaspard and François would be active in the challenges to Calvin's author-ity leading up to 1555. R. Consis. publ. 2, 134n133; Naphy, *Consolidation of the Genevan Reformation*, 96–104, 150–53.

household. Goujon, in turn, insisted that first the council needed to render a decision regarding his business with them. The consistory went on to admonish Goujon for not eating meat on Fridays—one of the most obvious ways to suggest to the Genevan authorities that one was still, in fact, Catholic. The case concludes with a long paragraph summarizing the consistory's recommendation: they sent Goujon on to the council, asserting that he cared only to profit from "worldly goods and not by the honor of God." Before dismissing him, they went on to question him about his religious practices, and he confessed that he had attended St-Pierre, the main cathedral of Geneva, at Christmas and had not taken communion. When asked if he had not promised to live according to the reformation of the gospel and of Messieurs, he responded that he had nothing else to say except that "he would like to conclude some business with Messieurs, and then to bring his wife and his children" to Geneva.[27]

The entries for Goujon's case convey the consistory's main concern quite clearly: no multiple residences. Genevans were to be entirely committed to living in Geneva, according to the Reformation, or they were not to live there at all. Anyone who could not make that commitment for himself as well as for his family and servants raised the suspicions of the consistory. In terms of giving us insight into *Goujon's* priorities in this situation, however, the consistory records are limited to the point of being misleading—until they are put together with the records of the city council, as the editing team for the consistory project has done in their notes for volume 2. Looking beyond the consistory records alone, we find that Goujon's struggle with the city council went back nearly twenty years and involved a fight over ownership of the assets of Goujon's former employer, Perrin Peyrolier, a wealthy supporter of the duke of Savoy who had left Geneva in 1526 and died that same year.

The governments of Bern and Fribourg, nearby Swiss cantons, had even become involved in the situation on Goujon's behalf. This lengthy dispute was finally resolved in 1546; in April of that year, the city awarded Goujon part of the amount that he had claimed as his inheritance from Peyrolier.[28] Although he continued to live in Geneva, he apparently did not follow through on his promise to relocate his

27. R. Consist. publ. 2:180–81 (R. Consist. 2:44v–45, April 1, 1546).
28. R. Consist. publ. 2:135n135.

family and household into the city. In February 1547, the consistory was still complaining to the council that Goujon "is a resident here and has gone several times to hear the Mass at La Roche." The council "resolved to ask him if he wanted to 'live according to the Christian Reformation' and, if not, to command him to retire to La Roche-sur-Foron."[29]

Goujon's case is an excellent source for observing the complex nature of Reformed Genevan relations with Catholics and the drawing of religious and political boundaries. It includes both pre-Reformation boundaries (supporters versus opponents of the duke of Savoy) and existing tensions that were made only worse by the Reformation. With the coming of the Reform, questions of political loyalty became matters of religious fidelity. Although consistory and council records do not let us fully know Goujon's thinking, the actions that they report make it clear that the religious distinctions between Protestants and Catholics did not weigh heavily on his mind. His priority was regaining his financial losses (or at least what he believed he was owed as his inheritance). If his financial complaint could be resolved to his satisfaction, Goujon was happy to relocate to Geneva, but he was in no way desperate to do so. Certainly he expressed no interest in abandoning his financial claims for the greater goal of living according to the Reform.

Goujon's case is somewhat unusual in the length of its records, but he was not unique in his nonchalance about negotiating life in both Catholic and Reformed places. As I mentioned earlier, one of the circumstances that most upset Calvin and his colleagues was when an individual promised to live according to the Reform in Geneva, then left the city, and subsequently returned, asking to be readmitted to the Genevan church. This type of situation recurs throughout the consistory records, as in the 1553 case of Estienne Brune from Provence. According to this entry, Brune "had lived in this city for a long time, and then he had returned to his cloister as a monk." Faced with this accusation, Brune responded that "he is repentant and says that he is a shoemaker." Although his response resolved the question of whether Brune could support himself financially—a significant factor in Geneva's acceptance of immigrants—it did not satisfactorily demonstrate his religious leanings. The consistory ordered him to return to them

29. R. Consist. publ. 2:181n391.

"before the next Lord's Supper to see if he is better edified and if he is more penitent."[30]

Two years later, in 1555, the consistory summoned Pierre de Laugre, called Germain, "because after having lived in this city and taken the Lord's Supper, he returned to Lyon and has confessed that he went to Mass there." Although de Laugre now wanted to return to Geneva, like Brune, the consistory held him in suspicion, sending him on to the council and excluding him from communion until "he shows other signs of Christianity."[31] Similarly, several weeks later, Pierre Nepveur of Lyon confessed to the consistory that "about eight years ago he had taken the Lord's Supper, and then he had returned to Provence, where he had attended Mass." Now Nepveur, too, was requesting that the consistory allow him to return to the Genevan church and community. Rather than welcome him with open arms, the consistory concluded that they would wait to "see how he behaves himself."[32]

That these particular cases represent a larger trend in the 1550s is demonstrated by the consistory's complaint to the council several years later, in 1558, about the problem of people renouncing the Reform and then returning to Geneva. The consistory requested that the council "put some order" to the problem of "those who renounce the gospel and the pure doctrine that they know to be for our salvation and [after having been in the] popery then return here." At the very least, said the consistory, "when such renouncers come and return themselves to the church, they should similarly repair their fault before the church in order to give an example to the others."[33] The following month, in September, the council responded to this request by resolving to establish a law for "all such renouncers, that upon exiting from the church they should make public reparations to provide an example to the others."[34]

The next spring, Jehan Chappelet of Champagne confessed to the consistory that he had "abjured God in Lyon" a week earlier. He

---

30. R. Consist. 8:29v., June 8, 1553. The transcription here is unclear. Although I have translated "moynene" as "monk," it is possible that the secretary meant that Brune had returned "to his cloister and his way of life."

31. R. Consist. 10:10v., March 21, 1555.

32. R. Consist. 10:18v., April 11, 1555.

33. R. Consist. 14:41v., August 30, 1558. The specific case involved Jehan Barral, who had returned from spending time in Lyon as a prisoner.

34. *SDG* 3:85 (RC 54, 273, September 1, 1558).

recognized his fault and "asked for mercy from God—and this was after having taken the Lord's Supper in this city." The consistory resolved to admonish him, and "as to the rest, because there is an edict regarding those who renounce God like this, it seems good to exclude him from the Lord's Supper and to send him to Messieurs on Monday" so that the council could take whatever action it deemed appropriate to "repair such scandal." But they also asked the council "to consider the fact that he came willingly to confess his fault."[35] Despite the frustrations involved in creating a godly community, neither the consistory nor Calvin himself expected Genevans to be sinless; their realistic hope was that faithful, Reformed Genevans would participate willingly in the disciplining of church and community.

Ultimately, the success of Geneva's reformation and its independent republic depended on the cooperation of its residents and their acknowledgment of the values of both the church leaders and the city government. Yet as these cases indicate, some Genevans shifted in their religious practices at the same time that they moved back and forth across the physical boundaries between Geneva and Catholic regions. The interest of such individuals in returning to the Reformed life of Geneva, and the ultimate willingness of the Genevan authorities to accept them back into the community after due investigation and testing, suggest a significant degree of porousness and flexibility in boundaries that, on paper and by reputation, appeared to be impermeable and rigid.

Conclusion

My discussion has only begun to illustrate the complexity of Reformed Genevan relations with Catholic people and regions. At the same time that it was adopting the Reformation, Geneva was a city grappling with the challenges of newly established political independence and the burdens and benefits of a large influx of immigrants. The consistory cases I have focused on here mostly involved immigrants and the particular challenges posed by their connections to their homelands. But the edicts I have discussed applied to all Genevan residents, temporary and permanent immigrants as well as native-born citizens.

35. R. Consist. 15:70, April 20, 1559.

Elsewhere I have begun to discuss the issue of native Genevans maintaining contacts with Catholic friends and relatives, another important aspect of Reformed Genevan interactions with Catholics. Both groups of people—immigrants and longtime inhabitants—posed challenges to Calvin's ideals of how a truly Christian community should operate. And both were significant parts of the Reformed Christian community as it really did operate—as a religious refuge, as a struggling merchant city, and as a community of faithful Christians living in regular contact with the un-Reformed world.

I will conclude with an edict of 1561. In April of that year, following a discussion about "the bourgeois who leave the city without permission," the city council declared that all "bourgeois suspected of wanting to leave" should be called before the council and "forbidden to leave without license, according to their oath." This phrasing strongly suggests that even the bourgeois of Geneva continued to travel outside of the city on a regular basis. But most interesting is the council's decision about how to deal with such rule-breakers: "If there are any who leave without asking, they should be noted in order to punish them if they return afterward. This is done in order not to give anyone occasion to say that we want to keep people in this city by force." That is, no member of the bourgeoisie would be physically restrained from leaving the city; rather, their departure would simply be noted so that justice could be meted out once they had returned of their own free will. The council was concerned not only that a reputation for overly strict control of its residents would deter people from moving to Geneva in the future, but also that "this city is open [*franche*] and free and that our bourgeois and residents are known to be such, and that there is no open city in which one is constrained and in such great subjection as to have to remain there perpetually despite one's affairs."[36] But how, exactly, could a city be both purely Reformed and open and free at the same time? After two and a half decades of reform, and despite the victory of Calvin's supporters in the government of Geneva, the model Reformed Church and city continued to struggle to find a balance between godliness and political independence, and between the desire to protect themselves from outside, Catholic influences and the need to interact with the Catholic world beyond Geneva's borders.

---

36. *SDG* 3:124–25 (RC 56, 169, April 1, 1561).

4

Rules of Engagement

Catholics and Protestants in the Diocese of Geneva, 1580–1633

Jill Fehleison

By the middle of the sixteenth century, Geneva had become the spiritual and intellectual center of the Reformed faith for the Francophone world, but neither Catholics nor their faith suddenly disappeared from the city's doorstep; rather, they maintained deep roots in the region. While the Roman cult faced major setbacks following Calvin's triumphs and the House of Savoy's failures, the last decades of the sixteenth century saw a resurgence of Catholicism, spearheaded by an activist clergy that included François de Sales, the future bishop and saint. With support from Rome, clerical leaders for the diocese of Geneva developed grand designs for the area, voicing publicly a desire to win back all of Europe for their faith, but most recognized that this goal was unattainable. François de Sales wrote of his aspirations to return the diocese to its pre-Reformation boundaries, but his actions reveal more immediate goals of reintroducing Catholicism into places where it had disappeared, winning a few prized converts, reviving existing parishes, and bringing clergy into line with Tridentine reform. As William Bouwsma has asserted, by the seventeenth century few in Rome held a realistic hope of winning back all the Protestants into the Catholic fold.[1] The more realistic aims were to revitalize the Roman faith and to weaken its rivals wherever possible, both psychologically and in numbers.

For much of the sixteenth century, the Catholic diocese of Geneva offered little response to the initial Reformed expansion as it steadily lost ground to the Swiss Protestant cities of Geneva and Berne, and the bishop took up residency in exile in Annecy. Savoy was a playground for the imperial aspirations of Spain and France, and Catholic revitalization was no more than a dream as the diocese tried to prevent further losses of its territory. Personnel inspired by a renewed vigor emanating from Rome assumed leadership of the diocese, beginning with the episcopate of Claude de Granier in 1579. He was part of a new generation of bishops who were receiving their education in Rome as the Council of Trent drew to a close in 1563. According to his biographer, Boniface Constantin, Granier studied philosophy as well as canon law under the Jesuit Francisco de Toledo, and he may have met Carlo Borromeo, archbishop of Milan.[2] Borromeo set a standard of renewal and reform within his diocese through pastoral visitations, diocesan synods, provincial councils, and the establishment of seminaries.[3] Whether or not there was a personal encounter, Borromeo's reputation would have been known to the young Savoyard cleric and would have provided a model to emulate for an active bishop. Bishop de Granier followed in the footsteps of Borromeo by conducting the first general visitation of his parishes since 1518; he challenged the status

1. William J. Bouwsma, *Venice and the Defense of Republican Liberty: Renaissance Values in the Age of the Counter Reformation* (Berkeley and Los Angeles: University of California Press, 1968), 294.

2. Boniface Constantin, *La vie du révérendissime et illustrissime evesque Claude de Granier: Religieux de Sainct Benoist, et predecesseur du B. François de Sales, en l'Evesché de Geneve* (Lyon: C. Rigaud & Philippe Bordes, 1640), 9, 12, 14, 24–26, 28–30.

3. John B. Tomaro, "San Carlo Borromeo and the Implementation of the Council of Trent," in *San Carlo Borromeo: Catholic Reform and Ecclesiastical Politics in the Second Half of the Sixteenth Century*, ed. John M. Headley and John B. Tomaro (Washington, DC: Folger Shakespeare Library, 1988), 67, 69.

quo by taking the initial steps toward placing the clergy and the laity under the increased scrutiny ordained by the Council of Trent.[4] The bishop's increased activity in the region not surprisingly coincided with a reduction of military conflict. As Granier and the clergy grew more engaged in the lives of the Alpine villages surrounding Geneva, there were more encounters with their confessional neighbors. Emboldened Catholics in the region began reasserting themselves.

Exchanges and encounters between Catholics and Protestants occurred on many different levels and could be social, economic, formal, or confrontational; supposedly regulated by treaties and formal agreements between sovereigns, the parameters of coexistence remained fluid in large part due to the close proximity and overlapping lives of the regions' inhabitants, making informal and private interactions inevitable. Local religious and secular leaders spent a great deal of time and energy trying to figure out a way to live with one another after years of conflict that disrupted and displaced everyone in the region. Few voices of progress and tolerance could be found among both groups of leaders, and in most cases rigid individuals remained married to their particular belief systems. Yet at times both sides of the confessional divide did choose pragmatism, if not toleration, over violence. Therefore, key questions emerge and inform the research that I have pursued on the Diocese of Geneva as its leaders followed a program of reform while navigating the complications that came with promoting Tridentine Catholicism near the epicenter of the Reformed faith. What were the realities of the biconfessional region around Geneva in the late sixteenth and early seventeenth centuries? With more contact came opportunities for more conflict, but were there corresponding opportunities for understanding? How did the two confessional communities perceive each other? Keith Luria has shown that Catholics and Protestants sharing communal space could reach acceptable compromises, but regular interactions between rival confessional communities could also heighten perceived differences rather than lessen them.[5]

4. Claude de Granier (or Granyer) spent part of each of the first three years of his episcopate touring the parishes of his diocese; Archives Départmentales de la Haute-Savoie, Annecy, France. (ADHS) 2Mi75: *Visites Pastorales du Diocèse de Genève: Visites par Claude de Granier. 1580–1582.*
5. Keith Luria, *Sacred Boundaries: Religious Coexistence and Conflict in Early-Modern France* (Washington, DC: Catholic University of America Press, 2005); see esp. xiv, 45, 57.

The examples I have chosen to highlight illustrate the ever-changing and multifaceted relationship of the religious rivals.

With the treaty of Nyon of 1589 between Savoy and Berne allowing for the reestablishment of the Mass and the relative peacefulness of the region, Catholic clergy became bolder in the 1590s as they engaged Protestants in and around Geneva.[6] The tandem missionary efforts of François de Sales and his cousin Louis de Sales in the fall of 1594, followed by the entrée of reinforcements three years later in the form of Jesuits and Capuchins, and the staging of public demonstrations of faith, including Forty Hours Devotions and Jubilees—all made the Catholic presence known in the region. The mission's efforts had significant success in winning back villages of the Chablais that were literally at the doorstep of Geneva. As a result, Catholic clergy challenged their status as personae non grata on the streets of the Reformed city.

Geneva was able to withstand the onslaught of the Catholic duke of Savoy's military forces during the *Escalade* (on the night of December 11 to 12, 1602), yet Catholics came openly as daily visitors through the city's gates, and the citizens of Geneva continued to interact with their Catholic neighbors. City leaders repeatedly addressed such actions and issued numerous ordinances in an attempt to control Catholic-Protestant interactions and comings and goings from the city. The city struggled with whether to view Catholic clergy who announced themselves at the gates of the city as enemies or as travelers passing through. City officials periodically revisited the issue since it proved difficult to create rules that applied to all Catholic visitors and to all encounters. Due to its geography, Geneva was a crossroads and remained the largest city in the region for commerce and the easiest way for diocesan officials to cut through the mountains and travel between Savoy-controlled Chablais and French-controlled Gex.

---

6. Paul Martin, *Trois cas de pluralisme confessionnel aux XVI et XVII Siècles* (Geneva: A. Jullien, 1961), 65; Alain Dufour, *La guerre de 1589–1593* (Geneva: A. Jullien, 1958), 94–96. A key turning point for the confessional composition of the region came with the treaty of Nyon of 1589 between Savoy and Berne. Charles-Emmanuel demanded that the treaty include a provision allowing for the reestablishment of Catholicism in the disputed areas. According to Dufour, Berne abandoned its alliance with its Protestant brethren of Geneva by acquiescing to the demands of the duke. This alliance left vulnerable the Protestants who found themselves under Savoy's secular rule and opened the door for the return of Catholicism to the Chablais in the 1590s.

François de Sales Visits Geneva

During his years in Savoy, François de Sales passed through the city gates of Geneva on several occasions, with one trip resulting in an encounter with Theodore Beza. At the beginning of 1597, de Sales and a fellow missionary, Capuchin Esprit de Beaume, hatched a plan to gain an audience with Beza with the expressed goal of counseling him to abjure the Reformed faith. De Sales was to try to obtain a meeting with Beza while Beaume, in Rome for a chapter meeting, was to obtain assurances from Pope Clement VIII that Beza would be welcomed into the Catholic fold if de Sales was successful in his conversion. De Sales recounted to the pope that he often visited Geneva under various pretexts before he was able to meet with Beza "alone and in secret" on the third festival of Easter. After the initial encounter, the young missionary claimed that he had used all his means to influence the Reformed leader but came to the conclusion that Beza was a bitter old man with a "heart of stone." However, this impression did not dissuade de Sales from hoping to meet with Beza again to persuade him to cross the confessional divide, noting that time was of the essence due to Beza's advanced age.[7]

The Catholic missionary's meeting with Beza did not go unnoticed, and rumors spread throughout Europe in the summer of 1597 that Beza had converted to Catholicism, forcing the spiritual leader of Geneva to publish a pamphlet addressing the gossip.[8] De Sales's visits were most likely the origin of these rumors. In the end de Sales was unable to convince Beza to convert, but easy entrée to the city and access to Beza are striking, and one wonders why the Reformed pastor was even willing to meet with de Sales. The missionary had little to lose and much to gain from this encounter, and if he had somehow been successful in his mission, it would have been a major coup of the Counter-Reformation. The rumors that forced Beza to defend himself may have been enough of a reward for de Sales's efforts. The

---

7. François de Sales, *Œuvres de Saint François de Sales*, 26 vols. (Annecy: J. Niérat, 1892–1932), 11:268–70; letter to Pope Clement VIII, April 21, 1597.

8. Scott M. Manetsch, *Theodore Beza and the Quest for Peace in France, 1572–1598* (Brill: Leiden, 2000), 318–20. Manetsch says that the Jesuits were the source of these rumors. The timing of the reports makes a convincing argument that de Sales's visit triggered the rumor.

attempted conversion, even if it had been nothing more than a rumor, illustrates clearly the potentially confusing personal encounters that could occur between Catholic and Protestants, in this case a conversation that might lead to greater understanding or rivalry between the two confessions.

Once de Sales became bishop, his visits to Geneva offered a more-significant statement, with broader religious and political ramifications. By 1608 de Sales was six years into his episcopate and had developed a reputation as a devout and able bishop, and he was well known in Turin, Rome, Paris, and, as we shall see, by his spiritual rivals in Geneva. King Henri IV offered the up-and-coming bishop a church position in France, which he seemed willing to accept, and de Sales had developed good relationships with French royal officials.[9] A post in France would have freed him from constantly balancing divergent interests of France and Savoy concerning his diocese. Whatever the case, de Sales did not leave Savoy permanently for a position in France. His twenty-year episcopate forced him to cross back and forth between contested territories, along the way encountering individuals from Geneva, France, and occasionally even Savoy who challenged his position and right to be there.

On a return trip from the French territory of the Pays de Gex in September 1609, de Sales—in a fit of what the bishop himself in hindsight called "impudent boldness"—passed through Geneva rather than taking a slower route back to Annecy. Claiming at the gates that he possessed the right to enter the city based on his predecessors' position as bishop-prince of Geneva, de Sales caught the attention of city leaders, who informed Duke Charles-Emmanuel; the duke was not amused at the bishop's claim of ancient privilege and accused de Sales of trying to retake temporal authority in the city.[10] If anyone was going to reclaim secular authority in Geneva, the duke reserved that

9. De Sales, *Œuvres de Saint François de Sales*, 14:9–10; letter to Antoine des Hayes, May 6, 1608. The bishop mentioned to Antoine des Hayes, master of the hotel of the king and governor and bailiff of Montargis, that the king had offered the bishop of Geneva a church position in France. De Sales said that he was very grateful for the offer and would accept it if the pope and king agreed; André Ravier, *Francis de Sales, Sage and Saint*, trans. Joseph Bowler (San Francisco: Ignatius Press, 1988), 112–13. Ravier claims that the position was the archbishopric of Paris and contends that de Sales was unwilling to leave Savoy.

10. De Sales, *Œuvres de Saint François de Sales*, 14:216; letter to Antoine des Hayes, December 4, 1609.

right for himself. No anonymous entrance into the city was possible for Bishop de Sales, such as he had accomplished ten years earlier in his encounter with Beza, and his use of his ancient title overstepped legal limitations and angered both the Reformed city and his Catholic sovereign.

Capuchins Visit Geneva

A biconfessional region meant that contact was unavoidable, and Catholics continued to have numerous reasons, legitimate and otherwise, to interact with their Protestant neighbors. Other clergy, particularly the Capuchins, did more than pass through Geneva, and their presence in the city raised suspicions among the leadership. The friars would present themselves at the city's gates, claiming a need to enter Geneva to purchase supplies and forcing the town officials to address the issue of Catholics entering the walls of its city.[11] Geneva had cause to be suspicious of its Catholic visitors, and more-frequent encounters did not engender better relations. In 1609 a Capuchin named Maurice on more than one occasion tried to preach at St-Pierre in Geneva, interact with members of the congregation, and dispute with students and syndics (magistrates). The Council of Geneva banned Maurice from entering the city on pain of physical punishment and began to scrutinize Catholic visitors more closely. Another Capuchin friar complained to the council about having his books confiscated on entering the gates of the city and requested a reimbursement, which the council granted.[12]

Geneva was not the only destination for roaming Catholics. Two preaching friars visited the nearby Reformed town of Lancy, which briefly detained them. There were reports that two Capuchins were preaching openly in Bossey, trying to charm the people with outrageous and scandalous claims.[13] Geneva and its environs was a Reformed

11. RC 109 Mi 478, n. 1: folio 75 (April 6, 1612).
12. RC 106 Mi B475: folio 153 (August 21, 1609); RC 106 Mi B475: folio 102v° (May 1609).
13. RC 106 Mi 475: folio 102v°, folios 106v°–107 (May 12, 1609), folio 153 (August 21, 1609); RC 108 Mi B477: folio 228 (August 9, 1611); RC 109 Mi 478, n. 1: folio 74v° (April 6, 1612).

island in a sea of Catholics, facing constant threats, both perceived and real, to its political and spiritual survival.

Although it proved impossible to prevent all contact with Catholic clergy, the leaders of Geneva believed that the presence of Capuchins in their city was a threat and took steps to ensure that the friars were monitored while passing through the city, limiting their contact with city dwellers. Not surprisingly, the measure met with resistance. The Capuchins widened the controversy into an international incident by complaining to France about their military escort through the streets of Geneva, triggering French Ambassador M. de Miron to forward a letter, arguing the friars' case, from King Louis XIII to the leaders of the city.[14] In an effort to defend its actions, the city council offered its side of the predicament to the French representative, informing Miron that the Capuchins had to be accompanied by soldiers because of their attempts to preach and other generally disruptive behavior while in the city. The ambassador agreed to forward Geneva's case to the king.[15]

Nevertheless, Miron continued to advocate on behalf of the Capuchins as he urged the council to allow the friars to walk about freely in Geneva. The council proposed a compromise: any Capuchin who entered Geneva must go to the house of a syndic to declare his intention, and then a guard rather than a soldier would accompany the friar to places of business but prevent him from preaching and entering homes.[16] Miron was successful in reducing some of the limitations on the Capuchins. By November 1618 the Capuchins could enter the city without a guard, but they still had to go to the house of a syndic to state the reasons for their visit.[17] This negotiated compromise failed to solve all the problems, and the consistory (council of ministers) continued to complain to the city council about friars' visits.[18] As long as Catholic clergy maintained commercial and personal relationships with citizens of Geneva, it remained difficult to regulate this sort of interaction; it appears to have been impossible for Geneva to completely exclude Catholic neighbors from passing through the city.

14. RC 117 Mi B484: folio 95v° (April 10, 1618).
15. RC 117 Mi B484: folio 98v° (April 14, 1618); Capuchins of St. Julien.
16. RC 117 Mi B484: folio 136v° (June 20, 1618).
17. RC 117 Mi B484: folio 259 (November 23, 1618).
18. L'Abbé Fleury, *Appendice à la Brochure Institulée le P. Chérubin et les Ministres de Genève* (Genève: Pfeffer & Puky, 1865), XLI.

Though the Catholic clergy may have had legitimate business to conduct in Geneva, the region's urban center, the leaders of the city had valid reasons to be mistrustful of Catholic clergy's visits. Capuchins continued to test both the spiritual and physical walls of Geneva, and occasionally their efforts had success, as was the case in late summer 1633, when reports reached the council that two young men had been visiting the Capuchins in nearby St. Julien. The syndics investigated the case, ordering the fathers of the two to appear before the council to explain the situation; by November it was evident that the two young men had been converted by the Capuchins. As a result, the council issued new ordinances attempting to reduce the friars' access to the citizens of Geneva.[19] Due to the close proximity of the city to revitalized Catholic centers, it proved impossible for the leaders of Geneva to shut off all contact between its people and its rival confession.

With the entrée of the religious orders into the mission project in 1597, one individual in particular became the focal point of the anxieties expressed by the leadership of Geneva. The consistory grew concerned that individuals were attending services conducted by Père Chérubin de Maurienne, an activity it viewed as dangerous, and vowed to single out for reprimand those who continued.[20] From his arrival in the Chablais, Chérubin became a lightning rod for intense encounters with the Reformed population because of his flamboyant demeanor and his willingness to confront his rivals directly rather than engaging in the more staid interactions that François de Sales tended to have.

Genevans Visit Catholic Villages

Catholics and Protestants perceived the situation around Geneva in strikingly different ways: the Catholics saw people as persons to engage, debate, and convert; the Protestants wanted to preserve their city and congregation by avoiding direct confrontations with their Catholic neighbors as much as possible. Despite prohibitions and warnings, some citizens of Geneva remained curious about their confessional rival decades after the Mass was banned in the city. Because of this

19. RC 132 Mi B499: folios 159 and 188 (August 26 and November 4, 1633).
20. RC 93 Mi B463: folio 183v° (December 12, 1598).

continued interest, city leaders tried to prevent the fraternization of Genevans with their Catholic counterparts, especially during religious celebrations. Yet all the interdictions failed to prevent at least a handful of Geneva citizens from venturing out of the city walls to see the Baroque celebrations nearby. As Thonon and Annemasse increasingly became the center of the Catholic mission in the Chablais, these two towns on the banks of Lake Leman (Lac Léman) drew the attention of many inhabitants of the region, regardless of confessional affiliation. By late summer 1597 both church and civic leaders grew concerned about the attention its citizens paid to the Catholic activities in the area, fearing that the various processions would distract Protestant townsfolk or, worse, were a guise for some shadowy plan hatched by the duke of Savoy to impose his secular and confessional domination on the city.[21]

For Geneva, the Catholics remained a spiritual threat that could always arrive with military force. The consistory punished a Pierre Besson for going to Annemasse, presumably to attend a Catholic service, sentencing him to prison on bread and water.[22] In the last years of the sixteenth century, the Catholic mission program ratcheted up its activities around Geneva. Between September 1597 and October 1598, the Catholics' celebration of the Forty Hours Devotions on three separate occasions, once in the village of Annemasse and twice in Thonon, gained the attention of Geneva's leadership. These celebrations attracted participants and audiences from across the region, including Cardinal Alexander de Medici and Duke Charles-Emmanuel, who both participated in the final one held in Thonon. The Company of Pastors noted that the Catholics were planning a great gathering to replant a cross in Annemasse, but the company did not seem to realize the full scale of the Forty Hours Celebrations until their completion.[23] Public displays like these served a twofold function of bringing Catholic visitors into the region and also exposing members of the Reformed faith to Baroque celebrations.

The success of the celebrations solidified the continued presence of Catholics in the towns around Geneva. In the weeks leading up to a Jubilee Celebration in Thonon in 1602, the ministers complained about vendors

21. *RCP* 7:72–73 (August 26, 1597).
22. RC 92 Mi B462: folio 118v° (August 4, 1597). The consistory was made up of both city council members and ministers, and its pronouncements were recorded by the city council, thereby giving them the force of law.
23. *RCP* 7:72–73 (August 26, 1597).

from Geneva going to Thonon to sell their wares, so the council passed an interdiction against this commerce. Furthermore, the council prohibited pilgrims from passing through Geneva on their way to Thonon.[24] As it had several years before with the Forty Hours Devotions, the council feared that the religious celebration would be a pretext for the duke of Savoy's military and political aspirations against Geneva. The council issued a further order prohibiting anyone from attending the Jubilee and ordered shopkeepers to keep their arms ready. But at the beginning of June, the council received a report from boatmen that individuals from Geneva were going to the Jubilee in Thonon; the council responded by issuing a fine of twenty-five florins to anyone caught attending.[25] Some risked the punishment for potential financial gain while others were curious about or attracted to the religious spectacle. The consistory sentenced one man named Guerin to three days on bread and water for leading a procession from Pont d'Arve to Annecy.[26] Geneva was trying to establish clear religious, political, and geographical boundaries, which came into conflict with the economic desires of the rank-and-file vendors and at least a few religious desires.

It proved impossible to foresee every possible encounter that might occur between the adherents to both confessions, and leaders on both sides tried to regulate these encounters in quite different manners. Catholic missionaries continued to engage Protestants in a variety of ways, viewing frequent interactions as offering more opportunities to win converts; meanwhile the Reformed leadership of Geneva tried to create rules restricting casual contact. Frequent contact did not help reduce suspicions on either side, yet both continued pursuing relations with the opposing confession.

Catholics and Protestants Meet for a Disputation

Another avenue for engagement was through formal negotiations between designated representatives. In theory, this format made it easier to regulate interactions between the two parties, but even this

24. L'Abbé Fleury, *St. François de Sales le P. Chérubin et les Ministres de Genève* (Paris: Librairie Saint-Joseph, 1864), 48.
25. RC 97 Mi B467: folios 71 and 79v° (May 18 and June 4, 1602).
26. RC 97 Mi B467: folio 88 (June 25, 1602).

type of contact proved difficult to control completely. Between 1597 and 1601 both sides participated in lengthy negotiations in efforts to stage formal debates, though only one brief disputation ever took place. These discussions revealed the very divergent goals of the two confessions. As William Reddy states in his work on the history of emotions, "Communities systematically seek to train emotions, to idealize them, to condemn others."[27] The Catholic missionaries wanted to have their message heard in as many public forums as possible; hence, it is not surprising that they appeared much more eager than the Calvinists to engage in an oral debate of confessional issues. The followers of the Reformed faith subscribed to a more internal and contemplative faith, which came from study and instruction, and they viewed flamboyant displays as more about "ardor" than "truth."[28] Second, the Calvinists continued to fear the duke of Savoy and did not want to antagonize him. Since his arrival in the region, François de Sales had believed in the potential benefit of a dialogue with the Calvinists, whether in one-on-one meetings or formal disputations; however, in the first months of the mission he could not organize a debate because he lacked the manpower, financial resources, and secular support.[29]

Emboldened by reinforcements in 1597, Provost de Sales mentioned to the papal nuncio in Turin that Père Chérubin was in contact with someone from Geneva, and he hoped a dispute would transpire with the Protestants. In an effort to justify such an event, de Sales cited the success of similar debates between the Jesuits of Tournon and the Protestants of Vivarais and Languedoc.[30] De Sales seemed to be acting on this evidence that public exchanges between the confessions could be efficacious for the diocesan goals in the region. In March, the exchanges came to the attention of the Company of Pastors in Geneva, who mistakenly thought a Jesuit was pursuing the disputation. A Geneva citizen had communicated with the Capuchin without

27. William M. Reddy, *The Navigation of Feeling: A Framework for the History of Emotions* (Cambridge: Cambridge University Press, 2001), 323.

28. *RCP* 7:114; and see n. 132 on the writing of company member Jean Pinault.

29. *Œuvres de Saint François de Sales*, 11:158–60; letter to Antoine Favre, September 18, 1595.

30. Ibid., 11:235–39 (February 21, 1597); 11:323–26 (March 17, 1598); letters to Jules-César Riccardi, archbishop of Bari and papal nuncio in Turin.

the company's consent, which it viewed as a "dangerous thing," warning against putting anything in writing and ordering a halt to further discussion with the presumed Jesuit.[31]

These negotiations continued, and the issue reached the full bodies of both the Council of Ten and the Company of Pastors by early summer. Jean Corajod, Geneva lapidary and member of the Council of Two Hundred, had issued some sort of invitation to Chérubin.[32] Theodore Beza convened a special meeting at his home to address the Capuchin's letters to Corajod and to uncover why Chérubin assumed that the lapidary possessed authority to negotiate a conference between the two confessions. Corajod and his accomplice Jacob Gradelle defended their actions, claiming that several pastors, including Charles Perrot, were well aware of their activities, but Beza acted as if he was not.[33] It is difficult to believe that the two men would have corresponded with Chérubin without at least tacit approval from a religious authority, which suggests disagreement among members of the company on how best to respond to Chérubin's overtures. The leaders of Geneva continued to finger point over who had responded to the missionary in the first place.[34] In his biography of Simon Goulart, Leonard Chester Jones asserts that from the Company of Pastors, Goulart, Perrot, and perhaps even Beza were involved in the initial negotiations with the Capuchin, and that Antoine de la Faye was the biggest opponent. Jones says that if la Faye could not lead the negotiations in his "mediocrity," then he did not want to proceed.[35] For many of the pastors, there was little to gain from an oral debate of their faith; yet one of their representatives succumbed to the Catholics' persistence.

On March 14, 1598, the Protestant professor of theology Herman Lignaridus, who had assumed his position in Geneva the previous July, arrived in Thonon and over the course of two days engaged in

31. *RCP* 7:63 (March 19, 1597). The Company of Pastors was composed of ordained ministers and directed the Reformed Church both in Geneva and beyond. The ministers worked closely with secular officials in Geneva and served on the consistory. Theodore Beza was leader of the company during this period, having assumed the position after the death of John Calvin.

32. *Œuvres de Saint François de Sales*, 11:236n1.

33. RC 92 Mi B462: folios 87, 89v°090; *RCP* 7:67–68 (June 12 and 17, 1597).

34. *RCP* 7:67–69 (March 19, 1597).

35. Leonard Chester Jones, *Simon Goulart, sa vie et son œuvre, 1543–1628* (Geneva: Albert Kündig, 1916), 113, 123, 125.

a disputation with Chérubin.[36] Lignaridus halted the proceedings and left for Geneva, but according to the Catholics, he signed a no-tarized statement promising to return.[37] The two sides offered quite different accounts of how the debate actually transpired. François de Sales reported to the papal nuncio in Turin that four people, including Lignaridus, came to Thonon from Geneva and engaged in a disputation that was recorded by witnesses. Not surprisingly, de Sales recounted that Chérubin performed with "great dexterity" and "embarrassed" the Protestant professor.[38] On the other hand, Beza denied that any formal debate was ever planned and claimed in a letter to the Reformed church in Lausanne that Lignaridus, in Thonon simply to refresh himself in the waters, had been accosted on the street by Chérubin. To maintain his honor in the face of the Capuchin's affront and at the urging of the people in the town, with Calvinists wanting to see their faith affirmed in public and Catholics hoping to see Chérubin best the Reformed theologian, Lignaridus in his "impudence" accepted the Capuchin's challenge.[39] The debate covered rather standard points of contention between the two con-fessions, including the interpretation of Scripture; the existence of purgatory; the authority of councils, tradition, and Scripture versus only Scripture; and the role of various church fathers.[40] Much of the debate centered on whether the books of Maccabees were canonical, as the Catholics claimed, or apocryphal, as argued by the Reformed tradition.[41]

36. RC 92 Mi B462: folio 22 (February 4, 1597), council addresses the hiring of Lignari-dus; and folio 105v° (August 4, 1597) mentions making payments to the Elector Palatine as a gesture of goodwill for Lignaridus. Charles of Genève, *Les trophées sacrés: ou, Missions des capucins en Savoie, dans l'Ain, la Suisse romande et la vallée d'Aoste, a la fin du XVIe et au XVIIe siècle*, ed. and foreword by Félix Tisserand (Lausanne: Société d'histoire de la Suisse romande, 1976), 86, 92–214; hereafter *Trophées sacrés*; also see *Œuvres de Saint François de Sales* 11:324–26; *RCP* 7:95–96.

37. *Trophées sacrés*, 186.

38. *Œuvres de Saint François de Sales*, 11:325–26; letter to Jules-César Riccardi, arch-bishop of Bari and papal nuncio in Turin, March 17, 1598.

39. *RCP* 7:317; letter from Theodore Beza to the Church of Lausanne, August 5, 1598.

40. *Trophées sacrés*, 132–61.

41. Antoine de Saint-Michel, Seigneur d'Avully, *Copie de la lettre du Seigneur d'Avully, touchant la dispute des ministres avec le R. P. Chérubin, prescheur de l'Ordre des Capucins* (Lyon, 1598), 14–15.

In the end neither disputant seemed to have accomplished much or changed many minds during the debate itself; but the manner in which each side handled the aftermath offers intriguing insight into the clash and coexistence of a biconfessional community. Chérubin insisted that the debate must continue as it was started, with live voices, and he continued to press the Protestants to send either Lignaridus or someone else to complete the task. Geneva appeared unhappy with the outcome of the dispute and seemingly tried to ignore the Capuchin's continued overtures.[42] By all accounts Chérubin was a powerful preacher and may have been better able to express himself than the theologian Lignaridus. The Company of Pastors maintained that the "dispute that he [Chérubin] requests before the people is only a vain thing and of no use unless our good conditions are met."[43] De Sales claimed, "If we are able to give to the cult the proper splendor, the head of the serpent will be broken."[44] The purpose of debating was quite different for each side: The Reformed leadership viewed it as a way to offer instruction in its doctrine, which could be done more effectively in writing. The Catholic mission preferred public displays that highlighted a few key emotion-evoking elements of its faith, such as the Eucharist, crucifix, and purgatory.

In the aftermath of the dispute, the Catholics put a much more successful public spin on the proceeding and pursued its continuation with much more enthusiasm than did their Protestant rivals. Geneva grew frustrated as it found it difficult to control even formal interactions. The Catholics let it be known that it was Geneva that chose not to continue the debate: they proclaimed victory from the pulpit, in published pamphlets, and on posted placards. One such publication was an open letter about the debate written by Antoine de Saint-Michel, Seigneur d'Avully, a former member of the Reformed faith who had converted under the tutelage of de Sales.[45] Avully portrayed Lignaridus as a lofty theologian who arrived in Thonon with his degree and books in hand

42. The company registers are silent on the matter until late summer 1598.

43. "Dispute qu'il demande devant le peuple ce n'est que chose vaines et de nul usage, sinon qu'il y eust de bonnes conditions commes la Seigneurie l'avoit demandé" (*RCP* 7:99 [August 18, 1598]). All translations are my own unless otherwise credited.

44. "Modo di farle splendidamente, il capo del serpente se ne va spezzato" (*Œuvres de Saint François de Sales*, 11:356–62; letter to papal nuncio, October 13, 1598).

45. *RCP* 7:98; n. 70 mentions the letter in *Copie de la lettre du Seigneur d'Avully*. Most of the published letter was included in *Trophées sacrés*, 129–32, 158–60.

to face Chérubin, who was armed with only his faith and passion.[46] To further this portrait of arrogance, Avully claimed that Lignaridus always interrupted Chérubin while he was making significant points and halted the proceedings, pleading the lateness of the hour, rather than letting the Capuchin have his full say.[47] In all of their propaganda, the Catholics portrayed the Calvinists as hostile and angry.[48] François de Sales asserted that the pastors of Geneva continued to fight not from courage or ardor, but out of rage and despair. He claimed that the Protestant ministers, "already fatigued from the idle talk that they produce, will easily open up their ears to the truth."[49] Despite the negative portrayal, de Sales continued to profess hope that the ministers would convert.

Regardless of the veracity of these portrayals, the Catholic message was effective and often drowned out the measured responses of the Protestants. William Reddy states that gossip and sermons can be "highly emotional and politically charged forms of communication."[50] When the Company of Pastors did react, it was always in writing, in an effort to counter some action or publication on the part of the Catholics. Herman Lignaridus tried to free himself from any further involvement in the situation by secretly negotiating a teaching position in Berne, and the only subsequent service he grudgingly completed for Geneva was providing a written account of the dispute as a rebuttal to Avully's letter that Geneva published at the end of 1598.[51] The city was unhappy with the written outcome of the brief encounter between Chérubin and Lignaridus, claiming that the Catholic-produced publications were inaccurate and caused a "great scandal."[52] While Beza instructed Lignaridus to address the theological points of controversy, the theologian's account instead provided his

46. *Trophées sacrés*, 131–32.

47. Ibid., 158–59.

48. Ibid., 115, 133.

49. "Già stracco delle loro ciancie, facilmente darà orecchio alla verità" (*Œuvres de Saint François de Sales*, 12:20; letter to papal nuncio in Turin, August 24, 1599).

50. Reddy, *Navigation of Feeling*, 46.

51. *Response de Herman Lignaridus, à certaine lettre imprimée, en laguelle le S. d'Avully s'est essayé de représenter la dispute entre iceluy Herman et Chérubin, moine de la secte des capuchins* (Geneva: Jean de Tournes, 1598); BPU.

52. MS Fr. 8, Pièces relatives à la Dispute entre le Conseil de Genève et le père Chérubin de Maurienne, capucin, "Conditions proposées par la Compagnie des Pasteurs pour participer la dispute" (September 24, 1598): folio 42° (BPU).

version of the dispute and responded directly to Avully's letter.[53] In his rebuttal, Lignaridus asserted that Geneva did not send him to Thonon; rather, he was mistaken for a disputer because he carried a book. He agreed to defend his faith only after the villagers begged him to. In an effort to counterbalance the portrait painted of him in the Catholic propaganda, Lignaridus described Chérubin as confused and lacking doctrinal erudition; he asserted that the Catholic belief system was "false and vicious."[54] But his response again demonstrates how the Protestants continued to let the Catholics take the offensive in the matter. Each side approached the matter quite differently, with the Catholics continuing to seek confrontations and the Calvinists wanting the more circumspect and less potentially inflammatory epistolary dialogue.

Correspondence between the two confessional camps escalated in late summer 1598, revealing the tentative nature of leadership in Geneva. Chérubin tried to widen the challenge by calling on other Swiss Protestant cities to send someone to dispute if Geneva would not.[55] The Reformed community was increasingly divided over the entire affair as the pastors of Geneva turned to their fellow ministers in Berne and Lausanne for advice and support.[56] The senior members of the Company of Pastors voiced frustration at the continued challenges from Père Chérubin; Beza, for example, proclaimed that the friar was more of a beast than a man.[57] Perhaps the advanced age of some of the Protestants lessened their enthusiasm for a confrontation with the robust Capuchin: after all, Beza was almost eighty; Antoine de la Faye, who would lead the Reformed Church after Bezas's death, was nearly sixty, as was Charles Perrot. These men had seen their confession face many assaults, including the devastation of the St. Bartholomew's Day Massacre (1572), and as Robert Kingdon has demonstrated, the memories of that violent confrontation surely remained with the Re-

53. *RCP* 7:98–100 (August 18, 1598).

54. *Response de Herman Lignaridus*, 6–7, 8, 12, 18–19.

55. MS Fr. 8: folios 1–2, summarizing the previous communications up to October 8, 1598, and mentioning that Chérubin is calling on both Geneva and Berne.

56. MS Fr. 8: Geneva waited for affirmation from Lausanne and, more importantly, Berne before they responded to the Catholics.

57. *RCP* 7:316–18, letter from Theodore Beza to the Church of Lausanne, August 5, 1598.

formed leadership, shaping its policies and actions.[58] In addition, the greatest protector of the Calvinists, Henri IV of France, had become Catholic, and his interest in the Savoy did not always prioritize the protection of Protestants there.

As negotiations continued, both sides proposed various conditions and parameters for a formal disputation but found little common ground. The sides could not agree on topics to be covered or the form for the disputation. Where the Catholics appeared to value spontaneity, the Protestants preferred a more structured agenda. The level of details in the accounts is striking evidence that neither side wanted anything left to chance; this is one of the reasons why there was so little progress made on setting a stage for formal interaction. Neither side was willing to risk being put in a position of weakness or even the appearance of it. Geneva offered a laundry list of nineteen conditions, reaffirming the travel complications, coordination of time and place, and costs associated with oral conferences. The pastors did not want the Capuchin friar performing for the crowd; they asserted that each disputer should propose his arguments clearly, without ambiguity and without "extravagant declarations." The disputers should not use "paroles injurieuses," including the terms *papist*, *heretic*, or *idolater*; instead, only *Roman Church* and *Reformed Church* were to be employed when referring to the opposing side. Location remained a thorny issue as well, with the pastors proposing Chambéry as a possible site given its position as a political and cultural center of Savoy.[59]

In the end Geneva's reticence could not be overcome because it remained fearful that Chérubin was sent by the duke of Savoy "to dissuade people from the true religion" and viewed any public engagements with him as risky.[60] The Berne clergy wanted no part of the affair, even asking the pastors in Geneva to not use their names in connection with the "dangerous quarrel."[61] In September 1598 the Company of Pastors proclaimed public prayers for their "brothers of Thonon," and the city council sent Jean Sarrazin on three missions to negotiate with the Catholics about the disputation as Chérubin continued to

---

58. Robert Kingdon, *Myths about the St. Bartholomew's Day Massacre* (Cambridge, MA: Harvard University Press, 1988).

59. MS Fr. 8: folios 42–45, "Conditions" (September 24, 1598).

60. "Pour desuoyer ce people de la vraye religion"; MS Fr. 8: folio 1.

61. *RCP* 7:96–97, 109–10 (March 19, 1597).

insist that the debate needed to be completed as it was begun, orally.[62] The Company of Pastors was well aware that in and around Thonon it was rapidly losing ground and acknowledged, "They [the Catholics] by their artifice and constraint have made the majority of the village into papists."[63] In fact, a Reformed leader on the ground even began to mirror the Catholics' demands in his desperation. In October, Claude Deprez, syndic (magistrate) of Thonon, dispatched urgent pleas to Geneva to continue the debate with Chérubin, reiterating the importance of a "dispute by live voice." He reminded the company that a written contest would benefit only those who could read and understand it. Deprez referred to "a time of desolation" and warned the Company of Pastors that if they did not aid Thonon, they could not blame the people if they turned to Catholicism.[64] Claude Deprez and his son left Thonon in exile after the Forty Hours Celebration and after the duke of Savoy revoked liberty of conscience for Protestants; they returned in 1599 and accepted Catholicism.[65]

Using Chérubin as its main go-between throughout the process proved to be a good strategy for the Catholic camp because it offered the appearance of a united front and provided a focus for the anger and frustration from the Reformed camp. From the initial secret negotiations between the Capuchin and Jean Corajod to the expanding list of individuals and bodies brought into the process on the Reformed side, the Protestants found it difficult to find a common voice. Geneva acknowledged this problem in the fall of 1598 by appointing Sarrazin to head their negotiations, but the process was coming to a close. By the beginning of 1599 formal negotiations ceased, probably to the relief of Geneva, and Chérubin, according to de Sales, fell "into a very lamentable illness."[66] Chérubin's zeal had led many to question the

62. MS Fr. 8: folio 19, declaration de J. Sarrazin, September 18, 1598; *RCP* 7:113 (September 29, 1598), 114–15, 120–23.

63. *RCP* 7:110 (September 27, 1598).

64. *RCP* 7:328, letter from Claude Deprez to the company, October 5, 1598; see MS Fr. 8: folios 31–34, Deprez's letters to Simon Goulart and Jean Gauthier, October 1598.

65. *Œuvres de Saint François de Sales*, 12:17–18nn1–11, 162–63n1. Protestants of the duchy of Chablais had been given liberty of conscience by Duke Emmanuel-Philibert in the Treaty of Lausanne of 1564 (from Joseph Brossard, *Histoire Politique et Religieuse du Pays de Gex* [1851; repr. Marseille: Laffitte Reprints, 1978], 279–80).

66. "Une tre lamentable infirmité" (*Œuvres de Saint François de Sales*, 12:4–5; letter to Claude de Granier, mid January 1599).

friar's mental health, and Duke Charles-Emmanuel had sent several officials to persuade him to leave the area immediately.[67] The Capuchin was sent to Rome on business in the winter of 1599, mostly likely at the insistence of the duke's officials, but the mission had enough momentum to continue without him. The topic of formal debate reemerged several years later, when François de Sales made another overture to Geneva for a disputation in the Chablais, mentioning the possibility of using the general confession of the Reformed Churches as a basis for a debate; but soon afterward, de Sales became bishop, and his attention shifted to other, more-pressing duties.[68]

Neither Reformed nor Catholic adherents could isolate themselves completely; this reality reminds scholars that the two communities need to be studied in concert because in many ways they remained one community. Inhabitants of the Chablais continued to engage with their confessional neighbors in significant ways despite decades of separation in religious practices, and these points of contact are crucial to our understanding of religious tolerance and intolerance. Despite official statements that the other was anathema, Catholic and Reformed remained important to each other, and this mutual valorization continued to shape both sides of the religious divide. They had to live together and could not resort to violence to resolve every encounter, thus making it necessary for both sides to continually reevaluate their perceptions, contacts, cooperation, and exclusion of the other.

---

67. Jules Vuy, ed., "A Propos de Saint François de Sales," repr. of a letter from the duke of Savoy to Governor Lambert, February 2, 1599, in *Revue savoisienne* 13 (1872): 13–14.
68. RC 96, Mi B466: folio 160v° (September 28, 1601).

5

In partibus infidelium

Calvinism and Catholic Identity in the Dutch Republic

Charles H. Parker

The Synod of Dordrecht (or Dort) that came to a close in 1619 carried important ramifications for the development of both Calvinism in the Dutch Republic and Reformed Protestantism in Europe. Within the Republic, the canons of Dort secured the triumph of predestinarian theology in the Reformed Church and ensured the prominence of Calvinism in public life. Across the international confessional landscape, the timing of the synod also proved fortuitous for Calvinists in the Netherlands to assume a greater leadership role in Reformed Europe. At that moment, French Huguenots were facing increased harassment under Cardinal Richelieu; German Calvinists were fighting a war with the Hapsburgs; English and Scottish Presbyterians were encountering hostility from the Stuart monarchy; and Genevan pastors had long lost their primacy in the Reformed world.[1] The success of the Counter-Remonstrant party at Dort signified the ascendancy of the Netherlands as the leading intellectual center of Reformed Protestantism.

Despite the victory for Dutch Calvinists, Reformed leaders in 1619 could hardly claim to have won over the hearts and minds of their fellow Netherlanders, since only 20 percent of the adult population had become church members. During the seventeenth century, the Reformed Church would gradually lay claim to a majority, a process known among Dutch scholars as "protestantization."[2]

Ironically, though, in a century characterized by growing Calvinist influence, Roman Catholicism also experienced a remarkable revival in the Dutch Republic. In 1622, Philip Rovenius, the vicar apostolic for the Netherlands, claimed, "Daily we see many run to the bosom of the church, abjure heresy, [and] pay no heed to danger and financial loss."[3] Rovenius's assertion was not an empty boast. For indeed, the Catholic Church—though prohibited by law, deprived of property, and bereft of priests—made an extraordinary turnaround and rivaled the size of the Reformed Church until the second half of the seventeenth century. In spite of a decline at the end of the 1600s, the Roman Catholic Church established itself as a permanent and substantial religious minority in the Netherlands.

Renewed growth in the Catholic Church was neither coincidental to the development of Calvinism nor simply corollary to the toleration for which the Dutch have become so famous. Rather, the ubiquitous presence of the Reformed Church and the particular characteristics of confessional coexistence in the Dutch Republic served as primary contexts for the resurgence of Catholicism in the seventeenth century. As the privileged church, the Reformed held a monopoly over public religious expression. Church buildings became the exclusive province for Reformed worship; many laws and customs carried a distinctly

1. Graeme Murdock, *Calvinism on the Frontier: International Calvinism and the Reformed Church of Hungary and Transylvania, c. 1600–1660* (Oxford: Clarendon, 2000), 147–49.

2. For an excellent discussion, see John P. Elliott, "Protestantization in the Northern Netherlands, a Case Study: The Classis of Dordrecht, 1572–1640" (PhD diss., Columbia University, 1990), 6–32.

3. A. van Lommel, SJ, ed., "Descriptio status in quo nunc est Religio Catholica in confoederatis Belgii-Provinciis anno 1622," *Archief voor de geschiedenis van het Aartsbisdom Utrecht* 20 (1893): 380. All translations are my own unless otherwise credited.

Reformed signature; schoolmasters and public officials were obliged to profess the Reformed faith. Ministers of the Reformed Church performed all public religious services, such as weddings, baptisms, and funerals. Though church membership was not compulsory (for nonholders of public office), Catholics nonetheless gained ample exposure to Calvinism. Even if most lay Catholics probably did not develop an appreciation for the subtleties of Reformed theology, it is more than likely that they acquired a basic familiarity with the church's doctrines.

The dynamics of confessional coexistence in the Dutch Republic mediated Catholics' exposure to Calvinism in this new Protestant society. The "freedom of conscience" proviso, first set forth in the Union of Utrecht (1579), protected Catholics and all Dutch people from prosecution for their private religious beliefs.[4] That protection, along with the state's refusal to compel affiliation with the Reformed Church, meant that Dutch citizens had a range of denominational alternatives not available to most other Europeans. Dutch people acted on those choices, as a variety of denominations thrived in the seventeenth century, including Reformed, Catholic, Lutheran, Mennonite, Remonstrant, and a host of spiritualist sects. Many people even chose not to affiliate with a church at all.[5] As a result, the Dutch Republic, especially the provinces of Holland and Utrecht, formed the most pluralistic religious environment in Western Europe.

Religious pluralism, however, was at odds with a basic assumption in seventeenth-century Europe, that religious unity was foundational to a stable political and social order. Few people, after all, questioned the principle of one temporal lord, one faith, one church. Dutch authorities, for their part, tried both to uphold a Protestant political order and to manage religious pluralism in the young republic. In areas with high concentrations of Catholics, magistrates allowed them to worship privately, provided they did so inconspicuously and paid a stiff fee. If a congregation intruded into public space or consciousness in any manner, however, local officials did not hesitate to crack down in a

4. M. E. H. N. Mout, "Limits and Debates: A Comparative View of Dutch Toleration in the Sixteenth and Seventeenth Centuries," in *The Emergence of Tolerance in the Dutch Republic*, ed. C. Berkvens-Stevelinck, J. Israel, and G. H. M. Postumus Meyjes (Leiden: Brill, 1997), 41.

5. See Judith Pollmann, *Religious Choice in the Dutch Republic: The Reformation of Arnoldus Buchelius (1565–1641)* (Manchester: Manchester University Press, 1999).

variety of ways. The interplay of accommodation and violence enabled political authorities to safeguard public space from religious pollution and granted Catholics a place on the margins of society.[6]

These circumstances—the public presence of the Reformed Church and the political management of pluralism—constituted critical factors in the development of Roman Catholicism in the seventeenth-century Dutch Republic. Institutionally, improvised ecclesiastical structures and innovative local operations derived their shapes from the political conditions spawned by the Reformation. In the realms of lived religious experience, the immediacy of heresy and a keen awareness of persecution fueled a clericalism and lay activism that gave Catholics a sharpened sense of their confessional heritage. Therefore, as Dutch Calvinism was gaining prominence among Reformed networks across Europe and growing into its public status in the Dutch Republic, it was also participating actively in the formation of Catholic identity.

Institutional Structures and Local Operations

The political settlements of the Calvinist Reformation left an unmistakable imprint on the institutional structures and local operations of the Catholic Church in the Netherlands. In 1573, the States General outlawed the Mass, and by 1581 it had banned all Catholic religious activity. During the 1570s, provincial and municipal governments appropriated all church properties and revenues to support the Reformed ministry, the poor, the parish fabric, and the war effort against Spain. Also during this time, all five Dutch bishoprics, as well as the archbishopric of Utrecht, fell vacant. The king of Spain held the patronage rights for these offices, but Philip II refused to approve any appointments until the rebellious provinces returned to political obedience. What little remained of the Catholic Church in the northern provinces in the early 1580s existed with no bishops, no property, no canonical parishes, and only a handful of active priests.[7]

---

6. Charles H. Parker, "Paying for the Privilege: The Management of Public Order and Religious Pluralism in Two Early Modern Societies," *Journal of World History* 17 (2006): 287–95.

7. P. W. F. M. Hamans, *Geschiedenis van de Katholieke Kerk in Nederland* (Bruges: Uitgeverij Tabor, 1992), 245; Jan Frederik van Beeck Calkoen, *Onderzoek naar den*

The success of the Calvinist Reformation in the Netherlands led Pope Gregory XIII to authorize a church structure to provide pastoral ministry and to reconvert those who had lapsed into heresy. He appointed Sasbout Vosmeer, a priest from a regent family in Delft, as the vicar general over the Netherlands in 1583. In order to augment Vosmeer's authority, Pope Clement VIII later named him vicar apostolic in 1592 and archbishop of Philippi *in partibus infidelium* (in the regions of unbelievers) in 1602. An office not utilized since the early Christian church, the apostolic vicariate endowed its holder with the authority of a delegated bishop, necessary in lands controlled by heretics, where the residence of an ordinary was not possible. Vicars apostolic possessed the highest canonical authority in the northern provinces, and they considered themselves as successors to the archbishop of Utrecht. Seven clerics served as vicars apostolic until the early eighteenth century, when the Jansenist schism divided the clergy into opposing camps.[8]

All the vicars apostolic comported themselves as resident archbishops formed in the mold of Trent, fighting heresy, shepherding the faithful, disciplining priests, and defending their own ecclesiastical prerogatives. A number of clerics involved in the Netherlands, however, did not share the same understanding of the vicar apostolic's authority. Jesuits and other religious orders who worked in the territories regarded the vicar as a superior of the secular clergy (diocesan priests), who held no jurisdiction over their activities. Vicars apostolic consistently and vigorously fought for their authority as archbishops, though the Jesuits never accepted this view. The Propaganda Fide (office overseeing Catholic missionary efforts) generally upheld the competence of the vicars apostolic over church affairs in the Netherlands.[9]

rechtstoestand der geestelijke en kerkelijke goederen in Holland na de reformatie (Amsterdam: J. H. de Bussy, 1910), 48–67, 279–83; Henk van Nierop, "Sewing the Bailiff in a Blanket: Catholics and the Law in Holland," in *Calvinism and Religious Toleration in the Dutch Golden Age*, ed. R. Po-Chia Hsia and H. F. K. van Nierop (Cambridge: Cambridge University Press, 2002), 105–6.

8. Hamans, *Katholieke Kerk*, 245–48; L. J. Rogier, *Geschiedenis van het Katholicisme in Noord-Nederland in de 16e en de 17e eeuw*, 3 vols. (Amsterdam: Urbi et Orbi, 1947–48), 2:23–114; Gian Ackermans, *Herders en huurlingen: Bisschoppen en priesters in de Republiek (1663–1705)* (Amsterdam: Prometheus / Bert Bakker, 2003), 14–15.

9. F. van Hoeck, SJ, *Schets van de geschiedenis der Jezuieten in Nederland* (Nijmegen: Dekker & van de Vegt, 1940), 118–26, 397–401; Rogier, *Katholicisme*, 2:60, 156–57.

Acting in his capacity as archbishop, Philip Rovenius, the vicar apostolic from 1614 to 1651, organized a church structure along the lines of an archdiocese, which eventually became known as the Holland Mission. In lieu of a bishop, an officer known as a *provicaris* oversaw pastoral care in each former diocese, all of which served under the vicar apostolic's authority. Beneath the *provicaris*, a deanery administered by an archpriest formed a local regional district, where either resident or itinerant priests attended to local congregations.[10] Thus the Protestant Reformation in the Netherlands created the conditions necessary for the construction of a missionary organization whose head proved more consciously attentive to diocesan prerogatives and responsibilities than many ordinaries in seventeenth-century Europe.[11]

The disenfranchisement of Roman Catholicism in the Dutch Reformation produced a critical shortage of priests that contained two far-reaching ramifications for day-to-day operations. First, significant numbers of regular priests, especially from the Society of Jesus, carried out pastoral work. In 1592, Vosmeer appealed to Pope Clement VIII for clerical support, and Jesuits, Franciscans, Dominicans, Augustinians, and other orders answered the call. The Jesuits formed the largest company of religious, comprising between 10 and 15 percent of all clergy in the Netherlands in the first half of the seventeenth century.[12] While many local congregations sang the praises of the fathers (priests), the presence of the Jesuits led to many rancorous conflicts with the secular clergy and the vicar apostolic. Jesuits made no secret that they neither held their secular counterparts in high regard nor readily acknowledged the broad authority of the vicar apostolic.[13] Consequently, persistent ecclesiastical discord beset the Catholic Church in the Netherlands and contributed to schism in the early eighteenth century.

Second, the chronic scarcity of priests gave laypeople opportunities to take on greater responsibilities in their congregations than

10. Hamans, *Katholieke Kerk*, 245–52.

11. See Philippus Rovenius, *Tractatus de missionibus ad propagandam fidem et conversionem infidelium et haereticorum instituendis* (Louvain: Henrici Hasteni,1626), 14–20, 42–47; Philippus Rovenius, *Reipublicae Christianae libri duo, tractantes de variis hominum status, gradibus, officiis, et functionibus in ecclesia Christi, et quae in singulis amplectenda, quae fugienda sint* (Antwerp: Arnoldum à Brakel, 1648), 74–77.

12. Hamans, *Katholieke Kerk*, 258.

13. Van Hoeck, *Jezuieten in Nederland*, 118–26, 397–401; Rogier, *Katholicisme*, 2:60.

would have been permitted otherwise. In the seventeenth century, approximately five thousand women opted to follow the religious life of a spiritual virgin (*geestelijke maagden*), a unique female vocation brought on by the closing of convents. Embracing the virtues of poverty, chastity, and obedience, spiritual virgins took no formal vows, yet they carried out an active apostolate in Catholic communities. Throughout the Netherlands, they performed such pastoral and liturgical tasks as catechizing children (and sometimes adults), attending at the altar during Mass, visiting the sick, helping the poor, and assisting priests in a variety of ways. Usually from elite families, spiritual virgins represented important entrées to patronage networks, and so they attracted a great deal of attention from clergy.[14]

Laity in local congregations also absorbed many important functions, including maintaining relief operations for the poor, providing patronage, managing the upkeep of the fabric (maintenance and repairs), protecting priests, and running orphanages and schools. Elite laymen, known usually as curators, represented the congregation in communications with the church hierarchy when it became necessary to negotiate about clerical staffing, complain about their priest, or seek church support for local needs.[15] Catholicism on the local level greatly benefited from the promotion, protection, and patronage by lay elites. For these elites, management of the religious community became a means to compensate for the loss of political status that accompanied the new Protestant regime. The Calvinist Reformation, then, sparked the formation of innovative ecclesiastical structures and lurked behind the organizational improvisations of local Catholic communities across the Netherlands.

14. Marit Monteiro, *Geestelijke maagden: Leven tussen klooster en wereld in Noord-Nederland gedurende de zeventiende eeuw* (Hilversum: Verloren, 1996), 49–109.

15. See A. van Lommel, SJ, ed., "Brevis descriptio status in quo est ecclesia Catholica in partibus Belgii ab haereticis occupatis anno 1616," *Archief voor de geschiedenis van het Aartsbisdom Utrecht* 3 (1874–75): 219, 224; idem, "Descriptio 1622," 358, 366, 368; idem, ed., "Relatio seu descriptio status religionis Catholicae in Hollandia etc. quam Roma collegit et exhibuit Alexandro septimo et cardinalibus congregationis de propaganda fide, Jacobus de la Torre, Kal. Septembris Anno 1656," *Archief voor de geschiedenis van het Aartsbisdom Utrecht* 10 (1882): 202, 226, 233; 11 (1883): 99, 126, 132, 172, 179–89, 191, 198; Archief van de Nederlandse Provincie der Jezuiten. Litterae Annuae Missionis Bataviae (hereafter cited as SJ. LA.), A.C. 2, 1659.

Heresy, Clerical Formation, and Clericalism

As the Roman faith made a comeback in the seventeenth century, the close proximity of Calvinism manifested itself in key features of Catholic identity. Induced in part by a need to counter heresy, a vigorous clericalism represented one defining element of a resurgent Catholicism in the Netherlands. The gravity of heresy for Catholics manifested itself not only in the public practice of Calvinism, but more importantly in the rise of a heretical government hostile to the Roman faith. Leaders of the mission consistently described the political settlement after the revolt as an occupation by a heretical regime. And that heretical government revealed its stripes by secularizing church property and by impeding priests from dispensing the sacraments.[16] The assault on Catholic devotion made it all the more expedient for church leaders to reestablish a corps of secular clergy in the Netherlands. To that end, Sasbout Vosmeer, Philip Rovenius, and Albert Eggius, dean of the Haarlem Cathedral Chapter, worked assiduously to organize institutions to train clergy. After experimenting with a variety of arrangements in the 1590s and 1600s, they founded two seminaries: Collegium Alticollense in Cologne in 1602 and Collegium Pulcheriae Mariae Virginis in Louvain in 1617. These seminaries operated throughout this period, though Alticollense relocated to Louvain between 1670 and 1683, where it became known more commonly by its Dutch name, Hogenheuvel.[17]

Clerical formation within the Holland Mission derived inspiration from two sources foundational to the Counter-Reformation: the Council of Trent and the Society of Jesus (Jesuits). As part of the campaign to reform the clergy, Trent called for the establishment of seminaries in every diocese under the authority of the ordinary. Seminary education was to include submission to disciplinary strictures, adherence to a devotional regimen, study of the humanities and church fathers,

16. See van Lommel, "Descriptio 1622," 351–52, 353; OBC, no. 168, Cort onderrecht vande heijmelijkcke exercitie der Catholijcke Religie inde vereenighde nederlantsche provintien.

17. Ackermans, *Herders en huurlingen*, 70–76; in the seventeenth century a few dozen Dutch clergy received training in institutions outside the Netherlands, such as the Paus College (Papal College, also College of Adrian VI) in Louvain, the Collegio Urbano in Rome, Oratorian colleges in France and the Southern Netherlands, and seminaries in Germany (72–76).

and training in the administration of sacraments. The reformers who crafted Trent's provisions sought to standardize and professionalize preparation for the priesthood in order to produce skilled preachers and scrupulous pastors.[18]

The directors and faculty in the Alticollense and Pulcheriae seminaries actively promoted the pastoral ethos of Trent, just as they stressed an uncompromising compliance with its canons. The standards for clerical formation in these colleges and for pastoral ministry in the field followed closely the framework set forth by Trent. Students had to pledge themselves to uphold the canons and to demonstrate an understanding of them. Similarly, the curriculum in both seminaries incorporated Tridentine standards for education in humanistic studies, church fathers, and pastoral ministry.[19]

Jesuit colleges, which wielded considerable influence by the end of the sixteenth century, provided the mission with working models for training priests. It might seem somewhat ironic that the mission hierarchy would utilize Jesuit pedagogy, given the bitter conflicts between seculars and regulars in the seventeenth century. Nevertheless, as Vosmeer, Eggius, Rovenius, and other Dutch clerics were working to develop a program for clerical education at the end of the sixteenth century, the widespread success of Jesuit colleges made an impression on them. A number of Jesuit colleges occupied locations just over the border of the Dutch Republic, in Nijmegen, Roermond, Maastricht,

18. James A. O'Donohoe, *Tridentine Seminary Legislation: Its Sources and Its Formation* (Louvain: Publications Universitaires de Louvain, 1957), 61; P. Decloeck, "Het seminarie decreet na Trent," *Collationes Brugenses et Gandavanses* 11 (1965): 13–19, 23–24, 36, 63–74, 89–93; R. Po-Chia Hsia, *The World of Catholic Renewal, 1540–1770* (Cambridge: Cambridge University Press, 1998), 116; Peter Schmidt, *Das Collegium Germanicum in Rom und die Germaniker: Zur Funktion einers römischen Ausländerseminars (1552–1914)* (Tübingen: Max Niemeyer, 1984), 12–14.

19. *Rectori collegii Sanctorum Willibrordi et Bonifacii multae gratiae et post hanc vitam magna gloria* (1603), in P. Gerlach, "Stukken betreffende de opleiding der geestelijkheid in de Hollandse Missie," *Archief voor de geschiedenis van het Aartsbisdom Utrecht 67* (1948): 58–62; Rovenius, *Tractatus de missionibus*, 26–27; Notarieel contract, in Gerlach, "Stukken betreffende," 21–23; Rijksarchief van Noord Holland, no. 225, Archief van het Kapittel (hereafter cited as Kapittel #225), no. 551, Statuta pulcheriae; Decloeck, "Seminarie decreet," 32–33; H. J. Schroeder, OP, ed., *Canons and Decrees of the Council of Trent* (St. Louis: Herder, 1941), 175–79; OBC, no. 248, van Neercassel to Blockhoven, September 7, 1678; no. 243, van Neercassel to Blockhoven, June 4, 1669; *Uittreksel uit het 3e exemplar van de "Historia Missionis Hollandicae Societatis Jesu sub Sasboldo Archepisc. Philippensi,* in Gerlach, "Stukken betreffende," 122.

and, most importantly, in Cologne, where the early organizers of the mission had set up their operations and their first seminary.[20]

Directed by Jesuit models and infused with the spirit of Tridentine Catholicism, Alticollense and Pulcheriae turned out a regular flow of priests by the 1620s, constituting a crucial factor in the revival of the Roman faith in the first half of the seventeenth century. The number of priests (including religious) in the mission grew from 165 in 1614 to 241 in 1635, and to a high of 442 in 1645.[21] The geographical dispersion of priests corresponded directly to the areas characterized by the largest growth of Catholics: the cities and towns of Holland and Utrecht. According to a pastoral report from 1629, Holland and Utrecht claimed 150 out of the 222 resident pastors (67 percent) in the mission. Of the remaining third, Friesland had 19 pastors, Twenthe 25, Gelderland 10, Overijssel 10, Groningen 4, Zeeland 4, and Drenthe none. This pattern remained consistent throughout the seventeenth century. A 1701 report listed 316 pastors, 220 (70 percent) of whom resided in Holland and Utrecht, 31 in Friesland, 15 in Twenthe, 17 in Gelderland, 16 in Overijssel, 12 in Groningen, 5 in Zeeland, and none in Drenthe.[22]

Compared to other territories of Catholic Europe, clerical reform got under way relatively quickly in the Netherlands. Seminary education did not become mandatory in all dioceses until the early eighteenth century, which helps account for the quite gradual and uneven pace of clerical reform across Europe. Many bishops faced major financial difficulties in establishing seminaries and encountered entrenched institutional interests indifferent or opposed to seminary training for priests. Thanks to the secularization of church property, vicars apostolic did not face these obstacles. The challenge in reestablishing a pastoral ministry also provided them with the opportunity to remake

20. Van Hoeck, *Jezuieten in Nederland*, 187–233; Paul Beghyn, SJ, "Uitgaven van Jezuïten in de Noordelijke Nederlanden 1601–1650," *Zeventiende Eeuw* 13 (1997): 294; B. A. Vermaseren, *De Katholieke Nederlandse geschiedschrijving in de 16e en 17e eeuw over de opstand* (Leeuwarden: G. Dykstra, 1981), 19–37; Hamans, *Katholieke Kerk*, 261; Rogier, *Katholicisme*, 2:44, 51–53; "Nadere aantekeningen op de statuten van het Keulse college, 1611–1612," in Gerlach, "Stukken betreffende," 94; OBC, no. 482, Erectio Collegii Germanus leges [early seventeenth century].

21. Hamans, *Katholieke Kerk*, 258n30.

22. Jonathan Israel, *The Dutch Republic, Its Rise, Greatness, and Fall* (Oxford: Clarendon, 1995), 389. This list accounts for neither itinerant priests nor religious orders, but represents the pattern of placement for resident secular priests.

the Catholic clergy from scratch. An unintended consequence of the Calvinist Reformation in the Netherlands was that it provided the impetus for expediting clerical formation in a timely manner, and it cleared the ecclesiastical landscape, giving vicars apostolic more control over clerical formation than in many areas of Catholic Europe.[23]

The presence of Calvinism, as well as other Protestant denominations, necessitated extensive academic training in apologetics for Dutch priests. The course of study for priests in Alticollense and Pulcheriae seminaries included training in combating Protestant teachings. According to pastoral and visitation reports, priests worked to confront Protestantism by the early seventeenth century, though the sources related to seminary education remain fairly meager until the mid-seventeenth century. By this time, a distinct neo-Augustinian approach to combating heresy had taken root in the seminaries. The study of Scripture, taught from a neo-Augustinian perspective, assumed a central place in Alticollense and Pulcheriae in the second half of the seventeenth century. During most mornings, students devoted study to the New Testament, though some days they worked in the Old Testament and the Psalms. Controversial soteriological and ecclesiological issues received primary attention in the morning lessons. In the late morning and early afternoon, seminarians shifted their study to moral and philosophical issues as addressed by Augustine and scholastic theologians, primarily Thomas Aquinas. On Saturdays students and faculty participated in disputations, and on Sundays they taught catechism lessons and carried out practical pastoral duties.[24]

After seminary, priests devoted much of their pastoral ministry to confronting Protestant teachings in their efforts to convert souls and to keep their flocks faithful. Visitation and pastoral reports from vicars apostolic, as well as from prefects of religious orders, give ample evidence that the work of converting heretics and reconciling lapsed

---

23. Marc R. Forster, *Catholic Revival in the Age of the Baroque: Religious Identity in Southwest Germany, 1550–1750* (Cambridge: Cambridge University Press, 2001), 177; Kathleen M. Comerford, *Ordaining the Catholic Reformation: Seminary Pedagogy in Fiesole, 1575–1675* (Florence: Leo S. Olschki, 2001), 108–9; Decloeck, "Seminarie decreet," 13; O'Donohoe, *Tridentine Seminary Legislation*, 6–12; Hsia, *Catholic Renewal*, 115.

24. Fred Smit and Jan Jacobs, *Vanden Hogenheuvel gekomen: Bijdrage tot de geschiedenis van de priesteropleiding in de kerk van Utrecht, 1683–1723* (Nijmegen: Valkof Pers, 1994), 80–81.

Catholics fully engaged the clergy. Almost without fail, each report during this period quantified the number of conversions, along with baptisms, confirmations, marriages, and communicants from every district. The data no doubt came from records kept by local priests, who relayed the numbers to the hierarchy as a means of marking growth and measuring clerical productivity.[25]

In addition to quantifying conversions, the reports regularly provided brief descriptions of priestly work in saving souls. A Dominican account from the 1630s cited the faithful work of Fr. Aegidius van Swieten for converting two hundred souls during his ministry of nineteen years in Leiden. The same report commended Fr. Louis Olislagers for his diligence in proselytizing in Dordrecht; the author claimed that the work there was especially difficult because many waver in their faith, fall into heresy, or turn to atheism.[26] The *Imago primi saeculi*, a seventeenth-century Jesuit history of the Society's work in the Low Countries, maintained that the fathers (priests) immersed themselves in the task of converting heretics in the Netherlands, leading thousands of Calvinists and Anabaptists back into the Roman fold.[27] Later in the century, the vicar apostolic Johannes van Neercassel described a mission he conducted in which he preached to a group in Gelderland, where he "demonstrated against the Calvinists that the true and real body of Christ is present in the Eucharist." He claimed that, as a result of his sermon, a number of heretics, some of whom were nobles, became drawn to the Catholic faith.[28] While sanguine appraisals such as these raise questions about the credibility of the reports, the same sources frequently conceded failure and ineffectiveness, suggesting a considerable degree of reliability. Regardless, the reports show unmistakably that priests in the Hol-

25. These reports are numerous; for a sampling, see A. van Lommel, SJ, "Descriptio 1616," 208–26; idem, ed., "Descriptio episcopatus Leovardiensis sive Frisiae ejusque stationum (anno 1640)," *Archief voor de geschiedenis van het Aartsbisdom Utrecht* 4 (1877): 90–107; idem, "Descriptio 1622," 349–81; idem, ed., "Kort verslag van den toestand der R. C. godsdienst der voormalige H. Z 1629," *Archief voor de geschiedenis van het Aartsbisdom Utrecht* 13 (1885): 245–58.

26. G. A. Meijer, ed., "Missie-verslagen der Dominicanen bij de Propaganda Fide," *Archief voor de geschiedenis van het Aartsbisdom Utrecht* 49 (1929): 147, 149–50.

27. [Johannes Bolland, SJ,] *Imago primi saeculi societatis Iesu a provincial Flandro-Belgica eiusdem societatis repraesentata* (Antwerp: Plantin, 1640), 800–801.

28. OBC, no. 223, Visitatierapporten, May 18 / June 18 / July 31, 1668.

land Mission went to great lengths to battle Protestantism by trying to convert heretics.

As Catholic clerics reached out to lost souls, they also reached inside their congregations to guard the faithful from the snares of heresy, an ever-present concern in a pluralistic land governed by Calvinists. Consequently, the mission placed a great deal of emphasis on educating the faithful about the dangers of heresy. In 1622, Rovenius highlighted the importance of teaching the fundamentals of the faith to ward off heresy: "The prosperity of the Republic and conversion of the Fatherland depends in good measure on the solid instruction of the youth in the basics of the faith." The stress on the teaching ministry of priests remained constant over the course of the seventeenth century. Van Neercassel in the 1660s demanded that priests provide reports on their work in explaining Scripture, answering doctrinal questions, refuting heresies, and teaching the catechism.[29]

In 1622, Rovenius established a standard catechism for use by the secular clergy: The Catholic Catechism, or a Short Instruction in Christian Doctrine (Catholijke Catechismus of Kort Onderwijs van de Christelijke Leeringe). It dedicated much attention to heresy and possessed a sharp polemical edge.[30] Question 5 asked, "Is heresy the worst plague that God has sent to people in this life?" The answer was obdurate and vociferous: "Yes, because heresy deprives the soul of all God's gifts and grace, and it contaminates the soul in a foul way." While this answer fit squarely within Catholic teaching across Europe, the catechism tried to expose catechumens to a full treatment of foul contamination: almost 10 percent of the work concentrated on heresy.[31] The leaders of the mission intended that the catechism would help Catholics navigate their way in a Protestant republic. In explaining his choice of the

29. OBC, no. 90, De geestelijkheid over het gebruik van het Rituale Romanum, en van een nieuwe catechismus, March 15, 1622; no. 235, Formula et modus [1663]; Johannes van Neercassel, *Constitutiones servandae a Presbyteris in Foederato Belgio Laborantibus* (Louvain: Guileilmi Stryckwant, 1668), 9–10, 13.

30. Philippus Rovenius, *Constitutiones Illustissimi ac Reverendissimi Domini D. Archepiscopi Philippensis et Vicarii Apostolici per Unitas Belgii Provincias* (Louvain: Apud Bernardium Masium, 1628), 4–5; J. F. Vregt, "Over katechismussen vroeger op de Hollandsche Missie in gebruik," *Bijdragen voor de geschiedenis van het Bisdom van Haarlem* 6 (1878): 359.

31. See Christiaan van den Berge, *Catholijke Catechismus of Kort Onderwijs van de Christelijke Leeringe* (Louvain: van de Wed. C Stichter, n.d., approved in 1633), 14–23, quote on 14–15.

catechism, Rovenius declared that it would enable "Catholics in these lands to mix more appropriately with non-Catholics."[32]

In the struggle against Protestantism, Catholics received additional support from a profusion of devotional materials, polemical treatises, and practical handbooks. Many of these works poured into the Dutch Republic from the Southern Netherlands. Calvinist consistories railed against this "papist" literature, just as provincial and municipal authorities reissued prohibitions against it throughout the seventeenth century.[33] Catholics also referred to books and pamphlets in their correspondence, which circulated among friends and acquaintances. Within this wide body of literature, a number of works targeted lay Catholics, to give them confidence in the Roman Church, to guide them in fending off Protestant attacks, and to help them defend their faith. For example, in the *Schildt der Catholijcken tegen de ketterijen* (Shield of Catholics against Heresies), the Jesuit Francis Coster advised Catholics that, when arguing with a Protestant, they should keep the discussion centered on a fundamental issue, such as the universal character of the Roman Church, and prevent the Protestant from changing the subject to frivolous issues. Coster repeatedly warned readers that heretics harbored great zeal for argumentation and slander, so they would certainly defame Christ and his church.[34]

Coster enjoyed significant influence among Dutch Catholics, though in the second half of the seventeenth century, neo-Augustinian handbooks became much more prominent. Brothers Peter and Adrian Walenburg and Hugo Francis van Heussen were leading controversialists who produced practical apologetic works for lay Catholics. The Walenburgs cowrote a treatise called *Den eenvoudigen Catholijck* (The Simple Catholic) to show laymen (and perhaps women) that they could refute Protestants

32. Philippus Rovenius, Ordonnantie, March 15, 1622, in Hugo Franciscus van Heussen, *Batavia Sacra; of, kerkelyke historie en oudheden van Batavia*, 3 vols. (Antwerp: Christianus Vermeij, 1715), 3:284; Vregt, "Katechismussen," 357–65.

33. Van Nierop, "Catholics and the Law," 106; Gemeente Archief te Delft, Archive van de Vroedschap, #1 Keurboek, vol. 3, folio 166r, September 6, 1573; *Groot Placaet-Boek, inhoudende de placaten ende ordonnantien van de Hoogh-Mog: Heeren Staten Generael der Vereenighde Nederlanden ende vande Ed. Groot Mog; Heeren Staten van Hollandt ende West-Vrieslandt, mitsgaders van Ed. Mog. Heeren Staten van Zeelandt*, vol. 1 ('s-Gravenhage: Weduwe ende erfgenamen van wijlen Hillebrandt Iacobsz. van Wouw, 1658), 193–94, 199–200, 203–4, 211–13, 217–18, 219–20, 223–24, 227–28.

34. Francis Coster, SJ, *Schildt der Catholijcken tegen de ketterijen* (Antwerp: Plantin, 1591), 3–4, 31–34.

and to give them strategies to confound their antagonists. Among other things, they cautioned their readers to steer clear of the conventional Protestant trap of inducing them to validate their beliefs from the Bible. Rather, they advised Catholics to put pressure on their opponents by making them demonstrate their own doctrines from Scripture, without relying on the Heidelberg Catechism or the Dutch Confession of Faith. For example, in a fictional dialogue between two laymen, one Catholic and the other Reformed, the Catholic pressed the Reformed partisan to show explicitly where Scripture prohibits the Mass. The latter was able to respond only weakly that the Heidelberg Catechism condemns it. The Catholic then observed that this was a strange answer from someone who holds to the principle of *sola scriptura* so strongly.[35]

Hugo Francis van Heussen's *Hand-en Huysboek der Katholijken* (Hand- and Housebook for Catholics) did not focus on debating with heretics, but it served the same ultimate purpose: to ground Catholics in their faith so that they would not fall prey to Protestant attacks. Van Heussen surveyed the long apostolic lineage of the Catholic Church, calling attention to popes, church councils, miracles, and saints, which all gave testimony to the truth of the Roman faith. He contrasted this pedigree with the innovations, fallacies, and deficiencies of contemporary sectarians and heretics.[36] The pervasive presence of Calvinism in the Netherlands, therefore, provided Catholics with ample motivation to become well schooled in the teachings that underlay their religious faith and practice.

Correspondence between local congregations and the Dutch mission hierarchy provides evidence that lay Catholics possessed a keen perception of the danger posed by Protestant heresy. This awareness frequently underlay exchanges between local congregations and the mission hierarchy about the need for an accessible priest. Throughout the seventeenth century, the lack of an adequate clerical presence represented one of the most consistent complaints from Catholic communities, especially in

---

35. Adrian and Pieter van Walenburg, *Den eenvoudigen Catholijck: Hier is achter by-gevoegt; Een klein werkje, met den naam van gesantschap* (Antwerp: Joannes Baptista, 1687), 4–33, 67–69.

36. H. Frans van Staden, *Hand-en Huysboek der Katholijken, waar in de voornaamste geloof-stukken klaar voorgesteld, Bondig bewezen, en Kragtig verdedigd worden; inzonderheid tegen de Hedendaagse Dwalingen der Protestanten* (Antwerp: Pieter vander Meersche, 1705), 44–96.

outlying areas, where priests were in low supply.[37] Given the sacramental nature of Catholicism, a priest was certainly essential to religious devotion and practice. Local leaders feared that, without a regular priestly presence, members were more vulnerable to the pull of Protestant churches. Leaders from Amersfoort, for example, complained in 1700 that the absence of a priest had led to "great difficulty and decline in religion, since many young people are going to other churches to marry, baptize their children, and receive other sacraments." Similarly, Catholics in Middleburg, a staunchly Calvinist city, lamented to the vicar apostolic in 1682 that their church languished in a "pitiful" state without adequate pastoral support. And a visitation report from 1668 claimed that the diligence of priests in the region around Arnhem was necessary to keep Catholics within the "ancestral faith."[38] According to laity and clergy alike, the best antidote for Protestant heresy was a capable and available priest. Oddly

37. For examples of lay expressions of requests for priests, affection for capable priests, or fears about the lack of a priest, see OBC, no. 8, Dronrijp to Vosmeer, May 14, 1607; no. 4, Coopmans to Vosmeer, March 4, 1599; no. 225, van Beeck to van Neercassel, August 11/21, 1671; Kapittel #225, no. 354, Machario to Eggius, March 7, 1605; OBC, no. 14, Pieters to Vosmeer, February 19, 1614; no. 230, Deventer to van Neercassel, August 18, 1682; no. 230, Deventer to van Neercassel, August 8/18, 1682; no. 230, Pieraet to van Neercassel, August 23, 1682; no. 230, Gorinchem to van Neercassel, November 15, 1682; no. 249, van Neercassel to Deventer, March 5, 1680; no. 252, van Neercassel to Krommenie, February 20, 1683, van Neercassel to Schuijt and Bock, December 15, 1683; no. 338, Amersfoort to Codde, June 19/29, 1690; no. 230, Zwolle to van Neercassel, March 3 / February 9, 1682; no. 231, Groningen to van Neercassel, June 6 / May 27, 1683; no. 229, Schagen to van Neercassel, [1680]; no. 337, Deventer to Codde, December 27, 1688 / January 6, 1689; no. 226, Amersfoort to van Neercassel, February 17/27, 1674; no. 229, Schagen to van Neercassel [1680]; no. 226, Zutphen to van Neercassel, August 25 / September 4, 1673; no. 11, Dircxzoon (Groenhout) to Vosmeer, February 20, 1610; no. 223, Jisp to van Neercassel, May 14, 1667; no. 229, Randenburg (Raamburg) to van Neercassel, February 5, 1680; no. 230, Deventer to van Neercassel, August 14, 1682; no. 230, Harlingen to van Neercassel, August 2/12, 1682; no. 230, Middelburg to van Neercassel, September 5, 1682; no. 252, van Neercassel to Oosterweer, January 25, 1682; no. 338, Kampen to Codde, September 16/26, 1690; no. 362, Codde to Goes, October 28, 1699; no. 8, van Mauden to Vosmeer, December 1, 1606; no. 248, van Neercassel to Harderwijck, May 6, 1677; no. 253, van Neercassel to Berkenrode, November 6, 1684.

38. OBC, no. 344, Amersfoort to Codde, January 11/1, 1700; no. 252, van Neercassel to Middelberg, August 16, 1682; no. 223, Visitatierapporten, May 18–June 18, July 31, 1668. See also Kapittel #225, no. 354, Fabritius to Eggius, March 12, 1605; no. 359, anonymous to Cats, September 1633; Kapittel #275, no. 69, Janssonius to Chapter, April 11, 1602; OBC, no. 10, Dordrecht to Vosmeer, March 22, 1609, Zeeland to Vosmeer, September 15, 1609; no. 238, Visitatierapporten, August 8, 1664; no. 248, van Neercassel to Ariens, December 28, 1677; no. 252, van Neercassel to Lingen, May 16, 1682.

enough, then, Calvinism in the Netherlands aided and abetted a vigorous clericalism among Catholics.

Heresy, Persecution, and Catholic Identity

A preoccupation with heresy also contributed to a deep appreciation among Dutch Catholics for both the distinct national traditions and the universal dimensions of Roman Catholicism. The vicars apostolic and other leaders in the Dutch mission promoted the veneration of national figures, most notably the cults of St. Willibrord and St. Boniface, the first missionaries to the Netherlands. Establishing the church's initial presence in the area in the late seventh century, Willibrord served as the first bishop of Utrecht. Vosmeer made Willibrord and Boniface the patron saints of Alticollense, and in 1603 the vicar apostolic instituted a sodality called the Fraternity of the Grace of God under the Protection of St. Willibrord and St. Boniface. The purpose behind the congregation was to bring together laity (men and women) and clergy and to instill within them a vision for reestablishing Catholicism in the Netherlands, a task that paralleled the apostolate of these two missionary saints. Though it is unclear how many Catholics joined the congregation, its reach did become fairly extensive in the Netherlands during the first half of the seventeenth century.[39] In addition to Willibrord and Boniface, the mission encouraged the veneration of other national figures. The most emblematic were the Gorcum martyrs, a group of nineteen Catholics, eleven of whom were Franciscans, who underwent torture and execution by Dutch troops in Brielle in 1572. Many stories, anecdotes, and legends made the rounds through congregations in the Netherlands, and indeed throughout Europe, about the signs and wonders that occurred after the execution and their ongoing intercession for Catholics under persecution. The martyrs, finally beatified in 1675, appeared widely in histories and martyrologies that crisscrossed the Netherlands, inspiring Catholics throughout the seventeenth century.[40]

39. OBC, no. 455, Catalogus confratrum sodalitatis gratiae Dei; Rogier, *Katholicisme*, 2:765–66.

40. Brad Gregory, *Salvation at Stake: Christian Martyrdom in Early Modern Europe* (Cambridge, MA: Harvard University Press, 1999), 315–41; Rogier, *Katholicisme*, 2:768–69;

The cultivation of local saints drew attention to Catholicism's long religious heritage, which Catholic writers contrasted sharply with Calvinism's recent vintage. The poet and priest in Delft, Jan Baptist Stalpert van der Wiele, put this fundamental point into verse: "One can hence find / still a kingdom inclined / that turns away from new religions / but that which is now Catholic / reaches long into the past / through the Roman Church."[41] Yet the emphasis writers placed on Dutch religious history and its emblems did not overshadow their promotion of Roman Catholicism's universal features, as many Dutch scholars have argued.[42] For most of the seventeenth century, Catholic writers highlighted Willibrord's connections to Rome and his role as a fighter of paganism and heresy. Stalpert van der Wiele observed that the founder of Christianity in the homeland was Roman Catholic, but the founder of Calvinism was a heretic. He wrote, "Though I want to ask of you, From where and from whom did he [Willibrordus] come? From Rome was his start / from there he did come / look now at this line: Willibrordus came from Rome, and Calvin came from Geneva."[43]

Hamans, *Katholieke Kerk*, 227; Willem Frijhoff, *Embodied Belief: Ten Essays on Religious Culture in Dutch History* (Hilversum: Uitgeverij Verloren, 2002), 131; Gijsbertus Hesse, "De oudere historiographie der hh martelaren van Gorcum," *Collectanea Franciscana Neerlandica* 2 (1931): 447–98.

41. Jan Baptist Stalpert van der Wiele, *Poëzie* (Haarlem: H. D. Tjeenk & Zoon n.v., 1954), 118.

42. See J. A. F. Kronenburg, *Maria's heerlijkheid in Nederland: Geschiedkundige schets van de vereering der h. maagd in ons vaderland, van de eerste tijden tot op onze dagen*, vol. 7 (Amsterdam: F. H. J. Bekker, 1904–31), 31–32, 57, 81–86, 94, 110, 127, 136; Rogier, *Katholicisme*, 2:762–69. For similar approaches that dichotomize national traditions and universal dimensions, see Marc Wingens, *Over de grens: De bedevaart van Katholieke Nederlanders in de zeventiende en achtiende eeuw* (Nijmegen: SUN, 1994), 26, 44; Frijhoff, *Embodied Belief*, 130; D. J. Schoon, *De Oud-Katholieke Kerk* (Kampen: Uitgeverij Kok, 1999), 16–21; B. A. van Kleef, *Geschiedenis van de Oud-Katholicke Kerk van Nederland* (Assen: Van Gorcus & Comp. n.v., 1953), 56–59; P. P. V. van Moorsel, "De devotie tot st. Willibrord in Nederland van ongeveer 1580 tot ongeveer 1750," *Ons Geestelijk Erf* 32 (1958): 337–69; P. Polman, "Het geestelijk leven der katholieken in Nederland onder de Apostolische Vicarissen," *Ons Geestelijk Erf* 20 (1946): 219.

43. Jan Baptist Stalpert van der Wiele, *Gulde-Jaer Ons Heeren Iesu Christi*, ed. B. A. Mensinck and J. A. Bömer (Zwolle: W. E. J. Tjeenk Willink, 1968), 116–20 (quote on 119). For other examples of the connection between Willibrord and the Netherlands, see Richard Verstegan, *Nederlantsche antiquiteijten met de bekeeringhe van eenighe der selve landen tot het kersten gheloove deur S. Willibrordus, apostel van Hollant, Zeelant, Sticht van Utrecht, Over-iisel, ende Vrieslant, met oock eenighe deelen van Gelderlant, Cleve, Gulich, Brabant, ende Vlaenderen* (Antwerp: Gaspar Bellerus, 1613), 35–89; [anonymous], *Chronijck ofte beschrijvinge behelsende de generale concilien mitsgaders den voortganck der*

Emulating Cesar Baronius's *Annales ecclesiastici*, other authors drafted extensive church histories to show that the venerable Dutch religious past belonged to the overarching narrative of Catholic Christianity's universal spread. Only in recent times, conversely, had the fatherland succumbed to heretical innovations. Dionysius Mudzaert, a Norbertine in Tilburg (Brabant), wrote, "The Dutch people have always been highly renowned because they have taken the Holy Apostle Peter as the Bishop, the father of their faith."[44] Likewise, Francis Coster argued that Willibrord's mission to the Netherlands came under the direction and authority of the pope in Rome.[45]

The widespread traffic in Catholic books and pamphlets suggests that these narratives found a broad audience in the Dutch Republic. One Amsterdam book house redistributed 50,000 guilders worth of Catholic literature from Antwerp in the first half of the seventeenth century. Other booksellers in Utrecht, Gouda, Haarlem, and Leiden conducted a substantial trade as well.[46] When authorities found prohibited books by Francis Coster on an apprehended priest in 1601, he defended himself, claiming that "since the books are well known in public, one concludes that they may be carried around."[47] Throughout the seventeenth century, Calvinist preachers found it scandalous that such books circulated so widely and denounced the traffic regularly from the pulpit.[48]

The coexistence of Calvinism and Catholicism in a political environment hostile to the Roman Church bred a strong sense of persecution

---

beldt-stormierijen (n.p.: J.P. Robijns weduwe, 1728), 2 (unpaginated); Dionysius Mudzaert, *Generale kerckeliicke historie van het begin der werelt tot het iaer onses heeren Iesu Christi 1624*, 2 vols. (Antwerp: Hieronymus Verdussen, 1624), 2:59–75.

44. Mudzaert, *Kerckeliicke Historie*, 2:4.

45. Coster, *Schildt der Catholijcken*, 73, 101–7; Francis Coster, SJ, *Catholicke Sermoonen opde evangelien van de sondaeghen naar sinxen tot den advent* (Antwerp: Ioachim Trognesius, 1598), 38–42.

46. F. J. M. Hoppenbrouwers, *Oefening in volmaaktheid: Zeventiende-eeuwse Rooms-Katholieke spiritualiteit in de Republiek* (The Hague: Sdu Uitgevers, 1996), 43; Lienke Pauline Leuven, *De boekhandel te Amsterdam door Katholieken gedreven tijdens de Republiek* (Epe: N.V. Drukkerij Hooiberg, 1981), 10–11.

47. Kapittel #225, no. 355, Eggius to unknown, July 1, 1601.

48. See, e.g., A. Ph. F. Wouters and P. H. A. M. Abels, *Nieuw en ongezien: Kerk en samenleving in de classis Delft en Delfland, 1572–1621*, 2 vols. (Delft: Eburon, 1994), 2:60–61; Herman Roodenburg, *Onder censuur: De kerkelijke tucht in de gereformeerde gemeente van Amsterdam, 1578–1700* (Hilversum: Verloren, 1990), 149–65.

among Catholics. The Dutch Republic, especially the cities of Holland, quickly acquired a reputation for religious tolerance across Europe, eliciting commentary from foreign merchants, diplomats, and other visitors.[49] Complaining regularly, Calvinist consistories also identified a laxity among political authorities in carrying out edicts against Catholic observances. Vicars apostolic also often reported to Rome that congregations in various locations enjoyed a relative degree of liberty to worship privately.[50] Unfortunately, until quite recently Dutch historians have anachronistically equated these observations with modern liberal notions of "religious freedom, which we define as a basic human right."[51] Only the most extreme free thinkers, roundly condemned by most religious, intellectual, and political figures, advocated such a concept. Calvinists and Catholics alike accepted the coercion of religious heterodoxy as vital to the health of the social order.

What religious liberality meant for Catholics in the Dutch Republic was a respite from the enforcement of laws that proscribed the practice of their faith. In the best of circumstances, as in Holland and Utrecht, Catholics paid exorbitant fees to attend Mass, often late at night in barns, attics, and private chapels. The "recognition fees" did not guarantee freedom from harassment when a sheriff (*schout*) wanted additional income or simply felt the inclination to disrupt the congregation. In provinces outside Holland and Utrecht, especially in Zeeland, Groningen, Overijssel, and Gelderland, the prosecution of Catholic activity was much more intense, which greatly limited growth in these areas. In all regions, Catholic worship was possible only if Catholicism did not infringe on the public Protestant domain. But

49. R. Po-Chia Hsia, "Introduction," in Hsia and van Nierop, *Calvinism and Religious Toleration*, 1–2.

50. See, for example, van Lommel, "Descriptio 1616," 219; idem, "Descriptio 1656," *Archief voor de geschiedenis van het Aartsbisdom Utrecht* 10 (1882): 195, 203; 11 (1883): 144, 151.

51. Benjamin J. Kaplan, "'Dutch' Religious Tolerance: Celebration and Revision," in Hsia and van Nierop, *Calvinism and Religious Toleration*, 9, 18–19. For examples, see John Lothrop Motley, *The Rise of the Dutch Nation* (New York: Harper & Brothers, 1883); Robert Fruin, "De wederopluiking van het Katholicisme in Noord-Nederland omstreeks den aanvang der XVIIe eeuw," in *Verspreide geschriften*, ed. P. J. Blok, vol. 3 (Den Haag: Martinus Nijhoff, 1901), 260–65; J. N. Bakhuizen van den Brink, J. Lindeboom, Cebus Cornelius de Bruin, et al., *Handboek der kerkgeschiedenis* (Den Haag: B. Bakker, 1965); J. N. Bakhuizen van den Brink, *Protestantse pleidooien uit de zestiende eeuw*, 2 vols. (Kampen: J. H. Kok, 1962).

authorities cracked down when a priest appeared openly, a spiritual virgin attracted notice, a congregational squabble became conspicuous, or the sights, smells, and sounds of religious observances somehow spilled out into the public realm. They took action against priests, imposed additional fines, and occasionally ransacked church property. In these situations, priests received the brunt of reprisals, since they were usually seized, sometimes beaten, incarcerated, ransomed, and then banished.[52]

Magistrates employed this combination of accommodation and violence as a tacit policy to line their own pockets, maintain the "cultural fiction" of religious unity, placate Calvinist consistories, and manage a pluralistic religious environment.[53] At war with Catholic Spain, Dutch political authorities could ill afford civil unrest, so a pragmatic approach to pluralism that ensured the loyalty of Catholics also made good political sense.

What for political authorities seemed like a pragmatic management of pluralism with a minimum of force felt like persecution to Catholics. A wide variety of sources, from correspondence and visitation reports to pastoral letters and internal institutional records, documented regular violent and repressive actions against Catholic communities. For example, two priests arrested in 1601 reported to Albert Eggius that authorities had stormed into Mass, snatched the priests, looked around for Sasbout Vosmeer, and then destroyed the altar and a number of religious objects.[54] Several years later, Rovenius remarked that the seizure and abuse of priests in Utrecht, which contained one of the highest concentrations of Catholics in the Republic, had generated there much apprehension among laity and clergy alike.[55] In the mid-seventeenth century, authorities in Leeuwarden (Friesland) seized a priest and dragged the furnishings of a chapel out into the street, setting the furnishings ablaze.[56] Though

52. Parker, "Paying for the Privilege," 287–93.
53. For an expansive analysis of this "cultural fiction," see Benjamin J. Kaplan, "Fictions of Privacy: House Chapels and the Spatial Accommodation of Religious Dissent in Early Modern Europe," *American Historical Review* 107 (2002): 1031–64, esp. 1036–39.
54. Kapittel #225, no. 354, Anthonij to Eggius, July 19/29, 1601.
55. Van Lommel, "Descriptio 1616," 216.
56. Van Lommel, "Descriptio 1656," 11 (1883): 191. For other reports of repressive actions, see idem, "Descriptio 1622," 356; idem, "Kort verslag 1629," 252; OBC, no. 3, Vermij to Vosmeer, April 11, 1598; no. 230, Blockhoven to van Neercassel, June 2, 1681; no. 249,

scholars recognize a general reduction in repression in the second half of the seventeenth century, complaints consistently appeared in Catholic sources throughout this period. The actions taken against priests and congregations occurred despite the fact that Catholics across the Netherlands were paying tens of thousands of guilders per year for the privilege of worshiping privately.[57]

These reports were neither simply lachrymose tales nor embellished accounts designed to elicit sympathy. Mission leaders readily acknowledged the times when and places where Catholics enjoyed a measure of liberality. In his 1622 report, Rovenius noted that Catholics moved about freely in Leiden, they possessed "moderate" freedom in Gouda,

---

van Neercassel to de Vanger, March 15, 1679; no. 254, van Neercassel to Makkum, April 20, 1686; Kapittel #225, no. 354, anonymous to Eggius, March 27, 1607; no. 353, Sillingius to Zaffius, December 4, 1608; Kapittel #275, no. 70, Beier to Cats, November 7, 1630; no. 66, Rovenius to Chapter, December 20, 1634; no. 69, de Jonge to Chapter, April 28, 1637; Kapittel #225, no. 359, Tiras to Hoorn, January 23, 1638; Kapittel #275, no. 60, Acta, January 15, 1647; January 19, 1649; February 8, 1650; October 11, 1650; no. 85, "Copiebook," Register, houdende afschriften van de statuten van 't bisdom Utrecht en van stukken betreffende de oprichting der bisdommen; onderhandelingen door de apostolische vicaris te Rome gevoerd, 42; no. 92, Persecutione; Kapittel #275, no. 70, Beier to Cats, November 7, 1630; no. 60, Acta, February 8, 1650; Meijer, "Missie verslagen Dominicanen," 148; Kapittel #225, no. 354, Copie [otherwise untitled condemnation of Albert Gerbrantszoon (Albert Eggius)], September 3, 1604; #275, no. 60, Acta, February 8, 1650; van Hoeck, *Jezuieten in Nederland*, 118; SJ. LA., A.C. 2, 1653 (Enkhuisen), 1654 (Delft), 1658 (Leiden), 1659 (The Hague), 1660 (Leeuwarden, Gouda), 1671 (Nieuwkerk, Zutphen), 1677 (Delft, Zutphen, Arnhem, Oudewater), 1683 (Utrecht), 1685 (Groningen), 1686 (Amsterdam, Leeuwarden), 1687 (Leeuwarden); A.C. 3, 1616 (Frisia); A.C. 4, 1677 (Gelderland), 1678 (Zwolle), 1681 (Nieuwkerk, Oudewater, Leeuwarden, Middelburg); OBC, no. 157, Sententie van schepenen van Leiden namens de centrale overheid tegen Rombout Medemblick, January 30, 1640; no. 158, Keur van Leiden, February 10, 1640; OBC, no. 238, Copiae litterarum missarum Romam, nuncios et episcopos vicinos, June 8, 1664. For examples of fear among Catholics, see OBC, no. 3, Vermij to Vosmeer, March 30, 1598; no. 1, Obijn to Vosmeer, May 5, 1583; no. 10, Dordrecht to Vosmeer, March 22, 1609; no. 10, Goes to Vosmeer, September 15, 1609; no. 252, van Neercassel to Zeeland, September 16, 1682; no. 231, van Neercassel [untitled status report, 1683]; van Lommel, "Descriptio 1656," *Archief* 10 (1882): 114–17, 181, 209; Kapittel #275, no. 206, Hagius to unknown, July 3, 1601; no. 354, Egbertszoon to Eggius, June 9, 1609; no. 354, anonymous to Eggius, April 26, 1610; OBC, no. 343, Petrus Codde [untitled], April 17 or 27, 1699; Kapittel #225, no. 359, Tiras to Hoorn, January 23, 1638; no. 351, Capitum Harlemensis exponit Nuncio Apostolico causam sacerdotam Strekanorum et religiosum sui laborantem in quibus componendum petit Vicario Harlemensis et Reverendissimo Vicario Apostolico fidem haberi quos commendat, 1617; no. 353, Sillingius to Zaffius, August 9, December 4, 1608; no. 354, Petri to Eggius, January 27 [1609]; OBC, no. 20, Vosmeer to Stalpert van der Wiele, July 2, 1613; no. 243, van Neercassel to Blockhoven, August 6, 1669; no. 252, van Neercassel to Zeeland, September 16, 1682.

57. Rogier, *Katholicisme*, 2:466–67.

and they benefited from connivance in Haarlem.[58] Consequently, the reports of harassment and violence offer a fairly reliable assessment from Catholics on the ground about the circumstances of confessional coexistence in the Dutch Republic.

Nevertheless for Catholics the specific incidents of mistreatment did not really comprise persecution per se as much as they manifested a general state of persecution that true Christians had to endure from heretics. A state of persecution existed in the Netherlands because a heretical government sought to deny Catholics access to the sacraments. The heretical regime did this by outlawing the Mass, which conferred grace, by banning the priests, who dispensed the sacraments, and by confiscating the properties that supported the priesthood. An anonymous treatise from 1640 argued that the highly touted principle "freedom of conscience" meant little for Catholics, since true freedom of conscience entailed the liberation from sin. Without property to provide for a pastoral corps, many Catholics could not experience a free conscience.[59] From a similar point of view, Johannes van Neercassel in 1684 accused a Catholic noble patron, the count of Warfuse, of persecuting Catholics in Schagen (north Holland) because he closed down a chapel in a dispute over patronage rights.[60] Lay complaints over the shortage of priests attest that laypeople recognized the centrality of the sacraments to a normative religious existence. A denial or interruption in the administration of the sacraments constituted persecution. Consequently, Catholics considered persecution as a fundamental state created and perpetuated by a heretical regime, which occasionally manifested itself in outbreaks of violence.

The sense of persecution among Catholics engendered a strong sense of commitment to Roman Catholicism. In most places for most people, remaining or becoming a loyal Catholic carried its share of hardships. Clergy had to operate surreptitiously and risked bodily harm, incarceration, and banishment. Dutch authorities did not execute any priests, though reports of physical abuse occurred with some frequency. Beyond religious deprivations, layfolk paid recognition fees but still experienced

58. Van Lommel, "Descriptio 1622," 363, 366.
59. OBC, no. 168, Cort onderrecht vande heijmelijcke exercitie der Catholijcke Religie inde vereenighde nederlantsche provintien [1640].
60. OBC, no. 253, van Neercassel to Warfuse [F. C. van Beyeren van Schagen], January 18, 1684.

additional fines, political disenfranchisement, and precarious worship environments. Provincial authorities in Groningen, Gelderland, Zeeland, and Overijssel mandated that Catholics marry in the public church and have their children baptized by Reformed ministers.[61] Certainly Dutch Catholics encountered far fewer dangers than their counterparts in England and religious minorities in other lands. Nonetheless, those who chose to remain loyal to Rome paid a price, which necessarily promoted a dedication to their faith. Correspondence between local congregations and church leaders reveals glimpses into this commitment, as layfolk donated enormous sums to the Holland Mission, carried out poor relief operations, demanded a certain level of pastoral skill, and cooperated with clergy in a range of ventures.[62]

Moderate levels of prosecution contributed to a strong sense of commitment, yet a more-rigorous enforcement of anti-Catholic legislation kept Catholic communities small. The various degrees to which authorities prosecuted the edicts played a significant role in the uneven density of Catholic populations in the Netherlands. The provinces of Groningen, Zeeland, Gelderland, Overijssel, and unincorporated Drenthe took a much more strict line against Catholic observances, and the numbers of Catholics in these territories remained low throughout the seventeenth century. Conversely, in the provinces with the highest Catholic density—Holland, Utrecht, and to a lesser degree, Friesland—authorities followed a more-moderate pattern of enforcement. It is difficult, however, to sort cause from effect, for the numbers of lay Catholic elites in Groningen, Zeeland, Gelderland, and Overijssel also dropped dramatically in the 1570s, before the more stringent anti-Catholic legislation appeared. At the same time, a sizeable elite presence persisted in Holland and Utrecht. Furthermore, the Holland Mission showed little inclination to send priests into lower-density areas because of the difficulty in obtaining financial support and political protection. Did

61. Manon van der Heijden, *Huwelijk in Holland: Stedelijke rechtspraak en kerkelijke tucht, 1550–1750* (Amsterdam: Uitgeverij Bert Bakker, 1998), 36–38; Joris van Eijnatten and Fred van Lieburg, *Nederlandse religiegeschiedenis* (Hilversum: Verloren, 2005), 196; Benjamin J. Kaplan, "'For They Will Turn Away Thy Sons': The Practice and Perils of Mixed Marriage in the Dutch Golden Age," in *Piety and Family in Early Modern Europe: Essays in Honour of Steven Ozment*, ed. Marc R. Forster and Benjamin J. Kaplan, St. Andrews Studies in Reformation History (Aldershot, UK: Ashgate, 2005), 7–8.

62. See Charles H. Parker, *Faith on the Margins: Catholics and Catholicism in the Dutch Golden Age* (Cambridge, MA: Harvard University Press, forthcoming in 2008), chap. 4.

prosecution produce small numbers of Catholics? Or did low Catholic density lead to more-rigorous enforcement? The most likely explanation is that in the late sixteenth century, political authorities adopted a stance on Catholicism that was based on the relative density of lay Catholic elites. Maintaining a strict policy in the low-density provinces thereafter kept priests out and the lay population small.[63]

Conclusion

The pluralistic religious environment in the initial decades after the Dutch Revolt against Spain compelled political authorities to endorse a Protestant public order, though still checking the theocratic tendencies of Calvinism, and to marginalize the practice of Roman Catholicism. Marginalization kept Catholicism out of public consciousness and allowed for private, quasi-clandestine religious observance through a combination of connivance and violence. This arrangement, along with the ubiquitous presence of Calvinism, influenced Catholic identity in the Netherlands in several important ways.

First, the secularization of church properties, the alienation of parishes, and the vacancy of bishoprics led to the creation of an effective organizational structure to direct Catholic communities *in partibus infidelium*. Directed by a vicar apostolic, the Holland Mission closely emulated the operation of a diocese and rigorously implemented Tridentine reforms in clerical formation and parish ministry. The Catholic Church in the Netherlands became infused with a Tridentine piety at a relatively early stage in the Counter-Reformation.

Second, the development of Catholicism in a Protestant environment produced vigorous lay activism and robust clericalism in local congregations. The chronic shortage of priests gave laymen and laywomen opportunities to perform organizational and pastoral duties not available elsewhere in Europe. These included catechizing children

63. Van Lommel, "Relatio 1656," *Archief voor de geschiedenis van het Aartsbisdom Utrecht* 11 (1883): 81–82, 99, 121–26, 132, 141, 160, 163, 172–76, 198, 374–93; Israel, *Dutch Republic*, 379, 383–84; Wiebe Bergsma, *Tussen gideonsbende en publieke kerk: Een studie over het gereformeerd protestantisme in Friesland, 1580–1650* (Hilversum: Verloren, 1999), 140–41; OBC, no. 10, Foeijt to Vosmeer, March 30 / April 9, 1609; Sherrin Marshall, *The Dutch Gentry, 1500–1650: Family, Faith, and Fortune* (New York: Greenwood, 1987), 88–89.

and youth, managing relief services to the needy, assisting with the liturgy, maintaining the fabric (physical facilities) of the congregation, and negotiating with the Holland Mission on various matters. Lay elites also played important roles in financing church operations and protecting priests from local officials. This lay activism went hand in hand with a strong clericalism fostered by the lack of priests and by the inculcation of Tridentine values.

Third, the ever-present threat of Protestantism led Dutch clergy to exert great energy in trying to convert people to Catholicism and to protect the flock from the snares of heresy. Throughout the seventeenth century, the Holland Mission made conversion a priority, revealed in the regular count of conversions in pastoral reports. Perhaps even more important, priests consistently warned their congregations about heresy, taught them the fundamentals of the Roman religion, and trained them how to interact with Protestants.

Fourth, the measures taken against Catholicism instilled a keen sense of persecution among Catholics. Persecution by a heretical regime functioned to validate the faith of those who chose to remain Catholic. They drew on national religious figures and the universal dimensions of the Roman Church to distinguish themselves as the true people of God, at odds with sectarian innovators.

The particular characteristics of confessional coexistence in the Dutch Republic warrant a dialectical approach to understand Catholic religious experience. The immediate presence of Calvinism created an urgency for reform and gave Catholics opportunities to define their belief system and sharpen their religious identity. In many respects that would no doubt dismay John Calvin, the advocates of Reformed Protestantism made important contributions to Catholic confessionalization.

6

John Calvin, Accidental Anthropologist

Carlos M. N. Eire

I n preparing this book, the volume editor asked us to "assess the degree to which Calvin might be seen as a Catholic theologian." John Calvin as a Catholic theologian? Surely this must be a Zen meditation, a koan of the highest degree. Square circles, red-hot icebergs, and the sound of one hand clapping might be easier to imagine.

How could one ever conceive of a Catholic theologian describing the Roman Catholic Church as a body in which "the entire true religion of God is sullied, mocked, trampled underfoot, contaminated, and even overturned and completely ruined, and . . . the poor people are villainously deceived, abused, and robbed through a thousand deceptions?"[1]

Yet this is exactly what we have been asked to ponder. The quote above comes from one of Calvin's earliest published treatises, an im-

1. John Calvin, *De fugiendis impiorum illicitis sacris, et puritate christianae religionis observanda* (1537), CO 5:288. All translations are my own unless otherwise credited.

passioned letter to his former friend, Gérard Roussel, who had chosen to play the Nicodemite as bishop of Oleron, in Nérac. Calvin knew that Roussel was a fully convinced evangelical and could not abide the thought of his onetime friend serving as a Catholic bishop. Calvin's parting words to Roussel were a harsh summation of his contempt for him and the Roman Catholic Church as a whole: "You deceive yourself if you think you have a place among the people of God, when you actually are a soldier in the army of the antichrist. You deceive yourself if you hope to partake in the kingdom of heaven with the Son of God, when you actually keep company with wretched brigands and take part in their robberies and depredations.... Think what you want about yourself: I, at the very least, will never consider you a Christian, or a good man. Farewell."[2]

Few other aspects of Calvin's thought are more anti-Catholic than his theology of worship, or his attitude toward Catholic symbols and rituals as "idolatry." So this subject, exactly, will be the focus of this essay, to examine Calvin's "Catholicity" in the harshest and strangest light possible. For if anything "Catholic" can be found in Calvin's theology of idolatry, at the very bottom of the hostile abyss that he imagined between himself and Catholicism, then surely one might be able to claim, at least, that Protestantism and Catholicism cannot be fully understood in isolation from each other.

Idolatry is a vast subject in Calvin, however, so the focus of this essay will be narrower: Calvin's understanding of the origins of religion, and the ways in which he was both an innovator and, paradoxically, still dependent on or even faithful to Catholic ways of thinking.

Calvin, Historian of Religion

Calvin knew Catholicism from the inside out. He had, after all, grown up Catholic and funded his entire education with income from ecclesiastical benefices. Writing as a Protestant reformer who despised the Catholic Church and his own past, he could not speak about Catholic piety with detachment. Yet his observations were always made with

2. Ibid., *CO* 5:310, 312. For more on Calvin's break with Roussel, see Carlos Eire, "Anti-sacerdotalism and the Young Calvin," in *Anticlericalism in Late Medieval and Early Modern Europe*, ed. Heiko Oberman (Leiden: Brill, 1993), 583–603.

a certain degree of clinical coldness, much like that which present-day anthropologists and ethnographers aim to achieve. In one of his most popular treatises, *The Inventory of Relics*, he made the following observation about Catholic piety in his native Noyon, when he was a child:

> I remember what I saw them do to images [*marmousets*] in our parish when I was a small boy. On the eve of the feast of St. Stephen, they would adorn all the images with garlands and necklaces, those of the murderers who stoned him to death (or "tyrants," as they were commonly known), in the same fashion as the martyr. When the poor women saw the murderers decked out in this way, they mistook them for Stephen's companions, and offered each of them his own candle. Even worse, they did the same with the devil, who struggled against St. Michael.[3]

It was precisely this kind of observation of Catholics as the "other"—as primitives of sorts vastly different from himself—that allowed Calvin to formulate a theory of the origins of "false" religion and of the difference between such falsehood and the "true" religion, which he believed he was defending. It is precisely this detachment, this ability to think of Catholics as "others," that made Calvin an accidental anthropologist, or as Jean Delumeau has argued, one of "the first armchair ethnographers of the Western world."[4]

Calvin's concept of religion is binary: religion exists among humans in two forms, either false or true. False religion, he contended, was a mere human invention, an extension of the natural world; true religion was derived straight from God and was therefore divine or genuinely supernatural. Calvin's binary understanding was quite traditional and Catholic, one might argue, but his conception of false religion was strikingly modern and certainly un-Catholic, as we shall see. At first sight his thinking on false religion might not seem like too radical a departure from traditional Catholic teaching, but if one digs deeper, it does not take too long to realize that Calvin is turning his back on a millennium and a half of Christian theology.

3. Calvin, *Inventory of Relics* (CO 6:452).

4. Jean Delumeau, "Les Réformateurs et la Superstition," *Actes du Colloque "L'Amiral de Coligny et son temps," Paris, 24–28 Octobre 1972* (Paris: Société de l'Histoire du Protestantisme Français, 1974), 471. See also J. Samuel Preus, "Zwingli, Calvin, and the Origin of Religion," *Church History* 46, no. 2 (June 1977): 186–202.

Calvin's own definition of true religion is simple enough and much in keeping with Zwingli, Bullinger, and the Reformed tradition: "Here indeed is pure and real religion: faith so joined with an earnest fear of God that this fear also embraces willing reverence, and carries with it such legitimate worship as is prescribed in the law."[5]

What Calvin says in the first few chapters of the *Institutes* is tightly woven around this series of facts: Scripture settles all questions and describes the truth in detail. What is this truth? That nature can lead to God, but only Scripture reveals God; that this revelation gives knowledge of God; and that genuine religion is the result of knowledge. As Calvin says, it is only through the fear of God evoked in Scripture that "we can learn to worship him."[6] There is no escaping this hermeneutical circle in Calvin: true religion can be found only in Scripture, and this is proved by Scripture alone. Calvin made the circle even tighter, asserting that real religion—genuine ritual as opposed to humanly devised idolatry—springs from the Bible itself, for the holy Scriptures are incapable of limiting discussion of God to a purely analytic level. All thinking about God, even the simplest mention of God's name, requires a response and, even more important, the right kind of ritual response: "As often as Scripture asserts that there is one God, it is not contending over the bare name, but also prescribing that nothing belonging to his divinity be transferred to another."[7]

Calvin, Historian of Idolatry

Calvin traces the origin of idolatry and false religion to humanity's fallen condition. He argues that fallen humanity is separated from God by a cognitive gulf that can be bridged only by grace and revelation, since human faculties have been impaired in two ways: our

5. *Inst.* 1960, 1.2.2. Ulrich Zwingli had developed this definition most clearly in *De vera et falsa religione commentarius* (1525). See *ZSW* 3:603.4; *LWZ* 3:46; ET: *Commentary on True and False Religion*, ed. Samuel Macauley Jackson and Clarence Nevin Heller (1929; repr. Durham, NC: Labyrinth, 1981). Heinrich Bullinger followed Zwingli closely in the three editions of his *De origine erroris circa invocationem et cultum deorum ac simulachrorum* (1528, 1529, 1539).

6. *Inst.* 1960, 1.10.2.

7. Ibid., 1.12.1.

natural gifts have been corrupted, and our spiritual gifts have been completely taken away.[8] Humankind's imperfection is greater in the spiritual dimension as a result of sin, since all things that pertain to the life of the soul are extinguished in us.[9]

As a result of the fall, humans have been placed in a hopeless situation.[10] There is still implanted in human nature a desire to search for the truth, but this desire can never be fulfilled. The human mind is dulled in its intellectual capacities, and the human soul is stripped of its original capabilities; hence, humans can only grope in the dark for the truth.[11] In this state of confusion, humans can move only in the direction of falsehood, evil, and self-destruction.[12]

Just as human nature retains an insatiable desire for the truth Adam once knew before the fall, so does it retain a longing for the relationship once enjoyed with God. Calvin identifies this innate desire as the *sensus divinitatis* (awareness of divinity) or the *semen religionis* (seed of religion).[13] By making this claim, Calvin begins to develop his anthropological theory of the history of religion, for he goes on to argue that all this is proved by the fact that there is not one nation on earth that lacks some form of religion.[14] Religion, therefore, springs from human nature itself, and the universal presence of idolatry and superstition are themselves the ultimate proof

8. Ibid., 11.2.12; 11.2.17.

9. Ibid., 11.2.12.

10. Hans Engelland argues that Calvin is torn between the rationalism of the humanists and the revelation theology of Christianity, in *Gott und Mensch bei Calvin* (Munich: Kaiser, 1943), 7–32, 46–59. See also Wilhelm Kolfhaus, *Vom christlichen Leben nach Johannes Calvin* (Neukirchen, Kreis Moers: Buchhandlung des Erziehungsvereins, 1949); G. Bockwoldt, "Das Menschebild Calvins," *Neue Zeitschrift fur Systematische Theologie und Religionsphilosophie* 10 (1968): 171–73; and Richard Stauffer, *Dieu, Création et la Providence dans la Prédication de Calvin* (Bern: Lang, 1978).

11. *Inst.* 1960, 11.2.12.

12. *Comm. on Ephesians*, on Eph. 4:17 (*CO* 51:204): "With respect to the kingdom of God, and all that relates to the spiritual, the light of human reason differs little from darkness; for, before it has pointed out the road, it is extinguished; and its power of perception is little else than blindness, for before it has reached its fruition, it is gone."

13. *Inst.* 1960, 1.3.1: "There is within the human mind, and indeed by natural instinct, awareness of divinity [*sensus divinitatis*]." Also 1.4.1: "God has sown a seed religion [*semen religionis*] in all men." Edward Dowey maintains that outside the *Institutes*, Calvin uses the term *semen religionis* most often (*The Knowledge of God in Calvin's Theology* [Grand Rapids: Eerdmans, 1994], 52n13). See also H. C. Hoeksema, "Calvin's Theology of the Semen Religionis," *Protestant Reformed Theological Journal* 8, nos. 25–37 (1975).

14. *Inst.* 1960, 1.3.1. Calvin cites Cicero on this point, in *De natura deorum* 1.16.43.

of the fact that there is some conception of God present in the mind of every human being.[15] But this is not a good thing. Ironically, this seed of religion does not bring us closer to God but further alienates us, for when this seed takes root, it brings forth only deformed and poisonous fruit due to the devastating effect of original sin on human nature.[16] The *sensus divinitatis*, therefore, is an unstoppable and corrupt instinct, the fountainhead of all false religion, superstition, and idolatry: "All have naturally something of religion born with them, but such is the blindness and stupidity as well as the weakness of our minds that our apprehension of God is immediately depraved. Religion is thus the beginning of all superstitions, not in its own nature, but through the darkness that has settled down upon the minds of humans, which prevents them from distinguishing between idols and the true God."[17]

Calvin's theological anthropology—his interpretation of human corruption—is thus one and the same with what we may call his scientific anthropology or history of religion. Idolatry is inborn in humans due to our innate corruption: our religious instincts, unaided by grace and revelation, cause us to conceive of our own fantasies as divine realities.[18] These false conceptions lead to the development of a vicious cycle wherein we drive ourselves ever farther from God and from true religion.

False religion, then, is embedded in the flesh itself, encoded in our genes. Calvin asserts that humanity, damaged by original sin, is continually drawn to the earthly and material. Forsaking the spiritual dimension, we become "creatures of the flesh" and fall prey to our own materiality and egocentricity. And this is the root of our worst problem and the origin of false religion.

15. *Inst.* 1960, 1.3.1.
16. Ibid., 1.4.1.
17. *Comm. on Psalms*, on Ps. 97:7 (*CO* 32:44). Johannes Ries, *Die natürliche Gotteserkenntnis in der Theologie der Krisis im Zusammenhang mit dem Imagobegriff bei Calvin* (Bonn: Hanstein, 1939), 34–35.
18. At times, Calvin attributes humans' perversion to the direct temptation of the devil, not to their corruption. Calvin believes that Satan's work among humans is to disrupt God's plan and to estrange them from God. See *Petit traicté* (*CO* 5:457) and *Comm. on Samuel* (*CO* 29:473).

As long as we do not look beyond the earth, being quite content with our own righteousness, wisdom, and virtue, we flatter ourselves most sweetly, and fancy ourselves all but demigods. Suppose we but once begin to raise our thoughts to God, and to ponder his nature, and how completely perfect are his righteousness, wisdom, and power—the straightedge to which we must be shaped. Then, what masquerading earlier as righteousness was pleasing in us will soon grow filthy in its consummate wickedness. What wonderfully impressed us under the name of wisdom will stink in its very foolishness. What wore the face of power will prove itself the most miserable weakness. That is, what in us seems perfection itself corresponds ill to the purity of God.[19]

Calvin further refines the theology of idolatry that had already been developed by Zwingli. Though Calvin's predecessors had also placed the blame for idolatry in human beings rather than in the material world, they had focused on this problem in isolation from the doctrine of the fall. Calvin weaves this teaching into the *Institutes* precisely at the point where it can be turned into a categorical judgment on the human condition: idolatry is inescapable in the fallen state, "for each man's mind is like a labyrinth."[20] The end result of this process is the "invention" of religion: "Surely, just as waters boil up from a vast, full spring, so does an immense crowd of gods flow forth from the human mind, while each one, in wandering about with too much license, wrongly invents this or that about God Himself."[21]

Because the "fault of dullness lies within us,"[22] Calvin says, the invention of religion is both personal and social, at once a welter of individual fictions and collective fantasies: "After we rashly grasp a conception of some sort of divinity, straightaway we fall back into the ravings or evil imaginings of our flesh, and corrupt by our vanity the pure truth of God. In one respect we are indeed unalike, because each one of us privately forges his own particular error; yet we are very much alike in that, one and all, we forsake the one true God for prodigious trifles."[23]

19. *Inst.* 1960, 1.1.2.
20. Ibid., 1.5.12.
21. Ibid.
22. Ibid., 1.5.15.
23. Ibid., 1.5.11.

Calvin thus speaks of the flesh as an obstacle that must be overcome,[24] but not in a spiritualistic or dualistic sense. What Calvin opposes is the egocentricity of humans, our attempt to worship God according to our own whims.[25] Or as Calvin also put it, our damnation rests on the fact that we who "precariously draw a fleeting breath from moment to moment" dare to devise our own religion.[26] Our "crass imaginations" and materialistic instincts always incline us "to try to circumscribe God's infinite essence, or to draw him down from heaven, and to place him beneath the elements of the earth."[27]

Calvin the anthropologist thus stumbled upon a theory of the origin of religion—as something distinct from genuine worship of God, and as something universal—by claiming that all humans are driven to invent false gods and to worship them: "Every one of us is, even from his mother's womb, a master craftsman of idols."[28] When awakened, the *semen religionis* thus necessarily leads to error.[29] It is no surprise, therefore, that Calvin refers to the *semen religionis* as "the beginning and source of idolatry."[30] Humanity persists in its search for a material divinity and refuses to accept God on his own terms.[31] "For this is the origin of idolatry, that when the genuine simplicity of God's worship is known, people begin to be dissatisfied with it, and curiously to inquire whether there is anything worthy of belief in the figments of men; for men's minds are soon attracted by the snares of novelty, so as to pollute, with various kinds of leaven, what has been delivered in God's Word."[32]

Finally, Calvin also makes it clear that there is no way that we could ever stumble upon true religion on our own, given our faulty impulses and the ontological gulf between us and the divine: "This single consideration, when the inquiry relates to the worship of God, ought to be sufficient for restraining the insolence of our mind, that God is so

---

24. *De fugiendis* (CO 5:243).

25. *De necessitate reformandae Ecclesiae* (CO 6:461).

26. *Inst.* 1960, 1.11.4.

27. *Comm. on the Last Four Books of Moses* (CO 24:392).

28. *Comm. on the Acts of the Apostles* (CO 48:562). Jean Delumeau stresses the point that Calvin, and the Reformers as a whole, were among the first armchair ethnologists of the Western world ("Réformateurs et la Superstition," 471).

29. *Comm. on the Last Four Books of Moses* (CO 24:423).

30. *Comm. on Isaiah* (CO 37:20).

31. *Comm. on Acts* (CO 48:153). Calvin also says elsewhere: "Le source d'idolatrie est que nous sommes charnelz et apprehendons Dieu selon nostre fantasie" (CO 10a:202).

32. *Comm. on the Last Four Books of Moses* (CO 24:282).

far from being like us, that those things which please us most are for him loathsome and nauseating."[33]

Calvin spends a considerable amount of time covering the history of idolatry to prove his point, and in the process he becomes a historian of religion. He begins by tracing how humans transferred the honor due to God to material objects.[34] Calvin believes this tendency developed in stages, starting with the honoring of heavenly bodies and earthly idols, and progressing "by ambition" to the heaping of divine honors on mortals, culminating in the invention of a pantheon of deities.[35] Calvin thus theorized that humans were inclined not only to seek God in the material world but also to scatter the honor due to God alone among various recipients.[36] Much like Max Weber, Victor Turner, or Clifford Geertz, Calvin was also inclined to see religion as a social phenomenon, an indispensable bonding agent closely tied to the need for cohesion. The inclination to commit false worship inherent in every individual is aggravated by society through mutual support and social conditioning.[37]

Moving from the history of the world in general to that of the chosen people, Calvin proposed that the example of the ancient Jews could serve as proof for his theory of the origin of religion.[38] Though God had revealed himself to them, they ended up worshiping the golden calf and lusting after the gods of the gentiles. Was there any proof of this more convincing than the constant struggles of the Old Testament prophets against the idolatrous impulses of the chosen people?[39] And what about the Christian church? Had it fared any better? Following in Bullinger's footsteps, Calvin the historian of false religion argued that early Christians had no images, relics, or any other type of improper

33. *Comm. on John's Gospel* (*CO* 47:90).

34. John H. Leith has remarked that "the history of religions becomes for Calvin the history of idolatry" ("John Calvin's Polemic against Idolatry," in *Soli Deo Gloria: New Testament Studies in Honor of William Childs Robinson*, ed. J. M. Richards [Richmond: John Knox, 1968], 114).

35. *Inst.* 1960, 1.12.3.

36. Ibid., 1.11.6 (Augustine, *City of God* 4.9; 4.31, trans. Henry Bettenson [London: Penguin, 1972], 145–46; 174–76). In a brief analysis three times removed from its original author, Calvin cites Augustine's use of Varro (a text no longer extant) in explaining the gradual corruption of religion.

37. *Comm. on Isaiah* (*CO* 37:38–39).

38. *Inst.* 1960, 1.11.8; here Calvin is commenting on the incident of the golden calf in Exod. 32:1: "We know not what has become of this Moses; make us gods who go before us."

39. *Inventory of Relics* (*CO* 6:450).

material worship.[40] Only when the purity of the ministry had degenerated, he averred, were images first introduced into Christian temples, and then only for decorative purposes.[41] But once inside the sacred space, the images themselves proved irresistible, drawing Christians to them and away from God.[42] And piling one disaster atop another, the consecration and worship of relics was both the product and cause of corruption and weakness within the church. Apparently unaware of the second-century text *The Martyrdom of Polycarp*, Calvin argued that the early church buried its saints and martyrs in hope of the resurrection, but without any veneration of their remains.[43]

The corruption of the early church, Calvin argued, was completed with the adoption of pagan practices.[44] Instead of abandoning the old idolatry, as the early Christians had been taught to do, new converts and old believers alike began to sanctify certain elements of pagan religion under the guise of Christian themes. Consequently, the old idolatry continued to be observed within the church, but under an aura of respectability. Echoing Erasmus, Zwingli, and Bullinger, Calvin argued: "So the priests of Gaul gave rise to the sacrifice of Great Cybele's celibacy. Nuns came in place of vestal virgins. The Church of All Saints to succeed the Pantheon [or the church of all gods]; against ceremonies were set ceremonies not much unlike."[45]

In the *Inventory of Relics*, Calvin explains in closer detail why the church abandoned itself to idolatrous practices, following closely a process that Erasmus had already outlined four decades earlier: "But

40. *Inst.* 1960, 4.4.1: Calvin gives a brief description of the condition of the early church; 4.10.19: he treats the accumulation of "useless" rites in the postapostolic church.

41. *Inst.* 1960, 1.11.13. Calvin was a strong proponent of the "consensus of the first five centuries." For more on this point, consult John Thomas McNeill, *Unitive Protestantism: A Study in Our Religious Sources* (New York: Abingdon, 1930), 271; Pontien Polman, *L'Elément historique dans la controverse religieuse du XVIe siècle* (Gembloux: J. Duculot, 1932), 74; Heinrich Berger, *Calvins Geschichtsauffassung* (Zurich: Zwingli Verlag, 1955), 168–70.

42. *Inst.* 1960, 1.11.6.

43. *Inventory of Relics* (*CO* 6:451): "Iamais ceste mal heureuse pompe de canonizer n'a esté introduicte en l'Eglise, iusques a ce que tout a esté perverty et comme profane; partie par la bestise des Prelatz et Pasteurs, partie par leur avarice, partie qu'ilz ne pouvayent resister a la coustume."

44. Heinrich Berger treats Calvin's polemic against images almost exclusively as a historical argument against the rebirth of paganism, overlooking other significant theological points (*Calvins Geschichtsauffassung*, 47–50).

45. *Comm. on Acts* (*CO* 48:325). Also see Heribert Schützeichel, "Calvins Einspruch gegen die Heiligenverehrung," *Catholica* 35, no. 2 (1981): 93–116.

the first vice, and as it were, beginning of the evil, was that when Christ ought to have been sought in his Word, sacraments, and spiritual graces, the world, after its custom, delighted in his garments, vests, and swaddling clothes; and thus overlooking the principal matter, followed only its accessory."[46]

Calvin tried to drive home the point that, regardless of the intentions behind it, the preservation of relics was a fatal error, caused by the innate, idolatrous drive of human nature. As soon as relics were admitted into the church, he argued, the faithful began to attach a spiritual value to them. It was a natural process, as irresistible as it was inevitable: "Men cannot look upon them, or handle them without veneration; and there being no limit to this, the honor due to Christ is forthwith paid to them. In short, a longing for relics is never free from superstition, nay, what is worse, it is the parent of idolatry, with which it is very generally conjoined."[47]

Calvin's Unique Anthropology

Like Zwingli and Bullinger, Calvin could think of religion only in binary terms, as either true or false, and of the definition of "true" religion as that which is revealed directly by God in the Bible. Like his Swiss mentors, Calvin, too, was not at all interested in any religion other than Christianity: whatever observations they made about religion were centered squarely on "false" Christianity or on the preconditions in the classical age that led to the corruption of the Christian church. In this respect, none of these theologians worked as a modern anthropologist might, with "others" outside their culture, seeking an empirically based global understanding of the world's religions. But oddly enough, in developing their very Christian theological anthropology, they all put enough distance between themselves and the religion practiced by Catholics to develop

46. *Inventory of Relics* (*CO* 6:409). Heinrich Bullinger had made this assertion in chap. 13 of his 1539 edition of *De origine erroris* (Tiguri [Zurich]: Froschover). Peter Brown has revived this theory, arguing eloquently for the function of the holy man as a cause of the acceptance of material worship in the early church (*The Cult of the Saints: Its Rise and Function in Latin Christianity* [Chicago: University of Chicago Press, 1981]).
47. *Inventory of Relics* (*CO* 6:410).

rudimentary theories of religion and what one might call scientific anthropology.

Indebted as he was to Zwingli and Bullinger, Calvin nonetheless went further than they did in conceiving of religion as something purely natural and human, as a *mere* invention, rather than as a phenomenon that somehow involved communing with the supernatural. Both Zwingli and Bullinger took a historical approach to religion, rather than a natural one, such as Calvin's. As Preus argued three decades ago, this approach entailed conceiving of "concrete, particular manifestations of religion elicited by specific divine activity."[48] In other words, Calvin's precursors could conceive of false religion only as stemming from some real encounters with divine agency in history, all of which were misconstrued by fallen human nature. Looking for the origin of religion, Zwingli thought he had found a key biblical clue in Genesis 3:9, where God calls out to Adam immediately after the fall: "Where are you?" "Here we see more clearly than day the origin of religion," Zwingli said. "It took its rise when God called runaway man back to himself, when otherwise he would have been a deserter forever."[49] All religion, therefore, derived from God and God's constant self-disclosure.

Like Calvin after him, Zwingli derived some of his thinking on religion from Cicero's *De natura deorum*, even citing it explicitly. Unlike Calvin, however, Zwingli refused to accept the Stoic idea of the "seeds" of religion (*semen religionis*) as some natural or permanent human characteristic. "All is futile and false religion that the theologians have adduced from philosophy as to what God is. If certain men have uttered certain truths on this subject, it has been from the mouth of God, who has scattered even among the heathen some seeds of the knowledge of himself, though sparingly and obscurely; otherwise it would not be true."[50]

In contrast, Calvin's thinking is much more anthropological, centered as it is in the twin notions that religious behavior is a natural phenomenon and that human nature is inherently corrupt. Calvin quotes the pagan authors Seneca and Cicero, but refuses to find any divine

48. Preus, "Zwingli, Calvin, and the Origin of Religion," 189.
49. *ZSW* 3:667.30–32; also *LWZ* 3:89: "Hic ergo religionem originem sumpisse luce clarius videmus, ubi deus hominem fugitivum ad se revocavit, qui alioqui perpetuus desertor futurus erat."
50. *Comm. on True and False Religion*, *ZSW* 3:643.20–24; *LWZ* 3:62.

self-disclosure in their texts or in any other nonbiblical manifestation of religion. As Calvin saw it, whatever springs from the *semen religionis* comes from within the human self, not from any divine source, much less from the *Logos Spermatikos*. The fact that even the most barbarous people have religion does not prove that God has disclosed himself; it proves only one fact: that nature itself has "engraved,"[51] or "implanted" and "inscribed"[52] on fallen human hearts the idea of the divine and the longing for it. In sum, as Calvin put it, all humans are "imbued with a firm conviction about God, from which the inclination toward religion springs as from a seed."[53]

Calvin's anthropology, then, goes beyond Zwingli's, both in a theological and in a social-scientific sense. And in various ways it is also further removed from Catholic tradition, especially in its denial of any concept of an indwelling, revealing Logos, or of a natural theology that can approximate the truth, or of a natural relation between certain elements of false and true religion. How, then, can any sense of Catholic continuity be found in Calvin? How can this Catholic-hating proto-anthropologist be thought of as somehow Catholic? Oddly enough, it is only by considering yet one more way in which Calvin differs totally from the Catholic tradition that a hidden, paradoxical homology can be suggested.

Calvin, the Devil, and the New World

One of the greatest ironies in all of Christian history is the fact that at exactly the same time that Protestants were attacking Catholic symbols and rituals as idolatrous, Catholics were engaged in a similar battle against the religions of the New World natives, destroying their "horrible" cultic objects and replacing them with "beautiful" Catholic ones. Reading Bernal Díaz del Castillo's account of the "horrible" idols and human sacrifices of the Aztecs alongside Protestant polemics against the "horrible" idol of the Catholic Mass can be an eye-opening experience, for it is impossible to deny that the rhetoric of both Catholics and

51. *Inst.* 1960, 1.4.5.
52. Ibid., 1.3.1.
53. Ibid., 1.3.2.

Protestants against "idolatry" and false religion is nearly identical.[54] In more ways than one, the sixteenth century was the age of idolatry, a special time when Europeans suddenly found themselves face-to-face with "false" religion, both at home and abroad.

In this one quite odd respect, then, Calvin shares something with Catholics of his age, for his commitment to a binary understanding of religion as either true or false and his attempts to vanquish idolatry were in essence indistinguishable from those of the Catholic Europeans, who engaged in an all-out war against the idols of the natives on the other side of the Atlantic Ocean.

Yet, even when we consider this, we have to take into account one of the most distinctively unique features of Calvin the proto-anthropologist: the fact that he removed the devil out of the picture and that this may be one of his most un-Catholic traits.

Since the earliest centuries, the devil had figured prominently in Catholic thinking about the origins of false religion and was definitely part and parcel of all medieval thinking. Though it is difficult to discern exactly which patristic or medieval texts Calvin might have read on this subject, there is no doubt whatsoever that he read Augustine's *City of God* and was thoroughly familiar with it. Augustine is quite clear on this issue, summarizing the prevailing opinion of the early church and passing it on to medieval Catholicism: demonic agency played a crucial role in the origin of religion. Speaking of the pagan elites who created and promoted false religions, Augustine had said:

> They made it their business not only to worship the demons but also to imitate them; for the demons' greatest desire is to deceive. The demons can only get control of men when they have deceived and deluded them; in the same way the leaders of men (who were not men of integrity, but the human counterpart of the demons) taught men as true, under the name of religion, things they knew to be false. By this means they bound them tighter . . . so that they might bring them under control. . . .

54. Bernal Díaz del Castillo, *Historia verdadera de la conquista de la Nueva España*; ET: *The Discovery and Conquest of Mexico, 1517–1521*, trans. A. P. Maudslay (New York: Octagon, 1970); François Antoine Marcourt, *Articles véritables sur les horribles, grandz et importables [insupportables] abuz de la messe papale, inventée directement contre la Sainte Cène de notre Seigneur, seul médiateur et seul Sauveur Jésus-Christ* (Neuchâtel: Pierre de Vingle, 1534).

What chance had a weak and ignorant individual of escaping from the combined deceits of the statesmen and the demons?[55]

Speaking of Porphyry's Neoplatonic view of demons, and of the "theurgic" rites of purification through which pagans claimed to commune with their deities, Augustine laid out very clearly and precisely what many earlier fathers had taught:

> That this is all the invention of lying demons must be clear to anyone who is not their wretched slave, and a stranger to the grace of the true liberator. . . . What a wonderful art is this "theurgy"! . . . The whole thing is in fact an imposture of malignant spirits. We must beware of it: we must abhor it; we must listen to the teaching of salvation. . . . For it is from the devil that these phantoms come. The devil longs to ensnare men's wretched souls in the fraudulent ceremonies of all those false gods, and to seduce them from the true worship of the true God.[56]

In other words, Augustine passed on the ancient Catholic tradition that false religion was based on real experiences with demonic agents, who deceived humans into thinking that they were deities. Since Calvin not only read the *Civitas Dei* but also quoted it fairly often, we can safely assume that he deliberately rejected this theory of the demonic origin of religion and forged ahead with a quite different hypothesis, which excluded demons altogether. This is exactly what Zwingli and Bullinger had done too, so in this respect Calvin chose to follow his Reformed mentors much more closely than Augustine or the Catholic tradition.

This is not to say that Calvin got rid of the devil altogether, but simply that he stripped him of responsibility for the creation of false religion. Calvin certainly accepted the reality of the devil and recognized the devil's role as tempter. Scripture itself demanded that. At times, Calvin attributes sin to the direct temptation of the devil rather than to human corruption. Calvin also believed that the devil's purpose, his very raison d'être, was to disrupt God's plans and to estrange humans from God.[57]

---

55. Augustine, *City of God* 4.32 (Bettenson, 176).

56. Augustine, *City of God* 10.10 (Bettenson, 385–86).

57. *Petit traicté* (CO 5:457); *Comm. on Samuel* (CO 29:473). The role of the devil in Calvin's thought and in the Calvinist tradition remains largely unexamined.

Moreover, Calvin also believed in demonic possession, and went so far as to argue that anyone who committed suicide was "possessed by the devil."[58] Speaking of those who kill themselves, Calvin argued: "We cannot help but conclude that the devil has put such a rage in them; such people are no longer themselves and no longer know what they are doing or saying."[59] What is most unique and perhaps also startling about Calvin's thinking on the origin of religion, especially as spelled out in the *Institutes*, is the way in which he removes the devil from the process of inventing false religion. And it is not just the *absence* of the devil that is remarkable, but also Calvin's unmistakably clear pronouncement, despite accepting the reality of the devil and his power, that all false religion stems from no source other than the human imagination: "In seeking God, miserable men do not rise above themselves as they should, but measure him by the yardstick of their own carnal stupidity. . . . They do not apprehend God as he offers himself, but imagine him as they have fashioned him in their own presumption."[60]

This demon-free Reformed interpretation of the origins of false religion stands in stark opposition not only to the Catholic tradition, but to contemporary Catholicism as well. Demons were alive and very active throughout the Catholic world, especially among the peoples whom Catholic Europeans were encountering beyond the confines of Christian Europe. Examples abound of the ways in which the devil and his minions were encountered head-on in the New World by the Spanish.[61]

One example alone sums up this experience: José de Acosta's *Natural and Moral History of the Indies* (1590), which gained wide circulation throughout Europe in various translations and was hailed as a pioneer-

58. World Presbyterian Alliance, *Supplementa Calviniana*, vol. 1, *Predigten über das 2. Buch Samuelis*, ed. Hanns Rückert (Neukirchen, Kreis Moers: Neukirchener Verlag der Buchhandlung des Erziehungsvereins, 1961), 515; cited in Jeffrey R. Watt, "Calvin on Suicide," *Church History* 66, no. 3 (September 1997): 463–76.

59. *Supplementa Calviniana*, 514.

60. *Inst.* 1960, 1.4.1.

61. See Fernando Cervantes, *The Devil in the New World: The Impact of Diabolism in New Spain* (New Haven, CT: Yale University Press, 1994); Robert Ricard, *The Spiritual Conquest of Mexico: An Essay on the Apostolate and the Evangelizing Methods of the Mendicant Orders in New Spain, 1523–1572*, trans. Lesley Byrd Simpson (Berkeley: University of California Press, 1974).

ing work of comparative ethnography and empirical observation of the natural history of the Americas, has recently been described as "a treatise on demonology."[62] The Jesuit Acosta, who was among the most learned and ostensibly "enlightened" of Catholic clerics—a "modern" priest, devoted to empirical study and to a contextual understanding of the pagan natives of the New World—was obsessed with demons and interpreted the history of Aztec religion as a satanic parody of Judeo-Christian salvation history. Acosta's view was an extension of Augustine's: He was intent on proving that demons had caused the New World natives to devise religious rites and institutions that were satanic inversions of Catholic Christianity. They, too, had amazingly perverse versions of baptism, the Eucharist, confession, the cult of the saints, and the priesthood. And the origin of these parallel inversions was clearly demonic.[63]

Viewing the origins of false religions as demonic was not just a question of scholarly opinion, limited to texts. The very process of converting and Christianizing the natives reflected this cosmic dualism. The devil was not only identified but also wrestled with, literally. Baptism and exorcism were normally one and the same thing. For instance, in his instructions to his missionary priests, Pedro de Villagómez, visitador of Peru, insisted they first gather all the natives under their charge and pray over them: "Unclean spirits, I exorcise you in the name of Almighty God, and Jesus Christ his Son, and the Holy Spirit, so you will withdraw from these servants of God, whom God our Lord wishes to free from your error and bewitchment."[64]

Conclusion

What a contrast we find in Calvin, who not only shuns this sort of dualism but actually thinks that humans *invent* religion, and that this

62. Jorge Cañizares Esguerra, *Puritan Conquistadors: Iberianizing the Atlantic, 1550–1700* (Stanford, CA: Stanford University Press, 2006), 120.

63. On other affinities perceived by the Spanish, see Jaime Lara, *City, Temple, Stage: Eschatological Architecture and Liturgical Theatrics in New Spain* (Notre Dame, IN: University of Notre Dame Press, 2004).

64. Pedro de Villagómez, *Carta pastoral de exhortación e instrucción acerca de las idolatrias de los indios de arzobispado de Lima* (1649), ed. Horacio Urteaga, Colección de Libros y Documentos Referentes a Historia del Perú 12 (Lima: Sanmarti, 1919), 255.

invention is wholly part of their fallen, materialistic bent. It matters little that Calvin's followers did not always follow his lead on this issue. Many of Calvin's Puritan heirs would find the devil in the Old and New Worlds, and hunt down witches and natives with equal ferocity, convinced that they were battling demons.[65] Social history aside, what matters most here is that Calvin took a giant step away from Catholic tradition; in the process he developed the intellectual framework for thinking of "religion" as a mere human invention.

Granted, Calvin himself would differentiate between true and false religion and affirm the existence of a numinous realm that could be approached only on God's own stringent terms. But by observing Catholics as "others" and by objectifying their religion as a purely natural, socially constructed figment of their imaginations, Calvin began to divorce religion from the supernatural, and to cast doubt on the possibility that religion per se always connects human beings to some numinous dimension. Banning the devil from the scene heightened human responsibility, too, and made religion seem even more illusory and less connected to the world of spirit, even a mere figment of the darkest recesses of the human mind and heart. Further steps would have to be taken to dismiss all religion as "false" and call it a delusion, along with the very idea of God, but Calvin opened that steep trail of doubt, so to speak. Two centuries later, thinkers such as Giambattista Vico, David Hume, the Baron d'Holbach, and Julien Offray de la Mettrie would follow that same trail to its summit, reaching more radical conclusions.[66] Three centuries later, secularizing theorists such as Émile Durkheim, Bronislaw Malinowski, and Arnold Van Gennep would look down from that high skeptical peak and try to map religion with *wissenschaftliche* (scientific) detachment and precision.[67] No matter how much their

65. See John Demos, *Entertaining Satan: Witchcraft and the Culture of Early New England* (New York: Oxford University Press, 1982); Stuart Clark, *Thinking with Demons: The Idea of Witchcraft in Early Modern Europe* (Oxford: Clarendon, 1997); E. William Monter, "Witchcraft in Geneva, 1537–1662," *Journal of Modern History* 43, no. 2 (June 1971): 179–204.

66. For an overview, see Alan Charles Kors, *Atheism in France, 1650–1729* (Princeton, NJ: Princeton University Press, 1990).

67. For an overview, see Fiona Bowie, *The Anthropology of Religion: An Introduction*, 2nd ed. (Oxford: Blackwell, 2006); Brian Morris, *Religion and Anthropology: A Critical Introduction* (New York: Cambridge University Press, 2006); Clinton Bennett, *In Search of the Sacred: Anthropology and the Study of Religions* (London and New York: Cassell, 1996).

work would displease Calvin, one must admit that they certainly should have thanked him.

Where does all this leave the Catholic Calvin? Where does it leave us, who were assigned the task of finding him? Are we irredeemably lost in a labyrinth of continuities and discontinuities?

Calvin always discerned a yawning abyss between his Catholic past and his life as a Protestant reformer. He never shrank back from identifying the faith of his forebears and neighbors as "other" and "false," especially with regard to symbols and rituals. Quite often, he surveyed Catholicism as a detached observer, coldly, though never free from feelings of revulsion. Calvin tended to think of himself as beyond his own Catholic past, that vile cesspool of idolatry from which God had plucked him. He was unable to see himself as we can, as a bricolage of traits that could be easily compartmentalized as Catholic or evangelical, and unable to identify any traces of Catholic surviving within himself. Calvin tended to place Catholicism outside of himself, out there, as something alien and false.

Dichotomies were essential to Calvin and the very structure of much of his thought, and so were paradoxes.[68] Five centuries later, we can discern this pattern clearly and puzzle over the dichotomies and paradoxes he loved so dearly. But we cannot afford to overlook the ultimate dichotomy in his life and thought: the distinction he made between true and false religion, which was at once Catholic in its steadfast defense of a single truth but anti-Catholic in its definition of it. And neither can we forget the ultimate paradox of all: that this man of faith, this accidental anthropologist, unintentionally developed a truly modern theory of religion that cast doubt on what he loved the most, simply by dismissing Satan from one of his traditional roles and replacing him with nothing other than the human imagination.

---

68. See William J. Bouwsma, *John Calvin: A Sixteenth-Century Portrait* (New York: Oxford University Press, 1988).

7

Revising the Reform

What Calvin Learned from
Dialogue with the Roman Catholics

Randall C. Zachman

John Calvin was a member of what he called the evangelical and orthodox church, which he claimed had emerged from the Roman Church just as the Jews had emerged from Babylon after their captivity. Since Calvin had concluded that the Roman Church was no longer the Christian church, he was forced to confront two crucial questions: How could the Christian church have disappeared from view during the ascendancy of the papacy? What are the distinguishing marks by which the true church may be recognized when it appears? Calvin addresses both questions in his Preface to Francis I that accompanied every edition of the *Institutes* from 1536 onward. Calvin identifies the two most effective questions that the Roman theologians put to their evangelical opponents. "Our controversy turns on these two hinges: first, they contend that the form of the church is always apparent and observable. Second, they set this form in the see of the Roman Church and its hierarchy."[1] To counter these objections, Calvin must establish that the church can in fact be hidden from view during certain times of its history and that its identifying marks are not to be found in the Roman see and the bishops in communion with Rome. "We, on the contrary, affirm that the church can exist without any visible appearance, and that its appearance is not contained within that outward magnificence which they foolishly admire. Rather, it has quite another mark, namely, the pure preaching of God's Word and the lawful administration of the sacraments."[2]

The form of the church is not to be found in the splendor of the Roman episcopacy, but rather in the Word and sacraments; this form is at times not seen in the world, as Calvin thought was the case before the emergence of Martin Luther in 1520. To defend his claim that the church can at times be hidden from view, Calvin appeals to the example of the church during the time of the prophets: "What form do we think it displayed when Elijah complained that he alone was left [1 Kings 19:10, 14]?"[3] To show that the church is not to be identified with the splendor of bishops in synodic communion, Calvin turns to the trial of Jesus before the Sanhedrin. "Was not such pomp manifested in that council where priests, scribes, and Pharisees assembled to deliberate concerning the execution of Christ [John 11:47–53, 57]?"[4] If the church is to be identified with its external form, then both Elijah and Jesus must be guilty of schism. "Now, let them go and cling to this outward mask making Christ and all the prophets of the living God schismatics; Satan's ministers, conversely, the organs of the Holy Spirit."[5] On the contrary, if the certain marks of the church are the pure preaching of the Word and the lawful administration of the sacraments, then the prophets and Jesus are members of the true church, even if its form was not visible in their day, and even if they were being persecuted and killed by those who claimed to represent the visible form and splendor of the church.

Even though Calvin will often describe the Church of Rome as though it were the antithesis of the true Christian and catholic church,

1. *Institutio 1536*, "Epistle Dedicatory to Francis I," *CO* 1:20C; *Inst.* 1536, 9.
2. *Institutio 1536*, "Epistle Dedicatory to Francis I," *CO* 1:20–21; *Inst.* 1536, 9.
3. *Institutio 1536*, "Epistle Dedicatory to Francis I," *CO* 1:21A; *Inst.* 1536, 9.
4. *Institutio 1536*, "Epistle Dedicatory to Francis I," *CO* 1:22A; *Inst.* 1536, 10.
5. Ibid.

he also holds that the true church was hidden in the Roman Church, only to emerge in his own day with the teaching of Luther. This means that the Roman Church contains within itself the true church, since God remains faithful in spite of human faithlessness. "Hence it arises, that our baptism does not need renewal, because although the Devil has long reigned in the papacy, yet he could not altogether extinguish God's grace; nay, a Church is among them; for otherwise Paul's prophecy would have been false, when he says that Antichrist was seated in the temple of God (2 Thess. 2:4)."[6] Thus Calvin is willing to grant to his opponents the truth of their claim that the church of God is with them, only he insists that it is hidden and is not to be seen in the public face of the Roman Church. "For when they thunder out with full cheeks—'We are the Church of God,' or, 'the seat of the Church is with us'—the solution is easy; the Church is indeed among them, that is, God has his Church there, but hidden and wonderfully preserved: but it does not follow that they are worthy of any honor; nay, they are more detestable, because they ought to bear sons and daughters to God; but they bear them for the Devil and for idols."[7]

If one looks at the mark that Rome holds out, the historic episcopacy in communion with the bishop of Rome, then the Roman Church is opposed to the true church of Christ. However, if one looks at the true marks of the church, such as baptism, then God has in fact preserved the true church in hiddenness in the Church of Rome, for otherwise the church of Christ would have perished. "For God always preserves a hidden seed, that the Church should not be utterly extinguished: for there must always be a Church in the world, but sometimes it is preserved miserably as in a sepulchre, since it is nowhere apparent."[8] The appearance of the evangelical and orthodox church in Calvin's day therefore represents the emergence of the true church from its time of hiddenness within the Roman Church, and not the beginning of a new church. "Since, then, the Lord wonderfully defends his Church, and preserves it in the world, so that at one time he seems to bury it, and then raises it from death; at one time he cuts it down as to its outward appearance, and then afterward he renews it; we ought to

6. *Comm. on Ezekiel*, on Ezek. 16:20, *CO* 40:354B; CTS 23:120–21.
7. Ibid.
8. *Comm. on Ezekiel*, on Ezek. 16:53, *CO* 40:387B; CTS 23:165.

take heed, lest we measure according to our own judgment and carnal reason, what the Lord declares respecting the preservation of his Church. For its safety is often hid from the eyes of men."[9] Alexandre Ganoczy therefore rightly claims that for Calvin, when one becomes an evangelical, one "does not break with the Church. Quite the contrary, in being converted one contributes to the purification of the Church in which one was baptized."[10]

The acknowledgment that the true church of Christ still exists in the Roman Church, even if in a hidden form, continually raises in Calvin's mind the question of the legitimacy of the evangelical and orthodox Christians separating from the Roman Church. One especially sees this in the discussion of the church in the 1543 edition of the *Institutes*, when he poses the question that his Roman opponents raise against his community. "Now they treat us as persons guilty of schism and heresy because we preach a doctrine unlike theirs, do not obey their laws, and hold our separate assemblies for prayers, baptism and the celebration of the Supper, and other holy activities. This is indeed a very grave accusation."[11] It is not surprising that Calvin addresses this question in 1543, for he had just participated in several colloquies (1539–41) between representatives of the evangelicals and those of the Roman Church, and the question of the continuity of the evangelicals with the older Catholic tradition must have become acute for Calvin during this period. Calvin had also been working closely with Martin Bucer and Philipp Melanchthon during this time, for whom the question of the catholicity of the evangelical churches was a central concern. Even though Calvin states that the accusation made against the evangelicals by the old Catholics can be easily answered by seeking true unity in Christ, nonetheless one can see in the 1543 edition of the *Institutes* several places where the impact of the dialogue with the Roman Catholics, possibly reinforced by the influence of Melanchthon and Bucer, leads Calvin to revise his earlier and more radical positions in the direction of the older Catholic tradition.

In what follows, I will examine four theological topics in particular in the 1543 *Institutes*: baptism, the holy Supper of the Lord, the laying

9. *Comm. on Hosea*, on Hos. 1:10, *CO* 42:217–18; *CTS* 26:65–66.
10. Alexandre Ganoczy, *The Young Calvin*, trans. David Foxgrover and Wade Provo (Philadelphia: Westminster, 1987), 266.
11. *Institutio 1543*; *Inst.* 1960 2:1046.

on of hands, and the offices of the church. I will frame the discussion of these issues in light of Calvin's position before 1543, in order to highlight any changes that were made at that time, and will also track these changes in his later writings, to see if they endure in his thought. The thesis I am arguing is admittedly circumstantial, since Calvin never states that he revised his positions in light of these dialogues. However, the changes Calvin makes in the 1543 *Institutes* strongly suggest that the dialogues with the Roman Catholics between 1539 and 1541 did have a significant influence on the direction in which he revised his earlier theological positions.

Baptism

In the first edition of the *Institutes*, in 1536, Calvin claims that baptism shows the faithful three things to confirm their faith. The first thing signified by baptism is the forgiveness of sin.[12] According to Calvin, the water is not an instrument of our cleansing and forgiveness, but rather the sacrament of baptism gives us the certain knowledge of our forgiveness by sealing the message of forgiveness. The forgiveness symbolized in baptism is not just for sins committed before baptism, but covers the whole life of the faithful.[13] The second thing signified by baptism is the mortification and vivification of the godly in Christ.[14] According to Calvin, this takes place not through our imitation of the death and resurrection of Christ by our putting sin to death within ourselves, but rather takes place by the participation in Christ through baptism.[15] Finally, baptism bears testimony to the unity with Christ that the faithful enjoy, together with all his blessings.[16] The right way to receive baptism is therefore to realize that "it is God who speaks to us through the sign," so that we see God as the one forgiving and renewing us, and uniting us with Christ and all his blessings.[17] The best way to come to the confirmation offered by baptism is by following the

12. *Institutio 1536* 4.12, *CO* 1:110A; *Inst.* 1536, 94.
13. *Institutio 1536* 4.14, *CO* 1:110–11; *Inst.* 1536, 95.
14. *Institutio 1536* 4.15, *CO* 1:111B; *Inst.* 1536, 95.
15. *Institutio 1536* 4.15, *CO* 1:111C; *Inst.* 1536, 95.
16. *Institutio 1536* 4.19, *CO* 1:114A; *Inst.* 1536, 98.
17. *Institutio 1536* 4.21, *CO* 1:114C; *Inst.* 1536, 99.

analogy between the sign and the thing signified.[18] However, Calvin once again denies that baptism itself is an "organ or instrument" by which the gifts of God are bestowed on us; instead, it is a pledge by which the will of the Lord is attested to us.[19]

In the Catechism of 1537/38, Calvin reverses the order of the gifts represented by baptism to place the primacy on participation in Christ, from which follows the grace of forgiveness and regeneration.[20] Calvin denies that the grace of forgiveness or regeneration inheres in the water, "but only that the knowledge of such gifts is received in this sacrament when we are said to receive, obtain, get what we believe to have been given us by the Lord."[21] The confirmation of faith provided by baptism has to do solely with our more-clear awareness of the grace of God in Christ, and not with the actual bestowal of that grace upon us in baptism. Calvin adds a lengthy appendix to his discussion of baptism in the second edition of the *Institutes* in 1539 to defend the practice of infant baptism against the objections of "certain fanatic spirits" who have disturbed the church over the issue.[22] Calvin is also very concerned not to ascribe to the water of baptism that which can be attributed only to the blood of Christ. The water is a symbol of forgiveness and mortification, but the blood of Christ is the reality that is attested by the water, and it alone cleanses our souls. The sacrament of baptism represents and attests the grace of Christ offered to us in the promise, to be received by faith. However, at this point in his career, baptism does not offer what it represents, nor does God act through baptism as through an instrument to effect in us what baptism represents and offers to us.

In the third edition of the *Institutes*, in 1543, Calvin accentuates the ecclesial nature of baptism. He inserts the ecclesial and corporate significance of baptism into the opening sentence of the discussion of baptism. "Baptism is the sign of the initiation by which we are received into the society of the church, in order that, engrafted in Christ, we may be reckoned among God's children."[23] From this point onward,

18. *Institutio 1536* 4.21, CO 1:115A; *Inst.* 1536, 99.
19. Ibid.
20. *Catechismus*, CO 5:350A; *Catechism*, 34.
21. Ibid.
22. *Institutio 1539* 11.19, CO 1:968B; *Inst.* 1960 2:1324.
23. *Institutio 1543* 17.1, CO 1:957C; *Inst.* 1960 2:1303.

Calvin will always combine the theme of our engrafting into Christ with the theme of our initiation into the society of the church. We cannot become members of Christ without becoming members of the body of Christ, nor can we be adopted as children of God without being initiated into the whole family of God. In the *Catechism of the Church of Geneva* of 1545, Calvin accentuates the ecclesial nature of baptism seen in the 1543 *Institutes* by describing baptism as "a kind of entry into the Church. For in it we have a testimony that we, while otherwise strangers and aliens, were received into the family of God, so that we are reckoned among his household."[24] Calvin repeats his concern not to have the sign of baptism eclipse the reality signified, which is the blood of Christ applied to us by the Holy Spirit.[25]

However, for the first time in his discussion of baptism, Calvin nonetheless insists that the reality signified by the water of baptism is truly offered by it, and is to be attached to it. "M: But do you attribute nothing more to the water than to be a mere symbol of ablution? C: I think it to be such a symbol that reality is attached to it. For God does not disappoint us when he promises us his gifts. Hence both pardon and newness of life are certainly offered to us and received by us in Baptism."[26] Thus unless we block the reception of these benefits, the water of baptism truly offers to us the reality it signifies, so that "we are fed with Christ and granted his Spirit."[27] From this time forward, Calvin will be concerned to emphasize the way the water of baptism, in conjunction with the Word, truly exhibits and offers the reality it symbolizes and represents.

In his *Commentary on 1 Corinthians*, in 1546, Calvin highlights the way Paul describes believers as all being baptized into one body, further emphasizing the meaning of baptism as incorporation into the society of the church. "Paul says: 'By baptism we are engrafted into the body of Christ, so that we are bound together, joined to each other as members, and live the one life. Therefore he who wants to remain in the Church of Christ must necessarily devote himself to this fellowship.'"[28] Calvin also emphasizes the way the efficacy of baptism

24. *Catechismus Ecclesiae Genevensis*, OS 2:133.12–16; *CTT*, 133.
25. *Catechismus Ecclesiae Genevensis*, OS 2:134.9–15; *CTT*, 133.
26. *Catechismus Ecclesiae Genevensis*, OS 2:134.16–20; *CTT*, 133.
27. *Catechismus Ecclesiae Genevensis*, OS 2:135.7–10; *CTT*, 134.
28. *Comm. on 1 Corinthians*, on 1 Cor. 12:13, *CO* 49:501C; *CNTC* 9:264.

lies not in the water, but in the power of the Holy Spirit.[29] However, unlike the *Commentary on Romans* (1540), which ascribes the presence of the reality of baptism to faith in the promise, Calvin here insists on the willingness of God actually to carry out everything that God represents to us in baptism.[30] Thus God not only represents our engrafting into the body of Christ in baptism, but also actually carries this out through baptism. "However, so that no one might suppose that this is effected by the outward symbol, Paul adds that it is the work of the Holy Spirit."[31]

In his *Acts of the Council of Trent with the Antidote*, in 1547, Calvin finally describes baptism as an instrument through which God freely works to bestow benefits upon us. "And not only do we strictly bind the faithful to the observance of it, but we also maintain that it is the ordinary instrument of God in washing and renewing us; in short, in communicating to us salvation. The only exception we make is that the hand of God must not be tied down to the instrument. He may of himself accomplish salvation."[32] Calvin is still concerned not to identify the efficacy of baptism with the water, but he no longer denies that the sacrament is an instrument that God ordinarily uses to confer grace upon us, even though God may give that gift without the sacrament. Calvin addresses this issue in even greater detail in his commentary on the Pauline Epistles, in 1548. God truly offers the reality figured in baptism to all who are baptized. Those who lack faith and repentance divorce the reality from the sign, whereas those who receive the sacrament with faith also receive what it figures. "The sacraments present the grace of God both to the good and to the bad; nor do they deceive in promising the grace of the Holy Spirit; believers receive what is offered."[33] In this way, Calvin thinks that he can prevent believers from binding the grace of God to the sacrament, while nonetheless viewing the sacrament as truly presenting and offering the reality it represents and figures. "In this way, what is proper to God is not transferred to the sign and yet the sacraments keep their power, so that they cannot be regarded as empty and cold spectacles."[34]

---

29. *Comm. on 1 Corinthians*, on 1 Cor. 12:13, *CO* 49:501C; *CNTC* 9:265.
30. Ibid.
31. Ibid.
32. *Acta Synodi Tridentinae cum Antidoto*, *CO* 7:499A; *TTRC* 3:180.
33. *Comm. on Galatians*, on Gal. 3:27, *OE* 16.87.15–17; *CNTC* 11:68.
34. *Comm. on Galatians*, on Gal. 3:27, *OE* 16.87.22–24; *CNTC* 11:69.

The Holy Supper of the Lord

The holy Supper of the Lord shares with baptism the role of being an exercise of faith that protects, arouses, and increases it (faith) throughout the life of the godly. In the first edition of the *Institutes*, in 1536, Calvin determines the meaning and purpose of the Supper by turning to the promise that it attests. Whereas the third benefit symbolized by baptism is our engrafting into Christ himself with all his benefits, Calvin makes our engrafting into Christ the primary benefit attested by the Supper.[35] The Supper is a proof and witness of the exchange Christ has made with us, which becomes effective in us when we are engrafted in him. Christ takes upon himself our sin, guilt, poverty, weakness, and mortality in order to pay our debt for us and bestow on us his wealth, power, and immortality.[36] In particular, the bread and wine of the Supper represent to us the body and blood of Christ, which were given for us, so that we may learn that they are the life and food of our souls. Such recognition takes place by means of the analogy between the sign and the thing signified.[37] However, at this point Calvin does not say that the signs of bread and wine actually offer the body and blood of Christ to us in the Supper. At this stage in his career, the sum of Calvin's teaching seems to be that the Supper of the Lord represents, attests, and exhibits the life we receive from Christ crucified, in order to remind us of the reality of our union with Christ and of our redemption by his death on the cross.[38]

By the second edition of the *Institutes*, in 1539, it is clear that Calvin no longer understands the testimony, offer, and exhibition in the Supper to represent the communion with Christ that believers always enjoy. Instead, he claims that God is not a deceiver and thus does not set forth an empty symbol before us. Thus "the breaking of the bread is a symbol; it is not the thing itself"; yet Calvin insists that "by showing the symbol the thing itself is shown."[39] The bread and wine of the Supper not only represent and figure the life-giving body and blood of

35. *Institutio 1536* 4.24, *CO* 1:118–19; *Inst.* 1536, 102.
36. *Institutio 1536* 4.25, *CO* 1:119A; *Inst.* 1536, 102–3.
37. *Institutio 1536* 4.26, *CO* 1:119C; *Inst.* 1536, 103.
38. *Institutio 1536* 4.33, *CO* 1:125C; *Inst.* 1536, 109.
39. *Institutio 1539* 12.18, *CO* 1:1002C; *Inst.* 1960 2:1371.

Christ; they also present and exhibit them.[40] Even as the godly ought to distinguish the symbol from the reality symbolized, so they ought always to join the reality to the symbol, for it is truly presented by the symbol.[41] From this point onward, Calvin insists that what God represents (*repraesentat*) in the symbol of the Supper, God simultaneously presents (*exhibeat*) in reality. However, Calvin also insists that the reality represented and exhibited by the Supper is present in heaven and must be sought there, and not in the symbols of the body and blood in the bread and wine.[42] Even though Christ's body and blood are in heaven, we enjoy true participation in them through the bond of the Holy Spirit.[43] Nonetheless, Calvin admits that he does not have the capacity to express the way that God offers us the reality when God shows us the symbol; he urges his readers to be ravished with wonder before the mystery, rather than to try too hard to express everything in words.[44]

In the *Short Treatise on the Holy Supper of Our Lord and Only Savior Jesus Christ*, in 1541, Calvin claims that even though the gospel offers the same participation in the life-giving flesh of Christ as does the Supper, God instituted the Supper out of accommodation to our weakness and infirmity.[45] The need for the visible representation of the promises becomes especially clear when we descend into ourselves and see how destitute we are of every good thing, and how full of sin and evil we are.[46] This mirror confirms our faith more fully than would the preaching of the gospel, even though both offer the same grace of Christ.[47] Since every good thing we lack can be ours only when we are joined with Christ, the Supper represents two things to us in particular: "Jesus Christ as source and substance of all good; and second, the fruit and efficacy of his death and passion."[48] Since our communion with Christ takes place especially by means of his flesh and blood, these are set before us in the symbols of the bread

---

40. Ibid.
41. *Institutio 1539* 12.18, *CO* 1:1002–3; *Inst.* 1960 2:1371.
42. *Institutio 1539* 12.29, *CO* 1:1009; *Inst.* 1960 2:1381.
43. Ibid.
44. *Institutio 1539* 12.15, *CO* 1:1000C; *Inst.* 1960 2:1367.
45. *Libellus de Coena Domini, OS* 1:505; *CTT*, 144.
46. *Libellus de Coena Domini, OS* 1:506; *CTT*, 145.
47. Ibid.
48. *Libellus de Coena Domini, OS* 1:507; *CTT*, 146.

and wine. As in the second edition of the *Institutes*, Calvin notes that the symbols take the name of the thing they symbolize, but now the reason given is that the bread and wine are the instruments by which Christ distributes the reality of his body and blood to us.[49] Once again, this takes place out of accommodation to our infirmity, by showing us a visible representation of our invisible communion with Christ. "For although it may be that the communion we have with the body of Christ is something incomprehensible, not only to the eye but to our natural sense, it is there visibly shown to us."[50]

However, the symbol not only represents the invisible reality to us, but also offers us the reality with the symbol.[51] Even as the reality ought to be distinguished from the symbol that represents it, so the reality ought always to be joined to the symbol, for God does not deceive with empty appearances.[52] Thus the bread and wine not only represent the reality of the body and blood of Christ and our communion with them, but also actually offer them to us so that we may participate in them. "We have to confess that if the representation which God grants in the Supper is veracious, the internal substance of the sacrament is joined with the visible signs; and as the bread is distributed by hand, so the body of Christ is communicated to us, so that we are made partakers of it."[53] The Supper is therefore both a symbol that represents and exhibits the body and blood of Christ to us, and also an instrument through which God distributes the body and blood of Christ to us. "For the chief thing is that he cares for us internally by his Holy Spirit, so as to give efficacy to his ordinance, which he has destined for this purpose, as an instrument by which he will do his work in us."[54] Nonetheless, Calvin cautions his readers that even though the reality is offered with the symbols of the Supper, it is not to be sought in the symbols themselves, but in heaven, even as it is made present to the faithful by the bond of the Spirit.[55] Calvin claims that this interpretation is not new with him, but rather is reflected in the eucharistic liturgy of the early

49. *Libellus de Coena Domini*, OS 1:508; *CTT*, 147.
50. Ibid.
51. Ibid.
52. *Libellus de Coena Domini*, OS 1:509; *CTT*, 148.
53. Ibid.
54. *Libellus de Coena Domini*, OS 1:510; *CTT*, 149.
55. *Libellus de Coena Domini*, OS 1:530; *CTT*, 166.

church. "Moreover, the practice always observed in the ancient Church was that, before celebrating the Supper, the people were solemnly exhorted to lift their hearts on high, to show that we must not stop at the visible sign, to adore Christ rightly."[56]

In the *Manner of Celebrating the Lord's Supper*, in 1542, Calvin combines the themes we have seen in the *Short Treatise* of 1541. On the one hand, he reminds the congregation that Christ does not deceive us with empty signs but will perform in our souls all that he represents to our eyes in the symbols of bread and wine.[57] On the other hand, Calvin encourages the congregation to lift up their minds and hearts to heaven, so that they seek the reality joined to the signs in heaven, and not in the signs themselves.[58] The faithful are to be guided by the Word of God, which has an inseparable relationship to the symbols of bread and wine, and to seek Christ in heaven so that they might be nourished by his vivifying flesh.[59] Christ will perform in our souls what the symbols represent to us—"to make us partakers of his own body and blood, in order that we may possess him entirely in such a manner that he may live in us and we in him"—only if we on our part seek Christ not in the symbols of bread and wine, but in heaven.[60]

In the third edition of the *Institutes*, in 1543, Calvin emphasizes the theme of accommodation to our weakness that he incorporated into his discussion of the Supper in 1541. "Since, however, this mystery of Christ's secret union with the devout is by nature incomprehensible, he shows its figure and image in visible signs. Indeed, by giving guarantees or tokens he makes it as certain for us as if we had seen it with our own eyes."[61] Calvin makes it clear that the analogy of the sign to the thing signified not only represents the spiritual blessings the faithful always enjoy in Christ, but also communicates those blessings to us in the Supper.[62] Moreover, Calvin accentuates the offer of communion with the life-giving flesh and blood of Christ in the Supper, over and above the offer we receive in the gospel.[63] Calvin makes it clear that Christ

---

56. *Libellus de Coena Domini, OS* 1:520–21; *CTT*, 159.
57. Ibid.
58. *La forme des prieres et chantz ecclesiastiques, OS* 2:48.24–29; *TTRC* 2:121–22.
59. *La forme des prieres et chantz ecclesiastiques, OS* 2:48.29–35; *TTRC* 2:122.
60. *La forme des prieres et chantz ecclesiastiques, OS* 2:48.5–7; *TTRC* 2:121.
61. *Institutio 1543* 17.1, *CO* 1:991B; *Inst.* 1960 2:1361.
62. *Institutio 1543* 17.3, *CO* 1:993C; *Inst.* 1960 2:1363.
63. *Institutio 1543* 17.5, *CO* 1:994C; *Inst.* 1960 2:1364.

not only offers himself and his benefits to us in the Supper, but also inwardly accomplishes what the Supper outwardly exhibits.[64]

Calvin claims that the church has always taught his distinction between the signs and the reality signified, as well as the need to see the reality offered and exhibited in the signs that represent it, thereby claiming catholicity for his teaching on the Supper. "I therefore say (what has always been accepted in the church and is today taught by all of sound opinion) that the sacred mystery of the Supper consists of two things: physical signs, which, thrust before our eyes, represent to us, according to our feeble capacity, things invisible; and spiritual truth, which is at the same time represented and displayed through the symbols themselves."[65] However, Calvin shows a willingness to allow for different ways of expressing the mystery he is describing, so long as such teaching "may neither fasten [Christ] to the element of the bread, nor enclose him in the bread, nor circumscribe him in any way (all which things, it is clear, detract from his heavenly glory); finally, such as may not take from him his own stature, or parcel him out to many places at once, or invest him with boundless magnitude to be spread through heaven and earth."[66] So long as Christ is not dragged out of heaven to be confined under the physical symbols of his body and blood, and his human nature is rightly understood as being in heaven, then Calvin is willing to "accept whatever can be made to express the true and substantial partaking of the body and blood of the Lord, which is shown to believers under the symbols of the Supper—and so to express it that they may be understood not to receive it solely by imagination or understanding of the mind, but to enjoy the thing itself as nourishment of eternal life."[67]

As in 1539, Calvin reiterates his inability to express this mystery in words, pointing to the experience of the reality in the Supper instead of to his own teaching. "Now, if anyone should ask me how this takes place, I shall not be ashamed to confess that it is a secret too lofty either for my mind to comprehend or my words to declare. And, to speak more plainly, I rather experience than understand it."[68] However,

64. Ibid.
65. *Institutio 1543* 17.19, *CO* 1:1003A; *Inst.* 1960 2:1371.
66. *Institutio 1543* 17.22, *CO* 1:1004C; *Inst.* 1960 2:1381.
67. *Institutio 1543* 17.22, *CO* 1:1005A; *Inst.* 1960 2:1382.
68. *Institutio 1543* 17.30, *CO* 1:1010A; *Inst.* 1960 2:1403.

essential to the right experience of this mystery is the need to seek the life-giving flesh and blood of Christ in heaven, and not in the symbols of bread and wine. Indeed, God gives us these symbols in accommodation to our weakness, to give us the assistance we need to seek Christ in heaven.[69] Once again, Calvin claims that this upward ascent is reflected in the eucharistic liturgy of the early church. "And for the same reason it was established of old that before the consecration the people should be told in a loud voice to lift up their hearts [*habere sursum corda*]."[70]

The most significant development that takes place in Calvin's understanding of the holy Supper of the Lord after 1539 regards his increasing emphasis on the Supper as a means by which to elevate the faithful from earth to heaven, where Christ dwells in glory. In this, Calvin is guided by the ancient Catholic practice of asking the people, "Lift up your hearts," at the beginning of the eucharistic celebration. Already in 1543, Calvin describes the chief purpose of the Supper as being a help by which we might raise our minds to heaven, in contrast to the Roman teaching of transubstantiation.[71] Calvin also describes the Supper as an accommodation to our weakness, whereby we are given the assistance we need to raise our minds and hearts to heaven.[72] In *The True Method of Giving Peace and of Reforming the Church*, in 1549, Calvin highlights the upward dynamic of the Supper, again in contrast to the Roman doctrine of transubstantiation.[73] To accentuate the purpose of the Supper in raising us to heaven, Calvin describes it both as a hand stretched out by Christ to lift us up to heaven, and as a ladder that Christ gives us so that we might ascend to him in heaven.[74] In the Supper, Christ reaches his hand down to us to draw us upward to himself, and assists our weakness by giving us ladders to climb to him. If we seek Christ in the symbols of bread and wine, we totally thwart this purpose.[75] Calvin uses the preface to the eucharistic prayer in the Roman Church against what he takes to be the earthbound attention

69. *Institutio 1543* 17.32, CO 1:1012A; *Inst.* 1960 2:1412.

70. Ibid.

71. *Supplex exhortatio ad Caesarem*, CTT, 205.

72. *Institutio 1543* 17.32, CO 1:1012A; *Inst.* 1960 2:1412.

73. *Vera christianae pacificationis et ecclesiae reformandae ratio*, CO 7:622C; TTRC 3:279.

74. *Vera ecclesiae reformandae ratio*, CO 7:623A; TTRC 3:279–80.

75. *Vera ecclesiae reformandae ratio*, CO 7:623A; TTRC 3:280.

directed to the sign of the bread. "And what meaning will there be in the ancient preamble, 'Sursum Corda,' which the Papists still chant in their masses, if our worship cleaves to the earth?"[76]

The Laying on of Hands

The laying on of hands is a symbol that arises in three different contexts for Calvin. The first has to do with the confirmation of those who had been baptized in infancy and now come to the profession of faith after catechesis. The second arises in the context of the public restoration of the penitent to full communion with the church in Calvin's consideration of whether penance is a sacrament. The third has to do with its use in ordaining presbyters and deacons for the office of ministry. For the sake of clarity, we will discuss each of these issues separately, since Calvin's position on each is distinctive and tends to develop dramatically by 1543, especially with regard to the issue of ordination.

As Confirmation

The laying on of hands plays a role in the controversy over whether confirmation ought to be considered a sacrament. In the first edition of the *Institutes*, in 1536, Calvin denies that the laying on of hands as practiced by the apostles was anything more than a rite of consecration.[77] Calvin is especially bothered by the Roman teaching that the grace of baptism is incomplete without the increase of grace in confirmation.[78] According to Calvin, this is a diabolical teaching that has the effect of leading the faithful away from the truth of their baptism.[79] Calvin again denies that the laying on of hands is a sacrament, since the ancient writers of the church mention only two sacraments. "The ancients speak of the laying on of hands, but do they call it a sacrament? Augustine openly affirms that it is nothing but prayer."[80]

76. *Vera ecclesiae reformandae ratio, CO* 7:623C; *TTRC* 3:280–81.
77. *Institutio 1536* 5.3, *CO* 1:142C; *Inst.* 1536, 125–26.
78. *Institutio 1536* 5.5, *CO* 1:144C; *Inst.* 1536, 127.
79. Ibid.
80. *Institutio 1536* 5.9, *CO* 1:146–47; *Inst.* 1536, 129.

Calvin does wish that the ancient practice of catechizing those baptized as infants could be restored, so that at the age of ten they could be examined about their faith before the whole congregation, and be taught anything about which they were still ignorant. But he does not mention the laying on of hands in this regard.[81]

However, in the third edition of the *Institutes*, in 1543, Calvin gives a fuller description of the practice of catechesis in the ancient church in order to indicate that it formed the completion of infant baptism by giving a fuller confession of faith. "Therefore, those who had been baptized as infants, because they had not made confession of faith before the church, were at the end of their childhood or at the beginning of adolescence again presented by their parents, and were examined by the bishop according to the form of the catechism, which was then in common form and definite use."[82] Calvin also stresses the more essential role the rite of the laying on of hands played in this ceremony. "But in order that this act, which ought by itself to have been weighty and holy, might have more reverence and dignity, the ceremony of the laying on of hands was also added. Thus the youth, once his faith was approved, was dismissed with a solemn blessing."[83] Calvin notes that it was customary, but not necessary, for the bishop to bless the child by the laying on of hands. "Therefore, I warmly approve such laying on of hands, which is simply done as a form of blessing, and wish that it were today restored to pure use."[84] However, Calvin repeats his objection to calling this form of the laying on of hands a sacrament, for to do so would denigrate the power of baptism.[85]

Calvin reiterates this position in his *Commentary on Hebrews*, in 1549. He thinks that Hebrews is referring to the rite of blessing catechumens when it speaks of "the teachings of baptisms, and of laying on of hands" (Heb. 6:2). Calvin claims that the passage shows that this rite came from the apostles, even though it was perverted by the Roman Church when it was defined as a sacrament conferring the spirit of regeneration, thereby mutilating baptism. "We should know that it was instituted by its first authors to be a solemn ceremony of

81. *Institutio 1536* 5.10, CO 1:147A; *Inst.* 1536, 130.
82. *Institutio 1543* 19.4, CO 1:1068C; *Inst.* 1960 2:1452.
83. Ibid.
84. *Institutio 1543* 19.4, CO 1:1069A; *Inst.* 1960 2:1452.
85. Ibid.

prayer, as indeed Augustine declares. By this sign they intended to confirm the profession of faith which adolescents make when they pass from their childhood, but they have planned nothing less than the destruction of the force of baptism."[86] However, in spite of this perversion of making the laying on of hands into a sacrament, Calvin still wants to restore its proper use as a solemn prayer of confirmation. "Today we must retain the institution in its purity, but we must also correct the superstition."[87] In his *Commentary on Acts*, in 1554, Calvin continues to endorse the laying on of hands in confirmation: "I do not condemn the use of the laying on of hands by men of old to confirm adults in the profession of the faith, so long as no one thinks that the grace of the Spirit is tied to such a ceremony, as Jerome asserts against the Luciferians."[88] Once again, however, Calvin denies that the laying on of hands in confirmation can be considered a sacrament without blaspheming against the power of baptism.[89]

As Public Restoration

Calvin engages in a lengthy discussion of the Roman teaching on penance in the first edition of the *Institutes*, especially the definition of penance as contrition, confession, and satisfaction. More germane to our concerns, he explicitly denies that it is a sacrament, for it lacks both a ceremony instituted by God and a promise to which it is appended as confirmation.[90] If his opponents do not like his definition of a sacrament, Calvin is willing to turn to the definitions provided by Augustine, all of which indicate that visual manifestation is essential to a sacrament but is lacking in penance.[91] However, if the Roman Church were to define the sacrament of penance in terms of the priest's absolution, Calvin thinks that a better case could be made for it being a sacrament.[92] In spite of this concession, Calvin denies that penance could ever be considered a sacrament, for "no promise

---

86. *Comm. on Hebrews*, on Heb. 6:1–2, *OE* 19.89–90; *CNTC* 12:73.
87. Ibid.
88. *Comm. on Acts*, on Acts 19:7, *CO* 48:443A; *CNTC* 7:152.
89. Ibid.
90. *Institutio 1536* 5.44, *CO* 1:175C; *Inst.* 1536, 157.
91. *Institutio 1536* 5.44, *CO* 1:176A; *Inst.* 1536, 157.
92. *Institutio 1536* 5.44, *CO* 1:1776B; *Inst.* 1536, 157.

of God—the only basis of a sacrament—exists," and because "every ceremony displayed here is a mere invention of men, although we have already proved that the ceremonies of sacraments can only be ordained by God."[93] For Calvin, as for Luther before him, baptism is the sacrament of penance, to which sinners return once they repent.[94] In the second edition of the *Institutes*, in 1539, Calvin confirms his description of baptism as the sacrament of penance by appealing to a work ascribed to Augustine.[95]

In the third edition of the *Institutes*, in 1543, Calvin presents a lengthy discussion of the practice of public or canonical penance under the bishops in the early church and thus makes a considerable addition to the beginning of his discussion of whether penance is to be considered a sacrament. "The ancients observed this order in public repentance, that those who had discharged the satisfactions enjoined upon them were reconciled by the solemn laying on of hands. That was a symbol of absolution by which the sinner himself was raised up before God with assurance of pardon, and the church admonished to expunge the memory of his offense and receive him kindly into favor. Cyprian very often calls this 'giving peace.' "[96] Calvin acknowledges that the laying on of hands was often done by bishops, as is also reflected in several canons of provincial synods. "However, Cyprian, in another passage, shows how not only the bishop laid on hands but the entire clergy as well."[97] By the time of Gratian, this practice was combined with private reconciliation, which became normative by Calvin's day. Although Calvin does not reject the efficacy of private reconciliation, he clearly wishes for the restoration of the laying on of hands in a public symbol of absolution. "I judge the ancient observance, which Cyprian mentions, to have been holy and wholesome for the church; and I would like to see it restored today."[98] However, Calvin acknowledges that this symbol of absolution is of human invention and therefore is neither a sacrament nor a necessary rite, only a desirable one from his point of view. "However it may be, we still see that the laying on of hands in

93. *Institutio 1536* 5.44, *CO* 1:176–77; *Inst.* 1536, 158.
94. *Institutio 1536* 5.44, *CO* 1:177A; *Inst.* 1536, 158.
95. *Institutio 1539* 16.17, *CO* 1:1078B; *Inst.* 1960 2:1465.
96. *Institutio 1543* 19.14, *CO* 1:1075C; *Inst.* 1960 2:1462.
97. *Institutio 1543* 19.14, *CO* 1:1076B; *Inst.* 1960 2:1462.
98. Ibid.

penance is a ceremony ordained by men, not by God, one that ought to be classed among the things indifferent and outward exercises—things that are indeed not to be despised, but that ought to occupy a lower place than those commended to us by the Lord's word."[99] The laying on of hands in public reconciliation would therefore be similar to the laying on of hands in confirmation, which in 1543 Calvin also wants to be restored.

As Ordination

Calvin first discusses the laying on of hands for ordination in the 1536 edition of the *Institutes*. He is especially concerned with the Roman view that the sacrament of ordination of itself bestows the Holy Spirit on those who receive it, while the oil of ordination bestows an indelible character on the souls of those who receive it. Calvin discerns three rites in the Roman sacrament of ordination. The first is insufflation, by which the bishop breathes on the ordinand and says, "Receive the Holy Spirit" (John 20:22). According to Calvin, Christ was not instituting a sacrament when he breathed on his apostles after the resurrection, but rather "used it as a symbol of a particular miracle."[100] By falsely imitating what Christ alone could do, the bishops act "like apes, which imitate everything wantonly and without any discrimination," while they also "mock Christ," for "they are so shameless as to dare affirm that they confer the Holy Spirit."[101] The second rite is anointing with oil, in imitation of consecration to the Aaronic priesthood. According to Calvin, such priestly consecration is an explicit denial of the sole Priesthood of Christ, and reflects the way that the Roman Church tends "to shape one religion out of Christianity and Judaism and paganism by sewing patches together."[102]

The third rite of ordination is the laying on of hands. Calvin admits that this symbol is in a different class than the others, as it was the practice of the apostles.[103] Calvin acknowledges that this rite was originally of Hebraic origin, by which the Israelites "presented to God by the lay-

---

99. *Institutio 1543* 19.14, *CO* 1:1076B; *Inst.* 1960 2:1462–63.
100. *Institutio 1536* 5.64, *CO* 1:189C; *Inst.* 1536, 169.
101. *Institutio 1536* 5.64, *CO* 1:189B; *Inst.* 1536, 169.
102. *Institutio 1536* 5.64, *CO* 1:1190C; *Inst.* 1536, 170.
103. *Institutio 1536* 5.65, *CO* 1:1190C; *Inst.* 1536, 170.

ing on of hands that which they wished to be blessed and sanctified."[104] Calvin claims that the apostles adopted this practice without returning to the shadows of the law, and more important, without the superstition that he thinks infects the Roman practice.[105] The key for Calvin comes in the prayer for the Holy Spirit that accompanied the laying on of hands, for it reveals that the apostles did not think that the symbol itself conferred the Holy Spirit, over against the Roman view. "To sum up: it was the symbol by which they commended to the Lord him for whom they wished to implore the grace of the Holy Spirit."[106]

The question for Calvin is, "Was it thenceforth continuously held to be a sacrament?"[107] According to Calvin, the laying on of hands is no more a sacrament than is kneeling, or the lifting up of hands to pray, or praying to the east, which the apostles also practiced. "In the end, all the gestures of the saints would turn into sacraments."[108] Therefore, Calvin categorically denies that the laying on of hands is a sacrament—even though it was a Hebrew custom that was also followed by the apostles—since there is no promise of God attested by the sign, which for Calvin is the definition of a sacrament. "In this rite one finds not even one syllable of any definite promise; hence, it would be fruitless to seek a ceremony to confirm the promise. Again, one reads of no ceremony ordained by God. Therefore, there cannot be any sacrament."[109] Calvin also explicitly denies that there is a dominical institution of the laying on of hands, or that the laying on of hands could bring the Holy Spirit. "If we use it to the end that we may confer gifts of the Holy Spirit, just as the apostles did, we are acting foolishly. For this mystery was neither committed to us by the Lord, nor was it established as a symbol by him."[110] However, so long as there was no expectation that the Holy Spirit is being given, Calvin would allow for the installation of a bishop by the laying on of hands.[111]

The *Institutes* of 1539 preserves this discussion of the laying on of hands from the first edition, including the categorical denial that it is

104. Ibid.
105. *Institutio 1536* 5.65, *CO* 1:1191A; *Inst.* 1536, 171.
106. Ibid.
107. Ibid.
108. *Institutio 1536* 5.65, *CO* 1:1191B; *Inst.* 1536, 171.
109. *Institutio 1536* 5.67, *CO* 1:192C; *Inst.* 1536, 172.
110. *Institutio 1536* 5.66, *CO* 1:192B; *Inst.* 1536, 171.
111. *Institutio 1536* 5.64, *CO* 1:191C; *Inst.* 1536, 170.

a sacrament.[112] Moreover, the *Draft Ecclesiastical Ordinances*, in 1541, seem to set forth a similar understanding, allowing for the practice if it is not viewed as a sacrament conveying the Holy Spirit, but denying its use due to the superstition surrounding it.[113] In the version of the article officially received by the magistrates of Geneva, all mention of the laying on of hands is removed.[114] Clearly, even as late as 1541, Calvin is so concerned with the Roman view that the Spirit is given through the ceremony of the laying on of hands that he will not allow it even when this belief does not accompany it.

A Change in View

However, in the third edition of the *Institutes*, in 1543, Calvin completely changes his position on the symbol of the laying on of hands and moves decisively in the direction of the older Catholic position that he had previously categorically rejected. In his discussion of the orders of ministry in the church, Calvin describes the rite of ordination in terms of the laying on of hands. "It is clear that when the apostles admitted any man to the ministry, they used no other ceremony than the laying on of hands."[115] Calvin repeats the 1536 discussion of the Hebraic roots of this rite; but far from denying its value as a sacrament, he claims that even its lack of clear dominical institution does not prevent it from being considered to be commanded by God. "Although there exists no set precept for the laying on of hands, because we see it in continual use with the apostles, their very careful observance ought to serve in lieu of a precept."[116] Calvin also denies that the laying on of hands is "an empty sign," provided it is restored to its true origin. "For if the Spirit of God establishes nothing without cause in the Church, we should feel that this ceremony, since it has proceeded from him, is not useless, provided it may not be turned into superstitious abuse."[117] The uniform practice of the apostles therefore takes the place of an explicit word instituting the rite of the laying on of hands, so that it

112. *Institutio 1539* 16.33–35, *CO* 1:1095–97.
113. *Projet d'ordonnances ecclesiastiques*, *CO* 10:18A; *CTT*, 59.
114. *Projet d'ordonnances ecclesiastiques*, *CO* 10:18C; *CTT*, 59–60.
115. *Institutio 1543* 8.50, *CO* 1:571B; *Inst.* 1960 2:1066–67.
116. *Institutio 1543* 8.50, *CO* 1:571C; *Inst.* 1960 2:1067.
117. Ibid.

can be considered to have proceeded from the Holy Spirit. Calvin accentuates this claim for authority in *The Necessity of Reforming the Church* of the same year. "It is absurd, therefore, to trouble us about the form of ordination, in which we differ neither from the rule of Christ, nor from the practice of the apostles, nor from the custom of the ancient Church."[118] Calvin also suggests that the Holy Spirit is conferred through this ceremony, by means of his paraphrase of 2 Timothy 1:6, in which Paul asks Timothy to rekindle the gift of God he received through the laying on of hands. "It is as if he said, 'See to it that the grace which you received by the laying on of hands, when I created you presbyter, is not void.'"[119]

In his discussion of the sacraments in 1543, Calvin indicates his willingness to consider the laying on of hands to be a sacrament, though it is not an "ordinary sacrament" for confirming the faith of all believers, as are baptism and the holy Supper of the Lord. "I am speaking of those which were established for the use of the whole church. I would not go against calling the laying on of hands, by which ministers of the church are initiated into their office, a sacrament, but I do not include it among the ordinary sacraments."[120] Therefore, in his discussion of the "false sacraments" of the Roman Church, Calvin willingly allows a place for the laying on of hands among the sacraments of the church. "For in it there is a ceremony, first taken from Scripture, then one that Paul testifies not to be empty or superfluous, but a faithful token of spiritual grace [1 Tim. 4:14]. However, I have not put it as number three among the sacraments because it is not ordinary or common with all believers, but is a special rite for a particular office."[121]

Calvin is aware that his Roman opponents will celebrate this complete reversal of his previous position as a vindication of their ministry, but Calvin adds the qualification that ministers are to be ordained as pastors to preach the gospel, not to be consecrated as priests to offer the sacrifice of the Mass.[122] He also removes entirely his sarcastic mockery of the apish imitation of every gesture of the apostles as constituting a sacrament and replaces it with this terse statement: "There remains

118. *Supplex exhortatio ad Caesarem, CTT*, 210.
119. *Institutio 1543* 8.50, *CO* 1:572A; *Inst.* 1960 2:1068.
120. *Institutio 1543* 16.20, *CO* 1:952–53; *Inst.* 1960 2:1296.
121. *Institutio 1543* 19.30, *CO* 1:1086C; *Inst.* 1960 2:1476.
122. Ibid.

the laying on of hands. As I concede that it is a sacrament in true and lawful ordinations, so I deny that it has a place in this farce [of Roman ordinations], where they neither obey Christ's command nor consider the end to which the promise should lead us. If they do not wish the sign to be denied them, they must apply it to the reality, to which it was appointed."[123] Thus by 1543 Calvin allows that the laying on of hands is a sacrament, with both a dominical institution (inferred from universal apostolic practice) and the efficacy of the Spirit bringing the reality of the sign, even though it is not numbered among the ordinary sacraments of the church.

We should observe that after 1543, Calvin uses the principle that universal custom serves as precept in order to explain how other rites of the ancient Israelite church could be considered to be sacraments. For instance, Calvin is convinced that the sacrifices offered by the patriarchs were symbols of the reconciling death of Christ after the expulsion of humanity from the Garden of Eden. However, there is no dominical institution of sacrifice during this time. To solve this problem, Calvin appeals to an oral tradition that must have existed from which Cain and Abel learned of the divine command to offer sacrifice. "For we must remember, that the custom of sacrificing was not rashly devised by them, but was divinely delivered to them."[124]

Similarly, when Calvin considers how David in Psalm 110 could have known that Melchizedek was a type of the coming messianic priest and king, he again appeals to an oral tradition handed down from the patriarchs to David. "David, indeed, does not propose a similitude framed by himself; but declares the reason for which the kingdom of Christ was divinely ordained, and even confirmed with an oath; and it is not to be doubted that the same truth had been traditionally handed down by the fathers."[125]

Finally, Calvin makes an appeal to oral tradition to find the divine institution of the rite of burial, which he interprets to be a symbol of the resurrection. "Indeed, I have no doubt that it was transmitted from the holy patriarchs, as if by hand, continuously through the generations, so that in death itself some visible representation might

---

123. *Institutio 1543* 19.33, *CO* 1:1094C; *Inst.* 1960 2:1479.
124. Ibid.
125. Ibid.

lift up the minds of the godly to a good hope."[126] Since the burial he is interpreting is that of Tabitha in the book of Acts, this oral tradition extended all the way from the patriarchs to the apostles.

Calvin reinforces his understanding of the laying on of hands as a sacrament in his *Commentary on First and Second Timothy*, in 1548. Calvin highlights Paul's statement that Timothy received the gift through the laying on of hands, insisting that it was not an empty symbol, but that the Spirit effected the reality signified by the symbol. "For we gather that the ceremony was not in vain, since God by his Spirit effected that consecration which men symbolized by the laying on of hands."[127] By accentuating the role of prayer in the ceremony, Calvin addresses his concern that the Spirit not be seen as automatically given with the symbol. "My answer is that all ministers ordained were commended to God by the prayers of the whole Church and in this way grace was obtained for them from God."[128] However, Calvin denies that this makes the ceremony itself meaningless, for it "was a faithful token of the grace they received from God's own hand."[129] This is not to say that Timothy had no gift of the Spirit before the laying on of hands, "but rather that it shone forth more brightly when the teaching office was laid upon him."[130]

In his *True Method of Giving Peace*, in 1549, Calvin explicitly allows that the laying on of hands is a sacrament, as it is understood to be by the Roman Church. "The laying on of hands, by which ministers are consecrated to their office, I do not quarrel with them for calling a sacrament."[131] However, Calvin denies that the Roman practice of consecrating priests to offer the sacrifice of the Mass is a sacrament, and he denies that the Spirit works through this symbol.[132] On the other hand, when laying on of hands is performed according to the purpose for which it was instituted, and when it is accompanied by the prayers of the community, the Spirit does work through the ceremony to join the reality with the symbol, in order to effect inwardly what the rite

---

126. *Comm. on Acts*, on Acts 9:37, *CO* 48:218B; *CNTC* 6:278–79.
127. *Comm. on 1 Timothy*, on 1 Tim. 4:14, *CO* 52:302–3; *CNTC* 10:247.
128. *Comm. on 2 Timothy*, on 2 Tim. 1:6, *CO* 52:349–50; *CNTC* 10:293.
129. Ibid.
130. Ibid.
131. *Vera ecclesiae reformandae ratio*, *CO* 7:632A; *TTRC*, 3:291.
132. Ibid.

outwardly represents. "We gather from this that the laying on of hands is a rite consistent with order and dignity, seeing that it was used by the apostles; not of course that it has any efficacy or virtue in itself, but its power and effect depend solely on the Spirit of God."[133]

The Order of Church Government

Related to Calvin's change of heart regarding the sacramental nature of the laying on of hands is his discussion of the orders of ministry in the church. In the 1536 edition of the *Institutes*, Calvin sarcastically dismissed the seven orders of doorkeepers, readers, exorcists, acolytes, subdeacons, deacons, and priests. He also rejects the use of the term "clergy" for this group of offices and satirizes the alleged holiness of the tonsure. Finally, he denies that there is any difference between presbyters and bishops. "Before devilish division arose in the church, and one said, 'I am of Cephas,' another 'I am of Apollos' [1 Cor. 1:12], there was no distinction between presbyters and bishops. Those to whom this distinction seemed to have been taken from the pagans reasoned much more correctly."[134]

When we turn to the discussion of "the order by which the Lord willed his church to be governed" in the 1543 edition of the *Institutes*, the picture is dramatically different. As is widely acknowledged, Calvin begins by showing how the order of teachers, pastors, elders, and deacons is established by the Word of God for the godly governance of the church. However, Calvin passes beyond the apostolic church to the ancient church of the patristic period, in order "to recognize in those characteristics of the ancient church the form which will represent to our eyes some image of the divine institution." Even though Calvin acknowledges that many of the early canons of the church express more than may be found in Scripture, he still insists that "they conformed their establishment with such care to the unique pattern of God's Word that you may readily see that it had almost nothing in this respect alien to God's Word."[135]

133. *Comm. on Acts*, on Acts 6:6, *CO* 48:122C; *CNTC* 6:163.
134. *Institutio 1536* 5.55, *CO* 1:184C; *Inst.* 1536, 165.
135. *Institutio 1543* 8.51, *CO* 1:572B; *Inst.* 1960 2:1068.

Calvin then goes on to argue that the church order of deacons, presbyters, bishops, archbishops, and patriarchs is as godly a form of governing the church as are deacons, elders, teachers, and pastors. According to Calvin, "Both bishops and presbyters had to devote themselves to the dispensing of Word and sacraments," and "at that time the character of the diaconate was the same as that under the apostles."[136] Calvin is at pains to defend the distinction between presbyters and bishops, and to acknowledge the relative authority of bishops over presbyters. "All those to whom the office of teaching was enjoined they called 'presbyters.' In each city these chose one of their number to whom they specially gave the title 'bishop' in order that dissentions might not arise (as commonly happens) from equality of rank."[137] He also defends the legitimacy of each province having an archbishop over the bishops, as well as a patriarch above the archbishops. "That each province had one archbishop among the bishops, and that at the Council of Nicaea patriarchs were ordained to be higher in rank and dignity than archbishops, were facts connected with the maintenance of discipline."[138] Far from taking their bearings from the pagans, Calvin claims that when they ordered the church in this way, "the bishops did not intend to fashion any other form of church rule than that which God has laid down in his Word."[139]

Calvin also defends the way that clergy were trained by bishops to become presbyters, even though he still thinks that the term "clergy" should be applied to all the faithful; he prefers instead to speak of future ministers as recruits being trained in the Lord's sacred army. "But the institution itself was particularly holy and profitable, for by it those who wished to consecrate themselves and their service to the church were brought up under the bishop's care."[140] Calvin commends the formation of such recruits under the care of the bishop whereby they are first made doorkeepers, then acolytes who serve the bishop, and then readers of Scripture from the pulpit, to accustom the people to seeing them in positions of public responsibility. "In this way, to

136. *Institutio 1543* 8.53, CO 1:573C; *Inst.* 1960 2:1070; *Institutio 1543* 8.55, CO 1:574C; *Inst.* 1960 2:1071.
137. *Institutio 1543* 8.52, CO 1:572C; *Inst.* 1960 2:1069.
138. *Institutio 1543* 8.54, CO 1:574B; *Inst.* 1960 2:1071–2.
139. Ibid.
140. *Institutio 1543* 8.59, CO 1:577C; *Inst.* 1960 2:1077.

prove their diligence in individual exercises, they were promoted by degrees until they were made subdeacons."[141] Calvin is clearly willing to acknowledge the legitimacy of the offices of doorkeeper, acolyte, lector, and subdeacon, so long as it is conceded that "these were more the rudiments of recruits than functions to be considered true ministries of the church."[142] He is also willing to concede that even though the ordination of presbyters and deacons takes place by the bishop acting in concert with his presbyters, yet "because the bishop presided and things were done under his auspices, the ordination was called 'his.' Accordingly, ancient writers often state that presbyter differs from bishop only in that the former does not have the power to ordain."[143] The contrast with his position in 1536 could not be more dramatic.

Conclusion

Both the concession that ordination is a sacrament, and that bishops, presbyters, and deacons are a form of church government sanctioned by the Word of God, clearly indicate that Calvin revised his understanding of church reform in the direction of older Catholic thought and practice in the years immediately following his dialogue with representatives of the Roman Church. His experience in these dialogues likely made Calvin vividly aware of the need to root evangelical and orthodox thought and practice more deeply in continuity with the orthodox and catholic tradition. It is hoped that these reflections might show that his dialogue with his Roman opponents had a more positive influence on Calvin than might otherwise be discernable in light of his continual polemic against them, and that he actually took the point of many of their criticisms of his earlier theological positions and changed his teaching accordingly, at times quite dramatically. If nothing else, the changes he makes in the 1543 *Institutes* support Alexandre Ganoczy's description of Calvin's own self-understanding. "He never stopped claiming his unshakable attachment to the unity of the Catholic Church which he did not want to replace, but to restore."[144]

141. *Institutio 1543* 8.59, *CO* 1:578B; *Inst.* 1960 2:1077.
142. Ibid.
143. *Institutio 1543* 8.66, *CO* 1:582B; *Inst.* 1960 2:1084.
144. Ganoczy, *Young Calvin*, 307.

8

Calvin and Sacramentality

A Catholic Perspective

Dennis E. Tamburello

Since fall 2003, the seventh round of the official Reformed–Roman Catholic Dialogue in the United States has been meeting twice a year, focusing on the theology of the sacraments. Before we delved into a detailed discussion of baptism—a conversation that proved to be more difficult than any of us expected, given that we already recognize each other's baptisms—we spent time at several sessions exploring the overall meaning of the word *sacrament.*

It did not take long before the Catholics started using the term "sacramentality," which sent up red flags for many of the Reformed participants. Some of them, like my late esteemed friend and colleague George Vandervelde, insisted that this notion was nowhere to be found in Calvin's thought.[1] I was George's nemesis in the discussion, because

1. George Vandervelde, a member of the Reformed–Roman Catholic Dialogue in the USA who died on January 19, 2007, taught at the Institute for Christian Studies in Toronto from 1977 to 2004. At the dialogue on October 26, 2005, he noted that "the Reformed center

I was convinced that Calvin's theology contained elements of what Catholics call sacramentality. At the time I was unable to put together a more systematic study of this question. But for me it has been the most burning issue raised by the dialogue sessions. The invitation to this conference, coinciding with a sabbatical, pushed me over the edge to pursue the matter more systematically. I suspect that George would disagree with much of what I am about to say. Nevertheless, I dedicate this essay to him, as the one who challenged me most strongly to prove my point.

On the face of it, relating John Calvin to the Catholic principle of sacramentality, as articulated in modern times by Edward Schillebeeckx and others, may seem to smack of anachronism. There is a legitimate concern that, in trying to make connections, we end up "accommodating" Calvin to modern theological constructs or ecumenical agendas. Many of us are familiar with Richard Muller's admonition in his book *The Unaccommodated Calvin* "to listen to Calvin, not to use him."[2]

However, the bigger tragedy would be that the writings of Calvin become dead letters and not be used as resources in contemporary theology. Just as Calvin "used" ideas from his predecessors to illuminate aspects of his own theological arguments, we can and should bring Calvin's ideas into dialogue with the theological discourse of our own day. It is certainly crucial that we use his ideas in a way that is attentive to and respectful of their historical and theological context—as Calvin generally succeeded in doing when he quoted his patristic and medieval forebears. In this way, we can be not only admirers of Calvin but also imitators of him, as theologians who incorporate the best of the past into our present thinking.[3]

To paraphrase a remark by my dissertation adviser Brian Gerrish, a good study of Calvin will sometimes do something for him that he did not do for himself. My dissertation on union with Christ in Calvin's theology tried to show how his notion of *unio mystica* had parallels

---

of gravity is more Word than Sacrament." He was disturbed that "the Catholic notion of sacrament seems to be *separate* from the Word." These and other comments provided much of the impetus for this essay.

2. Richard Muller, *The Unaccommodated Calvin* (New York: Oxford University Press, 2000), 188.

3. The ideas in this paragraph were originally presented in a paper, "Calvin and Spirituality: A Casualty of Post-Reformation Dogmatics?" given at the International Congress on Medieval Studies in Kalamazoo, Michigan, on May 7, 2005.

with the medieval notion of mystical union as found in Bernard of Clairvaux. In a similar vein, this essay will raise a key question: Is the notion of sacramentality as discussed in Roman Catholic theology in any way present in Calvin's thought? The answer, as in so many ecumenical questions, is a qualified yes.

Sacramentality in Contemporary Theology

Perhaps the most famous modern commentator on sacramentality is Edward Schillebeeckx, in his classic work *Christ the Sacrament of Encounter with God*. Schillebeeckx begins his study by noting that "personal communion with God is possible only in and through God's own generous initiative in coming to meet us in grace."[4] That statement certainly gets a dialogue with Reformed theology off on the right foot.

However, he immediately goes on to say that the sacraments are "the properly human mode of encounter with God."[5] I think a good Protestant would say that the *Word* is the properly human mode of encounter. Schillebeeckx recognizes this himself when he later talks about Protestant sacraments. He says that in Protestantism, "preaching remains primary; the sacraments underscore what the preaching has told me, that what Christ did once and for all on the Cross concerns me, the recipient of the sacrament, personally; and so the sacraments bring about and strengthen the act of faith in the grace-giving word of God."[6] We will need to ask whether this is an irreconcilable difference or a difference in emphasis.

Schillebeeckx defines a sacrament as "a divine bestowal of salvation in an outwardly perceptible form which makes the bestowal manifest; a bestowal of salvation in historical visibility."[7] For Schillebeeckx, Jesus Christ is the primordial sacrament, because in him "grace became fully visible; he is the embodiment of the grace of final victory."[8] More

4. Edward Schillebeeckx, OP, *Christ the Sacrament of Encounter with God* (New York: Sheed & Ward, 1963), 4.
  5. Ibid., 6.
  6. Ibid., 185.
  7. Ibid., 15.
  8. Ibid., 13.

specifically, "the man Jesus, as the personal visible realization of the divine grace of redemption, is *the* sacrament, the primordial sacrament, because this man, the Son of God himself, is intended by the Father to be in his humanity the only way to the actuality of redemption."[9]

This might seem to be a different starting point for sacramental theology than we find in the definition that Calvin gives in book 4 of the *Institutes*. There Calvin defines a sacrament as "an outward sign by which the Lord seals on our consciences the promises of his good will toward us in order to sustain the weakness of our faith; and we in turn attest our piety toward him in the presence of the Lord and of his angels and before [humans]." But he immediately qualifies this and says, "Whichever of these definitions you may choose, it does not differ in meaning from that of Augustine, who teaches that a sacrament is a 'visible sign of a sacred thing,' or 'a visible form of an invisible grace.'"[10] Although Schillebeeckx, as a good Dominican, quotes Thomas Aquinas more than he quotes Augustine, he could also argue that his definition is essentially the same as Augustine's.

Significantly, Schillebeeckx sees the spoken word as also constitutive of sacramentality, particularly in relation to the ritual sacraments. "The word," he says, "belongs to the intrinsic constitution of the presence of a supernatural reality among us."[11] That word in turn is intrinsically connected to faith. "Because a sacrament is a symbolic act of Christ in his Church, it is only through faith in Christ that the Church is able to make this spiritual signification manifest in her sacraments, and so the faith of the Church is necessary for the constitution of an outward sacramental sign."[12] Notice that Schillebeeckx refers to the faith of the church here, as opposed to the faith of individuals as such. However, he understands the church as embracing the community of all the individual faithful.[13]

Schillebeeckx begins with the notion of Christ as the sacrament of God, proceeds to discuss the church as sacrament of Christ, and finally treats the ecclesial ritual sacraments as expressing the church's

9. Ibid., 15.
10. *Inst.* 1960, 4.14.1; all translations of the *Institutes* in this chapter are from this edition; Latin sources from Calvin's works are referenced to *CO*, as here (*CO* 2:942).
11. Schillebeeckx, *Christ the Sacrament*, 99.
12. Ibid., 97.
13. Ibid., 48.

sacramentality. This emphasis on Jesus as the primordial sacrament suggests that sacramentality is directly tied to the theology of the incarnation.

However, liturgical theologians such as Kevin Irwin and Edward Kilmartin have argued that there is a more-general notion of sacramentality that has a long history, going back to the earliest days of Christianity. This notion is tied more to creation than to the incarnation. Irwin states that the ritual sacraments have their basis in the reality that "God is disclosed and discovered here and now on earth and in human life."[14] Irwin wants to recapture this earlier notion of sacramentality, the idea that "through materiality, the human, the fragile and the things of this earth we experience the divine." He thinks that this principle has in recent times been "eclipsed in favor of naming Jesus and the church as 'sacraments,'" to the detriment of Catholic sacramental theology.[15] If Irwin is correct, then Calvin's understanding of sacramentality is more Catholic than we may have thought.

Schillebeeckx is not alone among Catholic systematic theologians in using such sacramental language. David Tracy, in *The Analogical Imagination*, defines a sacrament as "nothing other than a decisive re-presentation of both the events of proclaimed history and the manifestations of the sacred cosmos."[16] Tracy speaks of two basic forms of religious expression, manifestation and proclamation, noting that in Christian theology these are usually formulated as "sacrament" and "word," the former emphasis being characteristic of Catholicism and Orthodoxy, and the latter of Protestantism.[17]

Tracy argues that manifestation and proclamation are equally important to a sound theology of the sacraments. On the one hand, losing the kerygmatic power of the Word leads to the sacraments becoming "magic, aesthetics, or even mechanics." On the other hand, if we lose the paradigmatic power of manifestation (i.e., cosmic and symbolic reality), "the deepest needs of our hearts and imagination are . . . dis-

14. Kevin M. Irwin, "A Sacramental World—Sacramentality as the Primary Language for Sacraments," *Worship* 76, no. 3 (May 2002): 201.

15. Ibid., 204.

16. David Tracy, *The Analogical Imagination: Christian Theology and the Culture of Pluralism* (New York: Crossroad, 1981), 216.

17. Ibid., 203.

carded and Christianity eventually retreats into a righteous rigorism of duty and obligation."[18]

The language of sacramentality has also filtered into more-popular Catholic literature, such as Fr. Andrew Greeley's book *The Catholic Imagination*. Greeley defines sacramentality simply as "the presence of God in all creation."[19] Father Greeley declares that we Catholics "find our world haunted by a sense that the objects, events, and persons of daily life are revelations of grace. . . . The objects, events, and persons of ordinary existence hint at the nature of God and indeed make God in some fashion present to us. God is sufficiently like creation that creation not only tells us something about God but, by so doing, also makes God present among us."[20]

We have come to expect this kind of language from Catholic writers, but recently I was quite surprised to see an endorsement of sacramentality from the prominent evangelical theologian Brian McLaren. In his book *A Generous Orthodoxy*, he comments:

> A sacrament is an object or practice that mediates the divine to humans. It carries something of God to us; it is a means of grace, and it conveys sacredness. I care little for arguments about how many sacraments there are (although I tend to prefer longer lists than shorter ones). What I really like about the sacramental nature of Catholicism is this: through learning that a few things can carry the sacred, we become open to the fact that all things (all good things, all created things) can ultimately carry the sacred: the kind smile of a Down's syndrome child, the bouncy jubilation of a puppy, the graceful arch of a dancer's back, the camera work in a fine film, good coffee, good wine, good friends, good conversation. Start with three sacraments—or seven—and pretty soon everything becomes potentially sacramental as, I believe, it should be.[21]

18. Ibid., 217.

19. Andrew F. Greeley, *The Catholic Imagination* (Los Angeles: University of California Press, 2000), 24.

20. Ibid., 15.

21. Brian McLaren, *A Generous Orthodoxy: Why I am a missional + evangelical + post/protestant + liberal/conservative + mystical/poetic + charismatic/contemplative + fundamentalist/Calvinist + anabaptist/Anglican + Methodist + catholic + green + incarnational + depressed-yet-hopeful + emergent + unfinished Christian* (Grand Rapids: Zondervan, 2004), 225–26. I am grateful to Richard Mouw of Fuller Theological Seminary for pointing out this reference in an unpublished paper he wrote for the Reformed–Roman Catholic Dialogue.

It was precisely this kind of statement that made me want to look deeper into this question from a Protestant, and especially a Reformed, standpoint. This essay will focus on two prominent twentieth-century theologians who have used similar language: Paul Tillich and Donald Baillie.

Paul Tillich, in volume 1 of his *Systematic Theology*, defines revelation as "the manifestation of what concerns us ultimately, . . . the ground of our being."[22] Regarding the mediums of revelation, he states:

> There is no reality, thing, or event which cannot become a bearer of the mystery of being and enter into a revelatory correlation. Nothing is excluded from revelation in principle because nothing is included in it on the basis of special qualities. No person and no thing is worthy in itself to represent our ultimate concern. On the other hand, every person and every thing participates in being-itself, that is, in the ground and meaning of being. Without such participation it would not have the power of being. This is the reason why almost every type of reality has become a medium of revelation somewhere.[23]

Tillich is emphatic that in these situations "it is not the thing or the event as such which has revelatory character; *they reveal that which uses them as a medium and bearer of revelation*."[24] In other words, they reveal the ground of being, or God.

Like Tracy after him, Tillich sounds a note of caution against overemphasis on the Word as "speech" in Protestant Christianity. He notes that both in the Bible and elsewhere, religious symbolism "uses sensing, feeling, and tasting as often as hearing in describing the experience of the divine presence."[25] Speaking specifically of the Christian doctrine of the incarnation, he says that it "includes the paradox that the Word has become an object of vision and touch."[26] He even goes so far as to say that misunderstanding of this doctrine is the Achilles' heel of Protestantism:

> The Word of God often is understood—half-literally, half-symbolically— as a spoken word, and a "theology of the Word" is presented which is

22. Paul Tillich, *Systematic Theology*, 3 vols. (Chicago: University of Chicago Press, 1951–63), 1:110.
23. Ibid., 118.
24. Ibid., 119, emphasis added.
25. Ibid., 123.
26. Ibid.

a theology of the spoken word. This intellectualization of revelation runs counter to the sense of the Logos Christology. The Logos Christology was not overintellectualistic; actually it was a weapon against this danger. If Jesus as the Christ is called the Logos, Logos points to a revelatory reality, not to revelatory words. Taken seriously, the doctrine of the Logos prevents the elaboration of a theology of the spoken or the written word, which is *the* Protestant pitfall.[27]

Tillich goes on to discuss six different meanings of the term "Word of God." One of them directly parallels the sacramental language of Schillebeeckx, Tracy, and Greeley. "The Word," he says, "is *the manifestation of the divine life in the final revelation. The Word is a name for Jesus as the Christ.*" Tillich insists that the Word "is not the sum of the words spoken by Jesus. It is the being of the Christ, of which his words and deeds are an expression."[28] From Schillebeeckx's perspective, Tillich's formulation would be roughly tantamount to saying that Jesus is the sacrament of encounter with God.

The notion of sacramentality has also appeared in the Reformed tradition. Theologian Donald Baillie, in his posthumously published *Theology of the Sacraments*, describes sacramentality as a basic need of both human and Christian life. Baillie asks: "What is there in human nature and human needs and our human situation, what is there in the Christian faith, the Christian Gospel, the Christian salvation, what is there in the nature of the divine grace and its ways of working, to demand this strange, visible, tangible expression, in material things and in perceptible actions, which we call sacramental?"[29]

Baillie finds grounding for this sacramental view of reality not only in the writings of twentieth-century theologians like Paul Tillich, but also in John Calvin's *Institutes of the Christian Religion.* He points to book 4, chapter 14, where Calvin writes a brief section on the sacraments in general. Calvin begins by explaining: "The term 'sacrament,' as we have previously discussed its nature so far, embraces generally all those signs which God has ever enjoined upon men to render them more certain and

27. Ibid., 157.
28. Ibid., 158, emphasis added. Tillich goes on to say: "Here the impossibility of identifying the Word with speech is so obvious that it is hard to understand how theologians who accept the doctrine of the Incarnation can maintain this confusion."
29. Donald Baillie, *The Theology of the Sacraments* (New York: Charles Scribner's Sons, 1957), 42.

confident of the truth of his promises. He sometimes willed to present these in natural things, at other times set them forth in miracles."[30]

As an example of the first category, Calvin discusses the tree of life in Genesis 2 and 3, and the rainbow after the flood in Genesis 9. These, Calvin claims, "Adam and Noah regarded as sacraments." Calvin is very clear that they were sacraments not in and of themselves, but because of the action of God's word upon them. His argument is worth quoting at length: "Not that the tree provided them with an immortality which it could not give to itself; nor that the rainbow (which is but a reflection of the sun's rays upon the clouds opposite) could be effective in holding back the waters; *but because they had a mark engraved upon them by God's Word, so that they were proofs and seals of his covenants.* And indeed the tree was previously a tree, the rainbow a rainbow. When they were inscribed by God's Word a new form was put upon them, so that they began to be what previously they were not."[31] Baillie is particularly taken by the following statement: "If [God] had imprinted such reminders upon the sun, stars, earth, stones, they would all be sacraments for us. . . . Cannot God *mark with his Word* the things he has created, that what were previously bare elements may become sacraments?"[32]

Note Calvin's insistence here on the Word component. In connecting these natural sacraments with the Word, Calvin anticipates the arguments of Tracy and Tillich, who caution against driving a wedge between word and sacrament. Following Calvin's lead, and paralleling the argument of Tillich, Baillie is emphatic that natural things are not in themselves sacraments: they become so when God uses them "as sacramental expressions of His mercy and faithfulness."[33]

Calvin also speaks of a second general category of sacraments, that of miracle. As examples, he cites the smoking fire pot that God showed Abraham in Genesis 15, and God's setting back the shadow of the sundial by ten degrees to promise safety to Hezekiah in 2 Kings 20. Calvin comments, "Since these things were done to support and confirm their feeble faith, they were also sacraments."[34] Thus Calvin, like Tillich and

---

30. *Inst.* 1960, 4.14.18 (*CO* 2:955).
31. Ibid., emphasis added.
32. Ibid., emphasis added.
33. Baillie, *Theology of the Sacraments*, 46.
34. Ibid.

Tracy in more-recent times, sees that both objects and events can be sacramental, as visible revelations of the divine presence.

The *Institutes* 4.14.18 is the only place I know where Calvin speaks explicitly of a wider notion of sacrament. Immediately after this section in the *Institutes*, he actually reminds readers that his present intention is "specifically to discuss those sacraments which the Lord willed to be ordinary in the church in order to nourish his worshipers and servants in one faith and the confession of one faith."[35] It is not entirely clear to this reader why he does not place this more general discussion of sacramentality earlier in the chapter. Perhaps it is because he does not want this understanding of sacrament to take primacy over the "ordinary" ritual sacraments.

When Calvin explicitly mentions a teaching only once or twice, the scholar would do well to be cautious about claiming too much importance for it in his overall thought. Having faced such a caveat before, in studying *unio mystica* (which is only mentioned a few times in Calvin's writings), I am inclined to make modest claims about Calvin and sacramentality. Nevertheless, a survey of other sections of the *Institutes*, as well as other relevant texts, reveals that what he says in book 4 is not just an isolated observation. The remainder of this essay will try to do two things: (1) discuss the notion of sacramentality as it appears in Calvin's teaching on creation, humanity, and the person of Jesus Christ; and (2) draw some tentative conclusions about Calvin's understanding of sacramentality in relation to the contemporary Roman Catholic understanding.

Sacramentality in Calvin's Thought

Creation

Let us begin with book 1 of the *Institutes*, "The Knowledge of God the Creator." By "knowledge of God," Calvin does not mean speculation

---

35. *Inst.* 1960, 4.14.19 (*CO* 2:956). Note that under the rubric of "ordinary sacraments," Calvin goes on to speak of certain Jewish ceremonies by which God revealed himself to humans. These include circumcisions, purifications, sacrifices, and other rites. These sacraments were abrogated at Christ's coming. See *Inst.* 1960, 4.14.19–21 (*CO* 2:956–58). The primary purpose of this essay, however, is to look at sacraments in a nonritual context.

about the mystery of the Godhead itself—such speculation is "idle" and worthless—but the kind of knowledge that teaches us "fear and reverence."[36] Thus Calvin will focus on God's revealing work or acts,[37] which can be fully known only in the context of piety.

Although Calvin spends the bulk of the *Institutes* talking about God as Redeemer, he wants to speak first of "the primal and simple *knowledge to which the very order of nature would have led us* if Adam had remained upright."[38] In other words, Calvin believes that there is something intrinsic in the order of nature that leads to the knowledge of God. Because of sin, humans do not have full access to this knowledge apart from grace. The crucial point is that there *is* a revelation in creation, even if it is, to use Edward Dowey's famous phrase, a "sin-negated natural theology."[39]

Chapter 5 gets to the heart of Calvin's teaching on how God is known through his fashioning of the universe. Sections 1–10 talk about how God is manifested in the works of creation. Calvin begins with a statement that would warm any Catholic's sacramental heart:

> [God] not only sowed in men's minds that seed of religion of which we have spoken but *revealed himself and daily discloses himself in the whole workmanship of the universe*. As a consequence, men cannot open their eyes without being compelled to see him. Indeed, his essence is incomprehensible; hence, his divineness far escapes all human perception. But *upon his individual works he has engraved unmistakable marks of his glory*, so clear and so prominent that even unlettered and stupid folk cannot plead the excuse of ignorance.[40]

Calvin goes on to introduce a metaphor that is characteristic of what he will later call this "general sacramentality" of nature. He comments that Hebrews 11:3 describes the universe as the appearance of things invisible because "this skillful ordering of the universe is for us

36. *Inst.* 1960, 1.2.2 (*CO* 2:35).
37. See the footnote regarding the title of book 1 in McNeill and Battles, *Inst.* 1960, p. 35n1.
38. *Inst.* 1960, 1.2.1 (*CO* 2:34), emphasis added.
39. This topic has been much debated, and there is no need to revisit it here. See esp. Günther Gloede, *Theologia naturalis bei Calvin* (Stuttgart: W. Kohlhammer, 1935). See also Edward Dowey, *The Knowledge of God in Calvin's Theology*, 2nd ed. (New York: Columbia University Press, 1965), 72–73.
40. *Inst.* 1960, 1.5.1 (*CO* 2:41), emphasis added.

a sort of mirror in which we can contemplate God, who is otherwise invisible."[41] The image of creation as a mirror of revelation appears at least nine times in book 1,[42] and also makes an appearance in books 2 and 4.[43]

Another metaphor that Calvin sometimes uses to describe the universe is that of a spectacle or theater of God's glory. He employs this image several times in the *Institutes* and in other works.[44] At the same time, Calvin laments that "however much the glory of God shines forth, scarcely one man in a hundred is a true spectator of it."[45] The missing link is faith, as Calvin explains in his commentary on 1 Corinthians 1:21:

> For it is true, that this world is like a theater, in which the Lord presents to us a clear manifestation of his glory, and yet, notwithstanding that we have such a spectacle placed before our eyes, we are stone-blind, not because the manifestation is furnished obscurely, but because we are *alienated in mind*, (Colossians 1:21) and for this matter we lack not merely inclination but ability. For notwithstanding that God shows himself openly, it is only with the eye of faith that we can behold him, save only that we receive a slight perception of his divinity, sufficient to render us inexcusable.[46]

41. *Inst.* 1960, 1.5.1 (*CO* 2:41).

42. The references are in *Inst.* 1960, 1.5.1; 1.5.3; 1.5.11; 1.8.7; 1.14.1; 1.14.5; 1.14.21; and two in 1.15.4 (*CO* 2:42, 43, 49, 65, 117, 121, 132, 138).

43. The relevant passages are in *Inst.* 1960, 2.12.6; 2.14.5; 2.14.7; 2.16.13; 4.8.5; 4.18.20 (*CO* 2:345, 356, 359, 380, 849, 1065). The majority of these use mirror imagery to describe Jesus Christ. This will be discussed below.

44. McNeill and Battles provides a partial list for this image of spectacle/theater, including *Inst.* 1960, 1.6.2; 1.14.20; 2.6.1; 3.9.2 (*CO* 2:54, 131, 247, 524); as well as *Comm. on Genesis*, on Gen. 1:6 (*CO* 23:18); and *Comm. on Psalms*, on Ps. 138:1 (*CO* 32:372).

45. *Inst.* 1960, 1.5.8 (*CO* 2:47).

46. CTS, vol. 20, *Comm. on 1 Corinthians*, trans. John Pringle, on 1 Cor. 1:21 (*CO* 49:326). Translations are from the series *Calvin's Commentaries*, originally published (1844–) by the Calvin Translation Society and reprinted by Baker Book House (1979–). Calvin characteristically employs several different Latin words for our English "manifestation." He sometimes uses *manifestatio*, but more often uses other words. Thus the Latin for this quotation reads: "Verum est enim, hunc mundum theatri instar esse, in quo nobis Dominus conspicuam gloriae suae figuram *exhibet*: nos tamen, quum tale spectaculum nobis ante oculos pateat, caecutimus, non quia obscura sit *revelatio*, sed quia nos mente alienati sumus: nec voluntas tantum, sed facultas etiam ad eam rem nos deficit. Nam utcunque Deus palam appareat, non alio tamen quam fidei oculo ipsum possumus adspicere: nisi quod tenuem divinitatis gustum concipimus, qui nos inexcusabiles reddat" (emphasis added).

Here Calvin sees this manifestation of God as completely clear in itself. The problem is that without grace, *we* cannot see it clearly.

All the themes we have discussed so far come together brilliantly in Calvin's commentary on Hebrews 11:3, a passage to which he often refers. Here Calvin, using the metaphors of both mirror and theater, speaks explicitly of how the invisible God is made visible in his works. Those who have been graced with the gift of faith see God's presence in every created thing:

> God has given us, throughout the whole framework of this world, clear evidences of his eternal wisdom, goodness, and power; and though he is in himself invisible, he in a manner *becomes visible to us in his works.*
>
> Correctly then is this world called the mirror of divinity; not that there is sufficient clearness for man to gain a full knowledge of God, by looking at the world, but that he has thus so far revealed himself, that the ignorance of the ungodly is without excuse. Now the faithful, to whom he has given eyes, see sparks of his glory, as it were, glittering in every created thing. The world was no doubt made, that it might be the theater of the divine glory.[47]

One final topic in book 1 of the *Institutes* that relates to sacramentality is providence, which Calvin sees in relation to creation. Calvin remarks that "to make God a momentary Creator, who once for all finished his work, would be cold and barren, and we must differ from profane men especially in that *we see the presence of divine power shining as much in the continuing state of the universe as in its inception.*"[48] Thus, the fact that the universe continues to exist from moment to moment is itself a visible sign of the power of God in creation. That power is also visible in the way God "sustains, nourishes, and cares for everything he has made."[49]

Let us look briefly at three other works where Calvin discusses his understanding of creation. In the "Argument" that introduces his *Commentary on Genesis*, Calvin reminds us that "Moses's intention in beginning his Book [Genesis] with the creation of the world is *to*

---

47. CTS, vol. 22, *Comm. on Hebrews*, trans. John Owen, on Heb. 11:3 (*CO* 55:145–46), emphasis added.

48. *Inst.* 1960, 1.16.1 (*CO* 2:144), emphasis added.

49. Ibid.

render God, as it were, visible to us in his works."[50] He goes on to state that to understand creation properly, we need to avoid two extremes: investigating and enjoying nature without reference to God, or engaging in idle speculation about the essence of the Creator rather than seeing God in his works.[51] Calvin is consistent here with what he says in the *Institutes*, that what we need to know about God is revealed in what God has done for us.

Here Calvin again uses the metaphors of both mirror and theater. In an interesting variation of phrasing, Calvin describes the world as "a mirror in which *we ought to* behold God." He wants to be clear that he is not asserting "either that our eyes are sufficiently clear-sighted to discern what the fabric of heaven and earth represents, or that the knowledge to be hence attained is sufficient for salvation."[52] Calvin does not say that faith *creates* the mirror, only that apart from the grace of faith we cannot see its contents clearly.

In his commentary on Psalm 19, Calvin gives a compelling argument for both the distinctness and inseparability of manifestation and proclamation. Commenting on verse 1, "The heavens declare the glory of God," Calvin claims that "Scripture, indeed, makes known to us the time and manner of the creation; but the heavens themselves, *although God should say nothing on the subject*, proclaim loudly and distinctly enough that they have been fashioned by his hands: and this of itself abundantly suffices to bear testimony to men of his glory."[53] In his comment on verse 2, he repeats this observation: "David, therefore, with the highest reason, declares, that *although God should not speak a single word to men*, yet the orderly and useful succession of days and nights eloquently proclaims the glory of God, and that there is now left

---

50. CTS, vol. 1, *Comm. on Genesis*, trans. John King, Argument, 58 (*CO* 23:6). Calvin goes on to refer to Heb. 11:3 and "the manifestation of things not apparent": "This is the reason why the Lord, that he may invite us to the knowledge of himself, places the fabric of heaven and earth before our eyes, rendering himself, in a certain manner, *manifest* in them [Haec ratio est cur Dominus, ut nos ad sui notitiam invitet, proponat nobis ante oculos coeli terraeque fabricam, et in ea se quodammodo *conspicuum* reddat]," Argument 59 (*CO* 23:7–8), emphasis added. Here we see Calvin using another word, *conspicuum*, for manifestation.

51. CTS 1:60 (*CO* 23:7–8).

52. CTS 1:62 (*CO* 23:9–10). The theater metaphor also appears here (*CO* 23:9–10, 11–12) and later in the *Comm. on Genesis*, on Gen. 1:6 (*CO* 23:18).

53. CTS, vol. 4, *Comm. on Psalms*, trans. James Anderson, on Ps. 19:1 (*CO* 31:195), emphasis added.

to men no pretext for ignorance."[54] Thus Calvin does not see the revelation in nature as itself dependent on the revelation in Scripture.

However, he also hones in on the phrasing of verse 1, "The heavens *declare* the glory of God." Calvin finds this phrasing more moving and effective than if the psalmist had said that the heavens "show" or "manifest" God's glory: "It is indeed a great thing, that in the splendor of the heavens there is presented to our view a lively image of God; but, as the living voice has a greater effect in exciting our attention, or at least teaches us more surely and with greater profit than simple beholding, to which no oral instruction is added, we ought to mark the force of the figure which the psalmist uses when he says that the heavens by their preaching declare the glory of God."[55] Calvin does not see any contradiction here. In fact, he sees the manifestation of God's glory in the heavens as a kind of language in itself. He explains: "The language of which mention has been made before [in the commentary on verse 1] is, as I may term it, *a visible language, in other words, language that addresses itself to the sight*; for it is to the eyes of men that the heavens speak, not to their ears; and thus David justly compares the beautiful order and arrangement, by which the heavenly bodies are distinguished, to a writing."[56] Calvin seems to reflect an awareness here of the intrinsic connection between manifestation and proclamation, a connection that has been stressed by our modern commentators, both Catholic and Protestant.

Finally, in his *Commentary on Romans*, on 1:20, Calvin gives an especially clear statement about the revelation of God in creation:

> God is in himself invisible; but as *his majesty shines forth in his works and in his creatures everywhere*, men ought in these to acknowledge him, for they clearly set forth their Maker: and for this reason the Apostle in his Epistle to the Hebrews says, that this world is a mirror, or the representation of invisible things. . . . Yet let this difference be remembered, that the manifestation [*demonstrationem*] of God, by which he makes his glory known in his creation, is, with regard to the light itself, sufficiently clear; but that on account of our blindness, it is not found

54. CTS, vol. 4, on Ps. 19:2 (*CO* 31:196), emphasis added.
55. CTS, vol. 4, on Ps. 19:1 (*CO* 31:195).
56. CTS, vol. 4, on Ps. 19:4 (*CO* 31:197), emphasis added. The mirror metaphor also appears in his comment on this verse.

to be sufficient. We are not however so blind, that we can plead our ignorance as an excuse for our perverseness. We conceive that there is a Deity; and then we conclude, that whoever he may be, he ought to be worshipped: but our reason here fails, because it cannot ascertain who or what sort of being God is.[57]

To this reader, all these statements about creation have a Catholic ring to them. A crucial question is whether Calvin is going to tie this sacramental language in any way to the incarnation.[58]

Humanity

Before Calvin articulates the manifestation of God in the created universe in book 1 of the *Institutes*, he speaks of a "natural endowment" by which the knowledge of God is implanted in the minds of humans. The *sensus divinitatis* and the *conscientia* are endowments that remain even after sin. They reveal to us two things: that God exists and that God's will is to be obeyed. However, apart from grace we do not have the power to accomplish God's will. Thus our very spiritual constitution as humans is revelatory of God, even if in an extremely restricted sense in the postlapsarian state.[59] Although these endowments are, in and of themselves, invisible, they are part of God's revelation to human nature as such. Whether we want to call them an expression of sacramentality probably depends on what side of the fence we find ourselves.[60]

57. CTS, vol. 19, *Comm. on Romans*, trans. John Owen, on Rom. 1:20 (*CO* 49:23–24), emphasis added. Note again Calvin's reference to the notion of manifestation, here using the Latin *demonstratio*.

58. One other image that Calvin uses, which does not appear elsewhere to my knowledge, is that "in God's individual works—but especially in them as a whole— . . . God's powers are actually represented as in a painting" (*Inst.* 1960, 1.5.10 [*CO* 2:48]).

59. For more on these endowments, see Dennis E. Tamburello, *Union with Christ: John Calvin and the Mysticism of St. Bernard* (Louisville: Westminster John Knox, 1994), 35–39.

60. Schillebeeckx (*Christ the Sacrament*, 9) speaks in similar terms of a kind of *sensus divinitatis* that is constitutive of all human beings: "All humanity receives that inward word of God calling men to a communion in grace with himself. This obscure call causes those among the heathen who listen to it in uprightness of heart dimly to suspect that there is a redeeming God who is occupying himself personally with their salvation." However, this vague sense of God's word is accompanied by distortion: "Precisely because [humanity's] religious motives] did not have the support of a special, a visible divine revelation, they became a mixture of true devotedness to God, of elements of an all-too-fallible humanity,

According to Calvin, the greatest proof of the divine wisdom that can be found in creation is humanity itself. He begins by acknowledging that "certain philosophers [he is thinking mainly of Aristotle] . . . long ago not ineptly called man a microcosm because he is a rare example of God's power, goodness, and wisdom."[61] Calvin quotes Psalm 8, explaining that David "not only declares that a clear *mirror* of God's works is in humankind, but that infants, while they nurse at their mothers' breasts, have tongues so eloquent to preach his glory that there is no need at all of other orators."[62]

Because of this, Calvin is astounded that anyone, "finding God in his body and soul a hundred times," can on this very basis deny the existence of God. The language Calvin uses in criticizing the philosophers is significant. He speaks of humans having "within themselves a workshop graced with God's innumerable works," yet they swell up in pride at their own excellence rather than attributing it to God. Speaking of how God variously works in humans, and the diverse gifts that they possess through God's generosity, Calvin asserts: "They are compelled to know—whether they will or not—that these are the *signs of divinity*; yet they conceal them within."[63]

At the end of his diatribe against the philosophers, Calvin reasserts his teaching on the manifestation of the divine in human nature: "Let us therefore remember, whenever each of us contemplates his own nature, that there is one God who so governs all natures that he would have us look unto him, direct our faith to him, and worship and call upon him. For nothing is more preposterous than to enjoy the very remarkable gifts that *attest the divine nature within us*, yet to overlook the Author who gives them to us at our asking. With what clear *manifestations* [*speciminibus*] his might draws us to contemplate him!"[64]

---

of dogmatic distortion, moral confusion and finally even of diabolical influence; yet in all of this there was a spark of real holiness which now and again managed to shine forth." Calvin would no doubt omit "true devotedness to God" in that mixture, since he believes that sin utterly destroys this capability. Here Schillebeeckx reflects a Catholic sense of anthropology, which takes a more optimistic view of the state of humanity after the fall. In my opinion, it is in the area of theological anthropology that the deepest differences between Catholic and Reformed theology lie.

61. *Inst.* 1960, 1.5.3 (*CO* 2:43).

62. Ibid., emphasis added.

63. *Inst.* 1960, 1.5.4 (*CO* 2:43–44), emphasis added.

64. *Inst.* 1960, 1.5.6 (*CO* 2:45), emphasis added. Here Calvin uses yet another word, a form of *specimen*, to talk about the divine manifestation.

Later in book 1, Calvin goes into more detail when he describes human beings as consisting of body and soul. Calvin believes that the soul is the principal part of humanity, and the proper seat of the divine image. He notes that "the many pre-eminent gifts with which the human mind is endowed proclaim that *something divine has been engraved upon it*."[65] Nevertheless, "although the primary seat of the divine image was in the mind and heart, or in the soul and its powers, yet there *was no part of man, not even the body itself, in which some sparks did not glow*."[66]

Here Calvin is talking about humanity in its pure, created state. *As created*, humans are a mirror or a sign of divinity. On the other hand, Calvin goes so far as to say that the fullest definition of humanity as *imago Dei* can be seen only in relation to redeeming grace: "We do not have a full definition of 'image' if we do not see more plainly those faculties in which man excels, and in which he ought to be thought the reflection of God's glory. That, indeed, can be nowhere better recognized than from the restoration of his corrupted nature."[67] Anticipating what he will later say about the incarnation, Calvin adds: "Now we see how Christ is the most perfect image of God; if we are conformed to it, we are so restored that with true piety, righteousness, purity, and intelligence we bear God's image."[68]

Before he proceeds to discuss how this manifestation of the divine presence in the world and in humanity is confused and distorted through disobedience, Calvin gives a masterful summary of his argument:

> We see that no long or toilsome proof is needed to elicit evidences that serve to illuminate and affirm the divine majesty; since from the few we have sampled at random, whithersoever you turn, it is clear that *they are so very manifest [prompta] and obvious that they can easily be observed with the eyes and pointed out with the finger*.... For the Lord manifests [*manifestatur*] himself by his powers, the force of which we feel within ourselves and the benefits of which we enjoy.... Consequently, we know the most perfect way of seeking God, and the most suitable order, is not for us to attempt with bold curiosity to penetrate to the investigation of his essence, which we ought more to adore than meticulously to search out, but for us to contemplate him in his works

65. *Inst.* 1960, 1.15.2–3 (*CO* 2:135–36), emphasis added.
66. *Inst.* 1960, 1.15.3 (*CO* 2:138), emphasis added.
67. *Inst.* 1960, 1.15.4 (*CO* 2:138).
68. *Inst.* 1960, 1.15.4 (*CO* 2:138–39).

whereby he renders himself near and familiar to us, and *in some manner communicates himself.*[69]

Calvin thus returns to the point he made at the beginning of book 1: we should not seek knowledge of the divine essence, but rather of what God has done for us, first in creating us, and more importantly in redeeming us. What is important for our purposes is Calvin's clear affirmation that God is in some sense made visible in the works of creation.

All this comes tumbling down when humanity chooses disobedience, as Calvin explains at length in book 2. However, in addition to the *sensus divinitatis* and the *conscientia*, which he described earlier, Calvin speaks here about several other natural gifts that are not lost by sin. Calvin makes a careful distinction between "earthly things" and "heavenly things." Earthly things are those that "do not pertain to God or his Kingdom, to true justice, or to the blessedness of the future life; but . . . have their significance and relationship with regard to the present life." Here Calvin includes "government, household management, all mechanical skills, and the liberal arts." Heavenly things include "the pure knowledge of God, the nature of true righteousness, and the mysteries of the Heavenly Kingdom."[70]

Calvin states that human competence in art and science "clearly testifies to a universal apprehension of reason and understanding by nature" implanted in humans. "Yet so universal is this good," he continues, that everyone ought to recognize in it *"the peculiar grace of God."*[71] Thus, the grace of God is visible in these natural human endowments. It is supremely important to note that these things have nothing to do with salvation (as opposed to the heavenly things), but even apart from grace, fallen humans are to some extent mirrors of the divine glory. Calvin goes on to say that the human mind, "though fallen and perverted from its wholeness, is nevertheless clothed and ornamented with God's excellent gifts."[72] Thus there are traces of the image of God remaining even in fallen humanity.

---

69. *Inst.* 1960, 1.5.9 (*CO* 2:47), emphasis added. In this passage, Calvin uses a form of the word *manifestatio* as well as the adjective *prompta*.

70. *Inst.* 1960, 2.2.13 (*CO* 2:197).

71. *Inst.* 1960, 2.2.14 (*CO* 2:198), emphasis added.

72. *Inst.* 1960, 2.2.15 (*CO* 2:198).

Jesus Christ and the Incarnation

What Calvin says about both the divinity and the humanity of Jesus also parallels the language we find in contemporary discussions of sacramentality. In book 1 of the *Institutes*, Calvin focuses on the doctrine of the Trinity and therefore emphasizes the divinity of Christ. In an argument on Hebrews 1:3 in which his main concern is to distinguish essence from person in the theology of the Trinity, he remarks: "Because the Father, although distinct in his proper nature, expresses himself wholly in the Son, for a very good reason is it said that *he has made his hypostasis visible in the latter.* In close agreement with this are the words immediately following, that the Son is '*the splendor of his glory*.'"[73] Although Calvin never uses the word *sacrament* to describe Jesus, this sounds very similar to Schillebeeckx's claim that Jesus is the primordial sacrament, in whom "grace became fully visible."[74]

It is in book 2 that Calvin speaks more specifically of the incarnation of Jesus. Here he makes an argument that is most intriguing in relation to sacramentality. In discussing Jesus's true humanity, he claims that in the period before the resurrection, Christ's divinity was temporarily hidden from view: "Although Christ could justly have shown forth his divinity, he manifested himself as but a lowly and despised man. For, to exhort us to submission by his example, he showed that although he was God and could have set forth his glory directly to the world he gave up his right and voluntarily 'emptied himself.' He took the image of a servant, and content with such lowness, allowed his divinity to be hidden by a 'veil of flesh.'" Thus "for a time the divine glory did not shine, but only human likeness was manifest in a lowly and abased condition."[75] So Calvin in effect sees the "hiding" of Christ's divinity as teaching us by example what it means to be a servant of others. We might also see it as another example of the marvelous accommodation of God to our weak understanding.

What is perhaps most striking in relation to our subject is that Calvin several times uses the image of a mirror—the same image we saw him use to describe creation in book 1—to describe Jesus's manifestation of divinity. Calvin speaks of the man Christ as the "mirror of God's

---

73. *Inst.* 1960, 1.13.2 (*CO* 2:90), emphasis added.
74. Schillebeeckx, *Christ the Sacrament*, 13.
75. *Inst.* 1960, 2.13.2 (*CO* 2:348–49).

inestimable grace."[76] Referring back to his earlier teaching on humanity being made in the image of God, Calvin proclaims that "whatever excellence was engraved upon Adam, derived from the fact that he approached the glory of his Creator through the only-begotten Son." In creating humanity in God's image, the Creator "willed that his own glory be seen as in a mirror. Adam was advanced to this degree of honor, thanks to the only-begotten Son."[77] Thus the only reason why Adam can mirror God's glory is because of Christ.

Conclusion

What are we to make of all of these texts? Is there a sense in which we can say that Calvin would find congenial the contemporary Catholic and Protestant discussion of sacramentality? It does seem that, in principle, Calvin is in agreement with our modern commentators that any created thing is capable of giving visible expression to the presence and power of God, provided that it is "marked" as such by God's Word. The metaphors that Calvin favors, which I would say are the closest parallels in his thought to the notion of sacramentality, are that of mirror, spectacle, and theater.

That being said, Calvin is also tireless in insisting that the sin of Adam and Eve has put us in a position where we cannot see clearly enough to give proper credit and glory to God. It bears repeating that Calvin does not think that the revelation in creation is somehow deficient or unclear. As Edward Dowey puts it, although "sin has blinded [us] to the revelation in creation, . . . the revelation itself is not harmed. [Our] *receiving apparatus* functions wrongly."[78]

Calvin also makes statements about Jesus that sound similar to Schillebeeckx's language of Jesus as the primordial sacrament. He speaks of Jesus as making God's glory visible, and he returns to his metaphor of the mirror to spell out the significance of the incarnation. Nevertheless, Calvin's notion of sacramentality seems to be tied more

---

76. *Inst.* 1960, 2.14.5 (*CO* 2:356–57). See also 2.14.7 (*CO* 2:359), where Calvin states: "For in the flesh that he received from us [Christ] is the only-begotten Son of God. Augustine sagely warns us that he is the bright mirror of God's wonderful and singular grace."

77. *Inst.* 1960, 2.12.6 (*CO* 2:345).

78. Dowey, *Knowledge of God*, 72–73, emphasis added.

to the theology of creation than to the theology of the incarnation. Schillebeeckx mentions the sacramentality of creation as such, but he wants to focus primarily on the Christ-church-ritual sacraments connection. Where this would break down for Calvin, I suggest, is in his discussion of the church. I think that Calvin would be loath to call the church "the sacrament of Christ," though he might be willing to tolerate such language when talking about the "invisible church" of the elect.[79] This is a topic for another day, or perhaps another five years of Reformed–Roman Catholic dialogue.

Calvin's creation-centered notion of sacramentality has much in common with the kind of language used by other Catholic authors like Tracy, Greeley, and Irwin. When describing the revelation in creation, Calvin strikingly uses several different words that translate as "manifestation," the word that Tracy favors so strongly in his thought.[80] Calvin would certainly be opposed to an uncritical assessment of this revelation in creation. As George Vandervelde put it at one of our Reformed–Roman Catholic Dialogue sessions, we must remember that "creation has turned against God, and grace makes things right."[81]

Kevin Irwin would agree. In his article "A Sacramental World," he states: "The world and all who dwell in it are termed 'sacramental,' meaning that the whole cosmos and all that dwell in it are regarded as not only reflecting God's glory but also in need of complete redemption." Irwin insists that "the rhetoric of sacramentality is always 'both . . . and' rather than 'either . . . or.' . . . In an 'either . . . or' framework sacraments offer escapes from the world and send us back to it charged to work more adequately in it for the cause of God's kingdom. In a sacramental world, it is the world itself that is, in the words of Gerard Manley Hopkins, 'charged with the grandeur of God,'"[82] but also, we might add, charged with rebellion against God.

It is probably fair to say that from a theological perspective, Catholics need to be cautioned against being overly optimistic about sacramentality, while the Reformed need to be cautioned about being too

79. See *Inst.* 1960, 4.1.7 (*CO* 2:752–53).

80. In addition to *manifestatio*, we have seen Calvin use *exhibeo, revelatio, demonstratio, specimen*, and the adjectives *promptus* and *conspicuum*.

81. Remark by George Vandervelde, Reformed–Roman Catholic Dialogue session, April 27, 2006.

82. Irwin, "Sacramental World," 204.

pessimistic about it. Perhaps Calvin's diatribes against fanatics and the ungodly in book 1 of the *Institutes* can help us Catholics to take more seriously the confusion and distortion that has led to our failure to recognize the glory of God in creation. Conversely, Catholics can sound a note of caution to our Reformed brothers and sisters not to forget that Calvin really believed that the world is charged with the grandeur of God, even if we cannot recognize this apart from grace.

In conclusion, we do well to remember this essay's earlier cautions about not co-opting Calvin for our own theological agendas, and not attaching too much importance to a teaching that Calvin mentions only occasionally. However, in answer to the question, "Does Calvin have a Catholic sensibility about the sacraments, despite his differences with the Roman Church in the sixteenth century?" this essay dares to answer yes, with the appropriate qualifications. I am not sure that my late colleague George Vandervelde would agree, but when it comes to his basic understanding of the notion of sacrament, I believe that Calvin remained firmly connected to his Catholic pedigree.

Name Index

Abels, P. H. A. M., 137n48
Ackermans, Gian, 123n8, 126n17
Acosta, José de, 160, 161
Alciati, Andrea, 60
Ambrose, 9
Anderson, James, 69n12, 206n53
Anselm, 7
Antoine, 93n26
Apollinaris, Sidonius, 35
Aristotle, 209
Augustine, 9, 153n36, 158, 159,
 159n55, 159n56, 181, 182,
 196, 213n76
Authin, Pierre, 79, 80, 80n1, 91

Backus, Irena, 10
Baillie, Donald, 16, 199, 200,
 200n29, 201, 201n33
Balesdens, Jean, 36
Balzac, Charles de, 46–47
Baronius, Cesar, 137
Barral, Jehan, 96n33
Battles, Ford Lewis, 203n37,
 204n44
Bauduin, François, 11, 33, 34,
 35, 36, 38, 39, 40, 41, 43, 44,
 46, 53, 55
Bayle, Pierre, 37, 37n32
Beaume, Esprit de, 103
Béda, Noël, 73
Beeck Calkoen, Jan Frederick
 van, 122n7
Beghyn, Paul, 128n20
Bellay, René du, 61
Bennett, Clinton, 162n67
Berengarius, 44

Berge, Christiaan van den, 131n31
Berger, Heinrich, 154n41, 154n44
Bergsma, Wiebe, 143n63
Berkvens-Stevelinck, C., 121n4
Bernard of Clairvaux, 195
Besson, Pierre, 108
Bethelier, Philibert, 56
Bettenson, Henry, 153n36,
 159n55, 159n56
Beza, Theodore, 11, 13, 26, 28,
 30, 32, 40, 45, 45n49, 54,
 58, 103, 105, 111, 111n31,
 112n39, 114, 115, 115n57
Blok, P. J., 138n51
Bockwoldt, G., 149n10
Bolland, Johannes, 130n27
Bolsec, Jerome, 11, 25, 26, 26n3,
 27, 27n5, 28, 28n6, 28n7,
 28n8, 28n10, 28n11, 29,
 29n12, 29n13, 30, 30n14, 31,
 32, 38, 41, 45, 48, 52, 54, 55,
 56, 57, 58
Bömer, J. A., 136n43
Boniface, 135
Borromeo, Carlo, 100
Bosio, Gulielmo, 53n65
Bourbon, Antoine de, 45n49, 74
Bourbon, Henry de, 77
Bourriquant, Fleury, 51
Bouwsma, William J., 58, 58n74,
 100, 100n1, 163n68
Bowie, Fiona, 162n67
Bowler, Joseph, 104n9
Briçonnet, Guillaume, 61, 74
Brink, J. N. Bakhuizen van den,
 138n51

Brossard, Joseph, 117n65
Brown, Peter, 155n46
Bruin, Cebus Cornelius de, 138n51
Brune, Estienne, 95, 96, 96n30
Bucer, Martin, 9, 42, 63, 64, 67,
 70, 76, 168
Bullinger, Heinrich, 9, 17,
 148, 148n5, 153, 154, 155,
 155n46, 156, 159
Buonarrotti, Michelangelo, 75
Bure, Idelette de, 42
Busch, Eberhard, 59n1, 60n2

Caluin, Jean, 56n69
Calvin, Charles, 41, 48, 49
Calvin, Gérard, 49, 53n65, 55
Calvin, Girard, 49n56, 50n60
Calvin, John, 7, 9, 10, 11, 12, 14,
 15, 16, 17, 25, 26, 27, 28, 29,
 30, 31, 32, 33, 34, 38, 39,
 39n36, 40, 41, 42, 43, 44, 45,
 46, 47, 47n53, 48, 48n55,
 50, 50n60, 51, 53, 54, 55, 56,
 57, 59, 60, 60n3, 61, 62, 63,
 63n8, 64, 65, 65n9, 66, 67,
 68, 68n11, 69, 70, 71, 75, 76,
 77, 78, 80, 80n1, 81, 84, 86,
 87, 89, 92, 93, 93n26, 95, 97,
 98, 99, 111n31, 144, 145n1,
 146, 146n2, 147, 147n3,
 148, 149, 149n10, 149n13,
 149n14, 150, 150n18, 151,
 152, 152n28, 152n31, 153,
 153n36, 153n38, 154,
 154n40, 154n41, 154n44,
 155, 156, 157, 158, 159,

217

160, 161, 162, 163, 165, 166,
167, 168, 169, 170, 171, 172,
173, 174, 175, 176, 177, 178,
179, 180, 181, 182, 183, 184,
185, 186, 187, 188, 189, 190,
191, 194, 195, 196, 196n10,
200, 201, 202, 202n35, 203,
204, 205, 206, 206n50, 207,
208, 208n57, 208n58, 209,
209n64, 210, 211, 211n69,
212, 213, 213n76, 214,
214n80, 215
Calvin, Richard, 53n65
Campion, Edmund, 55, 56
Capito, Wolfgang, 63, 64, 67
Carlstadt, 27
Carnesecchi, Pietro, 76
Cassander, George, 33, 71
Castillo, Bernal Díaz del, 157,
158n54
Cauvin, Antoine, 39
Cauvin, Charles, 48n55
Cauvin, Gérard, 48, 48n56, 55
Cauvin, Jean, 31, 49
Cervantes, Fernando, 160n61
Chaix, Paul, 80n1
Charles V (emperor), 34, 74, 75
Charles IX (king), 44
Charles of Genève, 112n36
Charles-Emmanuel (duke),
102n6, 104, 108, 118
Chermoluë, Antoine de, 47
Chérubin, Père, 110, 111, 112,
113, 114, 115, 115n55, 116,
117
Cherverny, Philippe Hurault
de, 34
Cibo, Caterina, 77
Cicero, 27, 35, 35n25, 43,
149n14, 156
Clark, Stuart, 162n65
Clement VII (pope), 75, 76, 77
Clement VIII (pope), 103, 103n7,
123, 124
Colladon, 11, 40
Colonna, Vittoria, 12, 60, 74, 76
Comerford, Kathleen M., 129n23
Constantin, Boniface, 100,
100n2
Constantine, 34
Contarini, Gasparo, 12, 72, 75
Cop, Nicolas, 62
Corajod, Jean, 111, 117
Coste, Hilarion de, 61, 61n6
Coster, Francis, 132, 132n34,
137, 137n45

Cottret, Bernard, 58, 58n74,
59n1
Courtin, Michel, 48
Cyprian, 9, 182

d'Albret, Jeanne, 74
d'Angestée, Charles, 48n55
d'Angoulême, Marguerite, 12,
61, 72, 73, 74
d'Espeville, Charles, 63, 63n8
D'Espinac, 29
d'Este, Alfonso II, 77n24
d'Estrée, Antoine, 48n55
d'Etaples, Jacques Lefèbvre, 62
d'Holbach, Baron, 162
de Sales, François, 12, 13, 99,
102, 103, 103n7, 103n8, 104,
104n9, 104n10, 105, 107,
110, 112, 113, 114, 117, 118
de Sales, Louis, 102
Debosc, Guillaume, 80
Decloeck, P., 127n18, 127n19,
129n23
Delumeau, Jean, 147, 147n4,
152n28
Demos, John, 162n65
Deprez, Claude, 117, 117n64
Desmay, Jacques, 46, 46n52, 47,
47n53, 48, 48n55, 49, 49n58,
50, 51, 52, 52n64, 53, 55
Dowey, Edward, 149n13, 203,
203n39, 213, 213n78
Duchemin, Nicolas, 60, 61, 62, 77
Dufour, Alain, 37n33, 45n49,
102n6
Dufour, Théophile, 31n15, 37,
53n65
Dupréau, 26
Durkheim, Émile, 15, 162
Dury, 56
du Tillet, Jean, 12, 62n7, 64, 66,
67, 68, 70, 71, 78
du Tillet, Louis, 11, 60, 62, 62n7,
63, 63n8, 65, 69, 77
du Tillet, Séraphin, 62n7, 63

Eggius, Albert, 126, 127, 137n47,
139
Eijnatten, Joris van, 142n61
Eire, Carlos, 10, 14, 15, 146n2
Elliott, John P., 120n2
Emmanuel-Philibert, Duke,
117n65
Engelland, Hans, 149n10
Erasmus, 15, 154

Erbe, Michael, 33n18, 33n19,
35, 35n24
Esguerra, Jorge Cañizares, 161n62
Estienne, Robert, 80n1
Eubel, Conrad, 61n5

Farel, Guillaume, 42, 63, 65,
69, 70
Fauvel, Antoine, 49, 50n60
Favre, Antoine, 110n29
Favre, François, 93n26
Favre, Gaspard, 93n26
Favre, Nicoline, 93n26
Fehleison, Jill, 10, 15
Ferrante, Marquis Antonio, 74
Ferrare, Anne de, 77n24
Ferrare, Louis de, 77n24
Ferrare, Renée de, 60, 62, 77,
77n23
Flaminio, Marcantonio, 76
Fontanini, Benedetto, 75, 76
Forster, Marc R., 129n23, 142n61
Foxgrover, David, 168n10
France, Charlotte de, 73
François I (king), 61, 62, 72,
74, 165
Friedrich III, Elector, 33
Frijhoff, 136n42
Fruin, Robert, 138n51

Gams, P. B., 61n5
Ganoczy, Alexandre, 10, 168,
168n10, 191, 191n144
Gardy, Frédéric, 26n2, 32n16
Gauthier, Jean, 117n64
Geertz, Clifford, 153
Gennep, Arnold van, 162
Gerlach, P., 127n19, 128n20
Germain, 96
Gerrish, Brian, 194
Gillot, Jacques, 36, 37
Gloede, Günther, 203n39
Gonzaga, Giulia, 12, 77
Goujon, Pierre, 92, 93, 93n26,
94, 95
Goulart, Simon, 111, 117n64
Gourlay, Philippe de, 47
Gradelle, Jacob, 111
Granier, Claude de, 100, 101,
101n4, 117n66
Gratian, 182
Greeley, Andrew F., 198, 198n19,
200, 214
Gregory, Brad, 135n40
Gregory XIII (pope), 123

Grosse, Christian, 82n5
Grynaeus, Simon, 42
Guggisberg, Hans R., 81n3
Guise, François de, 77n24

Hamans, P. W. F. M., 122n7, 123n8, 124n10, 124n12, 128n20, 128n21, 136n40
Harlay, François de, 46
Havart, Jean, 49, 50n60
Hayes, Antoine des, 104n9, 104n10
Headley, John M., 100n3
Heijden, Manon van der, 142n61
Heller, Clarence Nevin, 148n5
Hengest, Charles de, 48
Henri III (king), 29
Henri IV (king), 74, 104, 116
Henry II (king), 44, 77
Herminjard, A. L., 63n8
Heron, 60n2
Hesse, Gijsbertus, 136n40
Heussen, Hugo Francis van, 132, 132n32, 133
Hoeck, F. van, 123n9, 124n13, 128n20
Hoeksema, H. C., 149n13
Holtrop, Philip, 26n3
Hopkins, Gerard Manley, 214
Hoppenbrouwers, F. J. M., 137n46
Hsia, R. Po-Chia, 123n7, 127n18, 129n23, 138n49, 138n51
Hume, David, 17, 162

Irwin, Kevin M., 197, 197n14, 214, 214n82
Israel, Jonathan, 121n4, 128n22, 143n63

Jackson, Samuel Macauley, 148n5
Jacobs, Jan, 129n24
Jehan Chappelet of Champagne, 96
Jerome, 181
Johan, 65
John Chrysostom, 9
Jones, Leonard Chester, 111, 111n35
Jung-Inglessis, Eva-Maria, 75n22

Kaplan, Benjamin J., 138n51, 139n53, 142n61
Kilmartin, Edward, 197
King, John, 206n50

Kingdon, Robert M., 39n36, 80n1, 81n3, 82n5, 93n26, 115, 116n58
Kleef, B. A. van, 136n42
Kolfhaus, Wilhelm, 149n10
Kors, Alan Charles, 162n66
Kronenburg, J. A. F., 136n42

la Faye, Antoine de, 26, 111, 115
l'Allement, Richard, 52n64
Laing, James, 31
Lambert (governor), 118n67
Lambert, Thomas A., 82n5, 93n26
Lane, A. N. S., 9
Lara, Jaime, 161n63
Laugre, Pierre de, 96
LeFranc, Abel, 74n21
Leith, John H., 153n34
Leo X (pope), 77
Leuven, Lienke Pauline, 137n46
Le Vasseur, Jacques, 46, 47, 48, 49, 51, 52, 52n62, 52n63, 53, 53n65, 54, 55
Lieburg, Fred van, 142n61
Lignaridus, Herman, 13, 111, 112, 112n36, 113, 114, 115
Lindanus, 26
Lindeboom, J., 138n51
Lommel, A. van, 120n3, 125n15, 126n16, 130n25, 138n50, 139n55, 139n56, 141n58, 143n63
Louis XII (king), 62
Louis XIII (king), 106
Luria, Keith P., 82, 83, 83n6, 83n7, 101, 101n5
Luther, Martin, 9, 27, 54, 70, 76, 166, 167, 182
Lyon, Gregory B., 34, 34n21

Malinowski, Bronislaw, 162
Manetsch, Scott M., 103n8
Marcourt, François Antoine, 62, 158n54
Marlero, Antonio, 53n65
Marlière, Antoine de la, 53n65
Marshall, Sherrin, 143n63
Martin, Paul, 102n6
Masson, Jean-Baptiste, 35, 36, 37, 38
Masson, Jean-Papire, 11, 32, 33, 34, 34n23, 35, 35n26, 36, 36n29, 37, 37n34, 38, 38n35, 39, 39n37, 40, 41, 42, 43, 44,

45, 45n50, 48, 53, 53n65, 55, 57, 58
Maudslay, A. P., 158n54
Maurice, 13, 105
Maurienne, Père Chérubin de, 13, 107
McDonald, Wallace, 93n26
McDonnell, Killian, 10
McLaren, Brian, 198, 198n21
McNeill, John Thomas, 154n41, 203n37, 204n44
Medici, Alexander de, 108
Medici, Catherine de (queen), 77
Meijer, G. A., 130n26
Melanchthon, Philipp, 9, 72, 168
Mensinck, B. A., 136n43
Mesle, Antoine de, 53n65
Mesle, M. de, 47
Mettrie, Julien Offray de la, 162
Meyjes, G. H. M. Postumus, 121n4
Miron, M. de, 106
Monteiro, Marit, 125n14
Monter, E. William, 81n3, 86n11, 88n20, 90, 90n24, 162n65
Moorsel, P. P. V. van, 136n42
Morlet, Martin, 47
Morone, Giovanni, 75
Morris, Brian, 162n67
Motley, John Lothrop, 138n51
Mouchy, Antoine de, 51
Mout, M. E. H. N., 121n4
Mouw, Richard, 198n21
Mudzaert, Dionysius, 137, 137n43, 137n44
Muller, Richard, 194, 194n2
Murdock, Greme, 120n1

Naef, Henri, 81n3
Naphy, William G., 81n3, 82n5, 84n8, 85n9, 86n11, 90n23
Navarre, Antoine de, 44
Navarre, Henri de, 74
Navarre, Marguerite de, 60
Neercassel, Johannes van, 130, 131, 131n29, 141n60
Nepveur of Lyon, Pierre, 96
Neuser, Wilhelm, H., 70n13
Newman, John Henry, 7
Nicodemus, 60
Nicolas of Cusa, 74
Nierop, Henk F. K. van, 123n7, 132n33, 138n49, 138n51

O'Donohoe, James A., 127n18, 129n23

Oberman, Heiko, 146n2
Ochino, Bernardino Tomassini,
  12, 72, 75, 76, 77
Olislagers, Louis, 130
Owen, John, 205n47, 208n57

Parker, Charles H., 13, 14, 122n6,
  139n52, 142n62
Patin, Gui, 36
Paul III (pope), 61, 74
Paul IV (pope), 72, 78
Perrot, Charles, 111, 115
Peyrolier, Perrin, 94
Philip II (king), 122
Pinault, Jean, 110n28
Pius V (pope), 76
Plato, 28
Pole, Reginald, 75
Pollmann, Judith, 121n5
Polman, Pontien, 136n42,
  154n41
Porphyry, 159
Preus, J. Samuel, 147n4, 156,
  156n48
Pringle, John, 204n46
Priuli, Alvise, 76
Provo, Wade, 168n10

Quentin, Jean, 47

Raemond, Florimond de, 26
Ragnoni, Lattanzio, 76
Randoul, M., 47
Ravier, André, 104n9
Reddy, William M., 110, 110n27,
  114, 114n50
Regnard, Jacques, 48n55
Ricard, Robert, 160n61
Riccardi, Jules-César, 110n30,
  112n38
Richard, Lucien, 10
Richards, J. M., 153n34
Richelieu (cardinal), 11, 25, 46,
  54, 54n66, 55, 56, 57, 58, 119
Ries, Johannes, 150n17
Roget, Amédée, 89n20
Rogier, J. J., 123n8, 123n9,
  124n13, 128n20, 135n39,
  135n40, 136n42, 140n57
Ronzy, Pierre, 33, 33n17, 34,
  34n22, 34n23, 35, 35n24,
  35n25, 35n26, 35n27, 36n30

Roodenburg, Herman, 137n48
Roussel, Gérard, 12, 60, 61, 62,
  78, 146, 146n2
Rovenius, Philip, 120, 124,
  124n11, 126, 127, 127n19,
  131, 131n30, 132, 132n32,
  139
Rückert, Hanns, 160n58

Sadolet, Jacob, 42
Saint-Michel, Antoine de,
  112n41, 113
Sarrazin, Jean, 116, 117, 117n62
Savoie, Jacques de, 77n24
Schillebeeckx, Edward, 18, 19,
  194, 195n4, 196, 196n11,
  197, 200, 208n60, 209n60,
  212, 212n74, 213, 214
Schmidt, Peter, 127n18
Schoon, D. J., 136n42
Schroeder, H. J., 127n19
Schützeichel, Heribert, 154n45
Selderhuis, Herman J., 70n13
Seneca, 43
Servetus, Michael, 32, 41, 43, 44
Sigismund II (king), 71, 76
Simpson, Lesley Byrd, 160n61
Sleidan, 33
Smit, Fred, 129n24
Spierling, Karen, 12, 13, 81n4,
  82n5
Spijker, Willem van't, 70n13
Staden, H. Frans van, 133n36
Stapulensis, 12
Stauffer, Richard, 58, 58n74,
  149n10
Sturm, Jean, 33
Surius, Laurentius, 26
Swieten, Aegidius van, 130

Tacitus, 43
Taillepied, Noël, 27, 27n4
Tamburello, Dennis E., 10, 18,
  19, 208n59
Tavard, George, 10, 11, 12, 15,
  194
Thomas Aquinas, 129, 196
Thou, Christophe de, 34, 35
Tillich, Paul, 17, 199, 199n22,
  200, 200n28, 201
Toledo, Francisco de, 100
Tomaro, John B., 100n3

Torrance, T. F., 70n13, 71n14
Tracy, David, 16, 197, 197n16,
  199, 200, 201, 202, 214
Trémon, 47
Turchetti, Mario, 33n18
Turner, Victor, 153

Urteaga, Horacio, 161n64

Valdès, Juan de, 12, 75, 77
Valeri, Mark, 80n1
Valois, Marguerite de, 77
Vandervelde, George, 193,
  193n1, 214, 214n81, 215
Varro, 153n36
Vermaseren, B. A., 128n20
Vermigli, Pier Martyr, 27, 33, 76
Verres, 27
Verstegan, Richard, 136n43
Vico, Giambattista, 162
Villagómez, Pedro de, 161,
  161n64
Viret, Pierre, 65
Vosmeer, Sasbout, 123, 126, 127,
  135, 139
Vregt, J. F., 131n30, 132n32
Vuy, Jules, 118n67

Walenburg, Adrian van, 132,
  133n35
Walenburg, Pieter van, 132,
  133n35
Warfuse [F. C. van Beyeren van
  Schagen], 141n60
Watt, Isabella M., 93n26
Watt, Jeffrey R., 82n5, 160n58
Webb, Charmarie Jenkins, 77n23
Weber, Max, 153
Whittaker, William, 55, 56,
  56n69
Wiele, Jan Baptist Stalpert van
  der, 136, 136n41, 136n43
Willibrord, 135, 136, 136n43,
  137
Wingens, Marc, 136n42
Wouters, A. Ph. F., 137n48

Zachman, Randall, 15, 16
Zweig, Stefan, 58, 58n74
Zwingli, Ulrich, 15, 54, 148,
  148n5, 151, 154, 155, 156,
  157, 159

Subject Index

absolution, 181–82
accommodation
    of incarnation, 212
    Lord's Supper as, 174–75,
        176, 178
acolytes, 189, 191
Acosta, José de, 160–61
adultery, 39
Alciati, Andrea, 60
Ambrose, 9
Anabaptists, 41, 74, 76
Annemasse, 108–9
anointing with oil, 183
Anselm, 7
anthropologist, Calvin as, 147–63
anti-Calvin satirical literature, 54
antitrinitarianism, 44
Antoine de Navarre, 44
apologetics, Catholic, 14, 132–33
archbishops, 190
Augustine, 9, 129, 158–61, 179,
    181–82
Authin, Pierre, 79–80, 91
authority, 68, 71, 76
Aztecs, 157

*Babylonian Captivity of the
    Church* (Luther), 70
Baillie, David, 16, 199, 200–201
Balesdens, Jean, 36
Balzac, Charles de, 47
baptism, 167
    Calvin on, 15, 169–72
    and confirmation, 179–81
    by Roman Catholics, 71–72
Baronius, Cesar, 137
Bauduin, François, 11, 32–41,
    43, 53, 55

Bayle, Pierre, 37
Beaume, Esprit de, 103
Béda, Noël, 73
Berengarius, 44
Bergerac, Treaty of, 29
Bernard of Clairvaux, 195
Berne, 94, 100, 102, 115, 116
Berthelier, Philibert, 56
Beza, Theodore, 45, 54, 103–5,
    111, 112, 114–15
    life of Calvin, 11, 26–28, 32, 58
biography, vs. posthumous
    praise, 35
bishops, 16, 61, 189, 190, 191
body and soul, 210
Bolsec, Jerome, 11, 25, 26–32,
    45, 48, 52, 54, 55, 58
Boniface, 135
Borromeo, Carlo, 100
boundaries, religious and civic,
    82–83, 88, 95, 97
Bourbon, Antoine de, 74
bourgeois, 98
Brune, Estienne, 95–96
Bucer, Martin, 9, 63, 64, 67,
    70, 168
Bullinger, Heinrich, 9, 15, 153,
    154, 155, 156, 159
burial, rite of, 187–88

Calvin, John
    absenteeism from his charge,
        49–50
    alleged sexual degeneracy, 31,
        54, 55–57, 58
    anthropology of, 155–57

call to Geneva, 65
catholicity of, 14, 148, 157, 191
expulsion from and return to
    Geneva, 42
harm to France, 10–11, 40–41,
    44–45, 58
industriousness, 43
pride, 39
rumor of deathbed conversion
    to Catholicism, 50
sacramentality of, 16, 200–215
self-love of, 39
sexual depravity of, 31–32
temperament, 57
as tyrannical, 39, 40, 58, 76
vocation to ministry, 68, 70
youth and childhood, 47–50
Calvin Studies Colloquium
    (Notre Dame), 9
Campion, Edmund, 55, 56
Capito, Wolfgang, 63, 64, 67
Capuchins, 13, 105–7, 110,
    117–18
Carnesecchi, Pietro, 76
Cassander, George, 71
catechism, 87
*Catechism of the Church of Ge-
    neva*, 171
Catholic Catechism (Rovenius),
    131–32
catholicity
    of Calvin, 146, 157, 191
    of evangelical churches, 168
Cauvin, Antoine (Calvin's
    brother), 39

221

Cauvin, Charles (Calvin's brother), 41, 48–49
Cauvin, Gérard (Calvin's father), 48–49, 55
Chambéry, 116
Chappelet, Jehan, 96–97
Charles-Emmanuel, 102n6, 104, 108, 118
Charles V (emperor), 74–75
Charles IX (king), 44
Chermoluë, Antoine de, 47
Chérubin, Père, 13, 110–15, 116–17
Chester, Leonard, 111
Chrysostom, 9
church
    discipline, 97, 190
    form of, 166
    government, 189–91
    hiddenness of, 15, 166–68
    purification of, 168
    as sacrament, 196, 214
    unity of, 191
Cibo, Caterina, 77
Cicero, 43, 156
City Council of Geneva, 11, 57, 81, 84–91, 98
Clement VII (pope), 75, 76, 77
Clement VIII (pope), 103, 123, 124
clergy, Calvin on, 189
clericalism, 126–35, 143
Colladon, Nicholas, 11, 32, 40
Collegium Alticollense, 126–28, 135
Collegium Pulcheriae Mariae Virginis, 126–28, 129
Colonna, Vittoria, 12, 60, 74–75, 76
Company of Pastors (Geneva), 110–11, 113, 114, 115, 116–17
concupiscentia, 66
confirmation, 179–80
conscience, 83n7, 208, 211
consistory, of Geneva, 79–80, 91–97
Contarini, Gasparo, 12, 72, 75
Cop, Nicolas, 62
Corajod, Jean, 111, 117
Coster, Francis, 132, 137
Council of Nicaea, 190
Council of Trent, 75, 76, 126–28, 143
Counter-Reformation, 126–28, 143
Courtin, Michel, 48

creation, 16–17, 202–8, 214–15
custom, as precept, 187
Cyprian, 9, 182

d'Angoulême, Marguerite, 12, 60, 61, 72–74
d'Avully, Seigneur, 113–15
deacons, 16, 189, 190
debauchery, 39
demonic possession, 160
Deprez, Claude, 117
de Sales, François, 12, 13, 99–100, 102, 103–5, 110, 112, 114, 118
de Sales, Louis, 102
Desmay, Jacques, 46–51, 52–53, 55
d'Espeville, Charles (pseudonym), 63
d'Espinac, Pierre, 26
d'Etaples, Jacques Lefèbvre, 62
devil, 158–61, 162
dichotomies, in Calvin, 163
doorkeepers, 189, 191
Dubosc, Guillaume, 80
Duchemin, Nicolas, 60–61, 77
Dupréau, Gabriel, 26
Dury, 56
Dutch Calvinism, 14, 119–44
Du Tillet, Louis, 11–12, 60, 62–69, 70, 78

earthly things, 211
Edict of Coucy, 63
edicts, of Geneva City Council, 84–91, 98
education, in Geneva, 87
Eggius, Albert, 126, 127, 139
elders, 16, 190
Elogium, 35, 36, 37
emotions, 110, 114
England, 76
episcopal/papal ecclesial structure, 78
Erasmus, 15, 154
evil, 66
executions, of Calvin's political opponents, 89
exiles, from Geneva, 89
exorcists, 189

faith, 172, 206
fall, 148–49, 211, 214
false miracles, 40
false religion
    Calvin on, 13–15, 147–48, 150–56, 163
    Catholics on, 157–61

false sacraments, 186
false worship, 152–53
Farel, Guillaume, 42, 63, 65, 70
Fauvel, Antoine, 49
Ferrare, Renée de, 60, 62, 77
Flaminio, Marcantonio, 76
flesh, 152
Fontanini, Benedetto, 75–76
forgiveness, 169–70
fornicators, in Geneva, 79
Forty Hours Celebrations, 13, 102, 108–9, 117
France, Calvin's harm to, 10–11, 44–45, 58
François I (king), 61, 62, 72, 74, 165
freedom of conscience, 14, 141
French Catholics, sympathy with Calvin, 78
French immigrants, to Geneva, 89–90
Fribourg, 94

Geneva
    Calvin's call to, 65, 70
    Catholic diocese of, 99–118
    Du Tillet's despondency in, 63–65
    godliness and political independence of, 98
    and threat of Catholics, 13, 80–98
Gerrish, Brian, 194
Gillot, Jacques, 36–37
God
    glory of, 206–7, 215
    preserves church, 167
Gonzaga, Giulia, 77
Goujon, Pierre, 92–95
Gourley, Philippe de, 47
Gradelle, Jacob, 111
Granier, Claude de, 100–101
Gratian, 182
Greeley, Andrew, 198, 200, 214
Gregory XIII (pope), 123

Harlay, François de, 46
Havart, Jean, 49
heaven, 177, 178
heavenly things, 211
Heidelberg Catechism, 133
Henri IV (king), 74, 104, 116
Henry II (king), 44
heresy, heresies, 131–34, 135, 141
    of Calvin, 26, 30
    of Reformation, 44

hermeneutical circle, in Calvin, 148
Heussen, Hugo Francis van, 132–33
history, Bauduin on, 34–35
Hogenheuvel, 126
Holland Mission, 124, 126, 142, 143–44
Holy Spirit
    and laying on of hands, 184–87
    and Lord's Supper, 175
    and ordination, 188
    testimony of, 65–66
Hopkins, Gerard Manley, 214
humanism, 149n10
    of Masson, 42–43
humanity, sacramentality of, 17, 208–11
human nature, 149–50, 156
humility, 66

idolatry
    Calvin on, 14, 146, 148–55, 163
    Catholics on, 157–58
    of papacy, 60, 61, 71
image of God, 17, 210, 211
images, 153–55
imagination, and false religion, 152, 160, 161–63
immigrants, to Geneva, 89–90, 97
incarnation, 197, 199, 207, 210, 212, 213–14
Inquisition, 77
Institutes (Calvin), 165, 168–69, 191, 215
    on baptism, 15, 169–70
    on confirmation, 179–81
    on Lord's Supper, 173–78
    Masson on, 41, 43
    on ordination, 16, 183–87, 189–91
    on penance, 181–82
    on sacraments, 196, 200–202
insufflation, 183
Inventory of Relics (Calvin), 147, 154–55
invisible church, 214
Irwin, Kevin, 197, 214
Italian evangelicals, 75, 78

Jeanne d'Albret, 74–75
Jesuits, 14, 54, 103n8, 110, 124, 126–28, 130

Jesus Christ, as sacrament, 195–97, 200, 212–13
Jews, idolatry of, 153
Joint Declaration on the Doctrine of Justification, 78
Jubilee celebration, 102, 108–9
justification by faith alone, 12, 71, 72, 78

Kilmartin, Edward, 197
knowledge of God, 202–3

La Faye, Antoine de, 26, 115
laity, 16, 122, 125, 134, 135, 143–44
Laugre, Pierre de, 96
law, study of, 33–35
laying on of hands, 15, 16, 179–89
lectors, 191
Leo X (pope), 77
Le Vasseur, Jacques, 51–54, 55
Lignaridus, Herman, 13, 111–15
Lindanus, William, 26
Logos Spermatikos, 157
Lord's Supper, Calvin on, 15–16, 173–79
Luria, Keith, 82–83
Luther, Martin, 9, 54, 70, 166
Lyon, 80

manifestations, 204–5, 209, 210
martyrs, 135
Mass, 13, 188
Masson, Jean-Baptiste, 35, 36, 37–38
Masson, Jean-Papire, 11, 33, 34–46, 48, 53, 55, 57, 58
Maurice (Capuchin in Geneva), 13, 105
McLaren, Brian, 198
Medici, Alexander de, 108
Melanchthon, Philipp, 9, 72, 168
Melchizedek, 187
Mesle, M. de, 47
Michelangelo, 75
Middleburg, 134
ministry
    Calvin's theology of, 70–72
    Du Tillet on, 67–68
miracles, 40, 201
Miron, M. de, 106
mirror metaphor, 16, 17, 204, 205, 206, 209, 212–13
Morlet, Martin, 47
Morone, Giovanni, 75
mortification and vivification, 169–70

Mouchy, Antoine de, 51
Mudzaert, Dionysius, 137
mystical union, 194–95, 202

natural gifts, 149
natural revelation, 203, 206–7
Neercassel, Johannes van, 130, 141
neo-Augustinianism, 129, 132
Nepveur, Pierre, 96
Netherlands, and Reformed Protestantism, 14, 119–21
Newman, John Henry, 7
Nicodemites, 11, 59–60, 71, 76, 77–78, 146
Nicodemus, 60
Nicolas of Cusa, 74
Noyon, 31, 47–52, 55, 56, 57, 147
Nyon, Treaty of, 13, 102n6

Ochino, Bernardino, 12, 72, 75, 76
Olislagers, Louis, 130
oral tradition, 187–88
Oratory of Divine Love, 74, 76–77
Order of Fontevrault, 74
ordinary and extraordinary means of entering ministry, 71
ordination, 15
    Calvin on, 70–71, 182–89
    and laying on of hands, 179
    as sacrament, 68, 186–89, 191
original sin, 150

pagan religion, 154
papacy, 167
    abuses of, 64
    ascendency of, 165
paradoxes, in Calvin, 163
Paris, 74
pastors, 16, 190
patriarchs, 16, 190
Paul III (pope), 61, 74
Paul IV (pope), 78
penance, 181–82
Perrot, Charles, 111, 115
persecution, 135, 137–43, 144
Peyrolier, Perrin, 94
Pharisees, 30
Philip II (king), 122
Pius V (pope), 76
placards, 62
Plato, 28
pluralism, in Netherlands, 121–22, 139, 143

poetry, 74–75
Poland, 76
Pole, Reginald, 75
preaching, 87
predestination, 76
presbyters, 189, 190
priests, priesthood, 16, 61, 70–71
Priuli, Alvise, 76
private reconciliation, 182
promiscuity, of Calvin, rumors of, 31
Protestantism
  on sacramentality, 195
  on Word, 199–200
protestantization, of Netherlands, 120
providence, 205
Puritans, 162

Quentin, Jean, 47

Raemond, Florimond de, 26
Ragnoni, Lattanzio, 76
Randoul, M., 47
readers, 189
Reformed–Roman Catholic Dialogue, 193, 214
Regensburg, Colloquy of, 72
Registers, of Noyon, 47–51, 52–53, 55
relics, 153–55
religion
  as human invention, 161–63
  as social phenomenon, 153, 156
restoration, 179, 181–83
Richelieu (cardinal), 11, 25, 54–57, 58
Roman Catholicism
  as Babylonian captivity, 165
  as a church, 71–72
Roman Catholics
  biographies of Calvin, 25–58
  in Geneva, 12
  in Netherlands, 14, 120–44
  in New World, 15, 157–58
  scholarship on Calvin, 10
Ronzy, Pierre, 33
Roussel, Gérard, 12, 60, 61, 78, 146
Rovenius, Philip, 120, 124, 126, 127, 131–32, 139, 140

sacramentality, 16–17, 193–95
  in Calvin, 16, 200–215
  in contemporary theology, 195–202
sacraments, 186
sacrifice, 186, 188
Sadducees, 30
Sadolet, 42
Saint-Michel, Antoine de, 113
Sarrazin, Jean, 116, 117
satanic deception, and idolatry, 15, 158–61, 162, 163
Savoy, 102, 103, 116
Schillebeeckx, Edward, 16, 17, 195–97, 200, 208–9n60
schism, 168
Scripture, Calvin on, 148
semen religionis, 15, 149, 152, 156–57
seminaries, in Netherlands, 14, 126–29
Seneca, 41, 42, 43, 156
sensus divinitatis, 15, 149, 208, 211
Servetus, 32, 41, 43–44
sign, and thing signified, 173–75, 176–77
similitudo temporum, 34, 38
sodomy, 31
sola scriptura, 133
soul, 210
spectacle metaphor, 17, 204, 213
speculation, 202–3
spiritual gifts, 149
spiritual virgins, 125
St. Bartholomew's Day Massacre, 77, 115
Stoicism, 156
St. Pierre, 13, 94, 105
Strasbourg, 42, 65, 70, 76
Sturm, Jean, 33
subdeacons, 189–91
supernatural, 162
superstition, 150, 155
Surius, Laurentius, 26
sursum corda, 178–79
Swieten, Aegidius van, 130
Synod of Dort, 12, 14, 119

Tacitus, 43
Taillepied, Noël, 27
teachers, 16, 190

theater metaphor, 16, 17, 204, 205, 206, 213
Thomas Aquinas, 129
Thonon, 108–9, 111–12, 116–17
Tillich, Paul, 16, 199–200, 201
Toledo, Francisco de, 100
toleration, 92, 101
Tracy, David, 16, 197, 200, 201, 214
transubstantiation, 178
true church
  Du Tillet on, 64, 65, 67
  hidden in Roman Catholic Church, 166–68
  marks of, 165–66
true religion, Calvin on, 147–48, 155, 163

Union of Utrecht, 121
union with Christ, 169–70, 194
usurers, in Geneva, 79

Valdès, Juan de, 12, 75, 77
Vermigli, Peter Martyr, 33, 76
vicars apostolic, 14, 123–24, 135, 138, 143
Villagómez, Pedro de, 161
Viret, Pierre, 65
Virgin Mary, 75
Vita Calvini (Masson), 35, 36, 37
vocation, of ministry, 65, 67–68
Vosmeer, Sasbout, 123–24, 126, 127, 135, 139

Walenburg, Adrian, 132
Walenburg, Peter, 132
Wars of Religion, 11, 29, 40, 44–45
Whittaker, William, 55, 56
Wiele, Jan Baptiste Stalpert van der, 136
Willibrord, 135, 136–37
witches, 162
women, education of, 76–77
Word and sacraments, 166, 190, 197, 201
worship, Calvin on, 146, 152

Zurich, 76
Zwingli, 15, 54, 151, 154, 155–57, 159